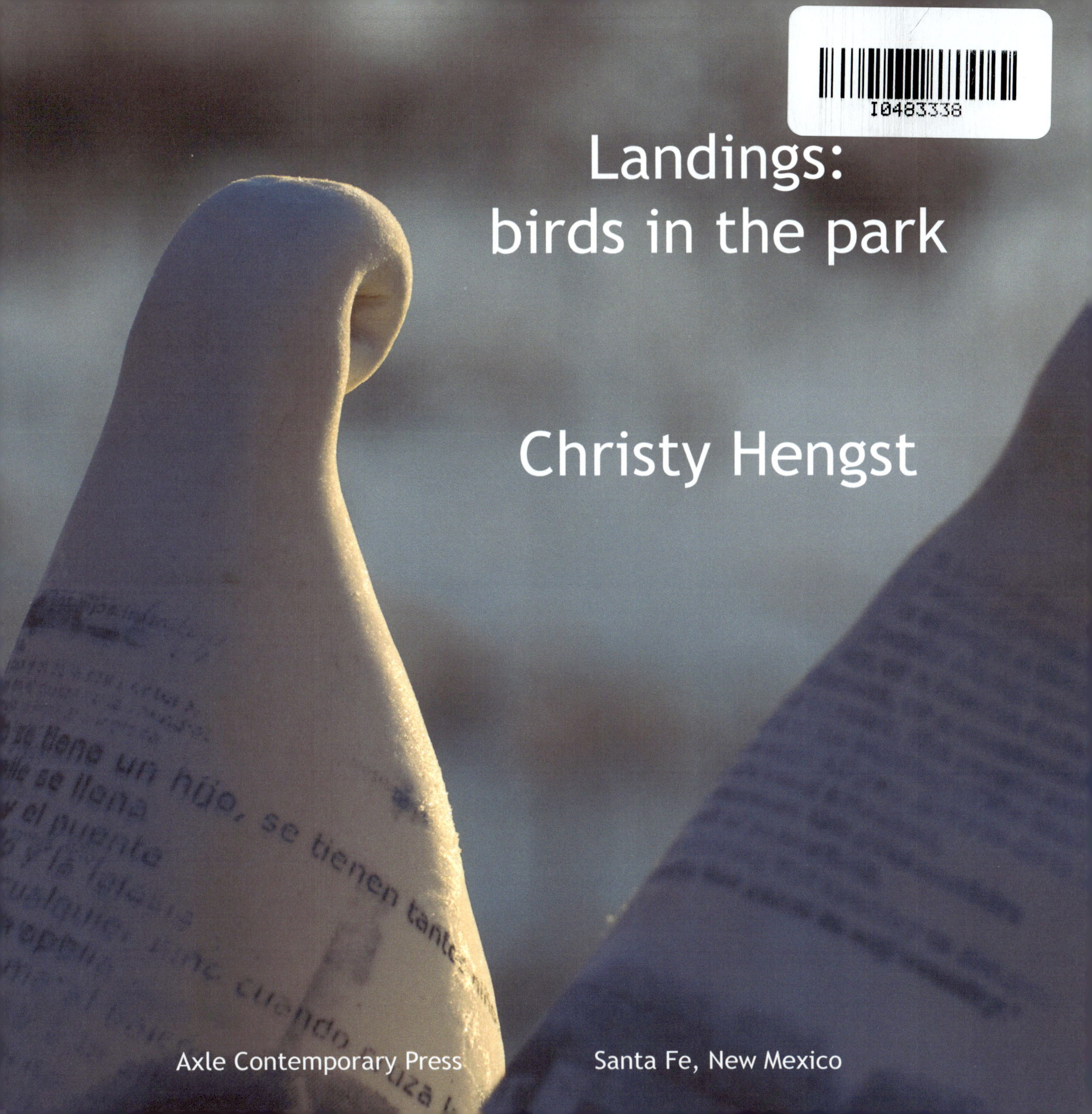

Landings: birds in the park

Christy Hengst

Axle Contemporary Press Santa Fe, New Mexico

Published by
Axle Contemporary
P.O. Box 22095
Santa Fe, New Mexico 87502
www.axlepress.com

ISBN: 978-0-9858116-1-7

www.christyhengst.com
Edited by Rebecca Morgan
Designed by Christy Hengst and Matthew Chase-Daniel

Preceding page photo: Maria De Las Casas
Front cover: Central Park, New York, NY.
Back cover: Santa Barbara, CA. Photo: Helmut Hillenkamp
Unless otherwise specified, all photos taken by Christy Hengst.

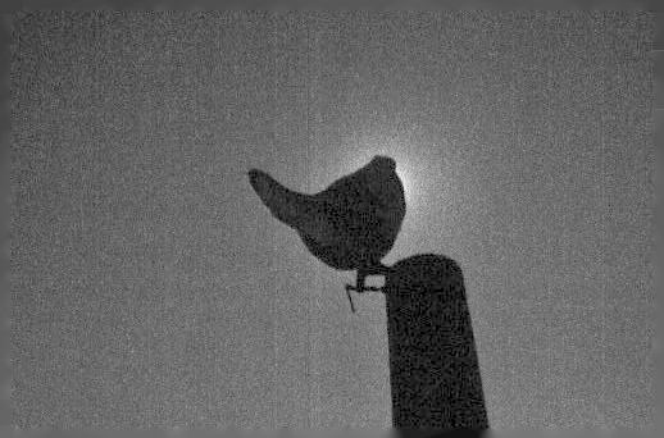

LANDINGS: b i r d s i n t h e p a r k

Contents

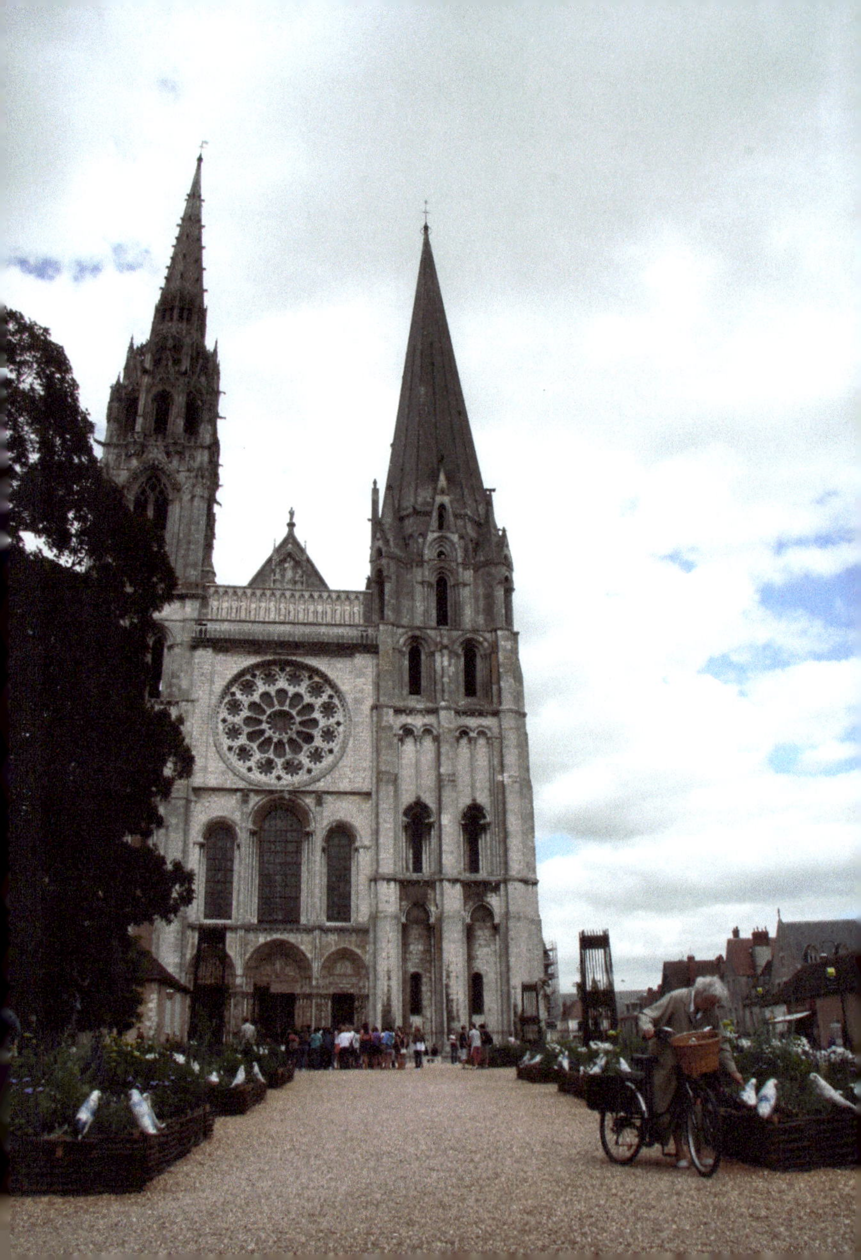

LANDINGS

In the Abrahamic faiths the holiest bird is the dove. The Holy Spirit comes as a dove, bringing peace and inspiration to the heart and mind of humanity. Ever since Noah set the dove loose from the Ark over the face of the deep, and it came back bearing an olive twig in its beak, the dove has been a symbol of the hope of homecoming, of return to our true home, a place within each of us that is always at peace, always in love.

Christy Hengst's inspired art project Landings has served as a reminder to people around the world of our deepest longing - to be truly at home. This flock of remarkable birds, made of fine porcelain, silk-screened with messages and images of all kinds - poetry, newspaper print, images of childhood and war, weapons plans, courting letters and recipes from grandparents - have been "landing" in iconic and unexpected places for the last two years. Their itinerary has included the Washington Mall, civic plazas around the American Southwest, the Galapagos Islands, the Cathedral in Chartres, Aachen in Germany. They are well-travelled. Like Noah's dove, they have floated a long way across the face of the earth.

But wherever they land they have the same effect, they bring the same message: they make people stop and look. And then talk with one another, and ask questions: what are these beautiful birds doing here? What does it say on this one, that one? What is the image on this one's back? Who made them? Who brought them here? Pretty soon the flock of birds is mingling with a crowd of people happy to have had their day interrupted, expanded, changed by this unexpected arrival.

Now their journey continues within the pages of this book, perhaps traveling even further than they have so far. Give these birds a moment: let them land in your heart with their message of peace, and change your day.

-Henry Shukman, Santa Fe, 2012

birds in the park

Birds in the Park is a traveling public art project that I started in 2008. Both event and exhibition, it involves a flock of porcelain birds which appear in the early morning hours at a particular location, are available for interaction during the day, and disappear by nightfall. The birds have cobalt images and text silk-screened and fired onto them, investigating aspects of humanity, with a focus on war and peace.

With their initial landings in Santa Fe, the birds have flown to over sixty locations, including Central Park and the United Nations Headquarters in NY; beaches along the coast of California; a sculpture garden in New Orleans; the National Mall and the Capitol in Washington D.C.; Chartres Cathedral in France; Peenemünde, Germany; the weapons lab town of Los Alamos, New Mexico; the Netherlands; Cuenca, Ecuador; and have even migrated as far as the Galapagos Islands.

At first sight, the sculptures are often mistaken for oddly still pigeons. They are, in a sense, carrier pigeons, as the forms carry images and text on their backs. The message they bear is an exploration of the beautiful and the horrible side by side. The content originated with the shock and dismay I felt as the US government began its second war with Iraq, and expanded to consider the phenomenon of war in general. The questions posed by the birds are about the humanness of us all, how we are all connected, and the unthinkable ways in which that bond is disregarded.

The specific material on the birds includes images of children playing, love letters, poetry, recipes and prose, layered with newspaper articles and photographs of the lead-up to and beginning of the second Iraq war, as well as other war-related documents. Placing images of life and intimacy in such close proximity to images of death and destruction leads us to ask the question, "How can people do that to each other?!" Further, we may consider critically how the initiation of a war is "sold" to regular people, and how discussions about the cold facts of war, (weapons capabilities, etc.) can become detached from the human reality on the other end, creeping into everyday life as something normal, like birds in the park.

The content material has developed over time and in response to the places the birds have or will be visiting. In addition to personal photography and drawing, and images and text borrowed from public media, I have collaborated with writer and Vietnam War veteran Tim Origer, Iraq veteran Alex Smith, English poet Henry Shukman, Venezuelan photographer Maria De Las Casas, and my father, Werner Hengst, who was a child in WWII Germany. One of the most significant landings during the project was in July of 2010, in Peenemünde, Germany, the site of the V-1 and V-2 rocket development during WWII. My grandfather was working there as a scientist then, and photographs of the weapons lab town before and after its bombing, as well as quotes from Germans (such as Goering) during that time, were integrated into the birds that landed there.

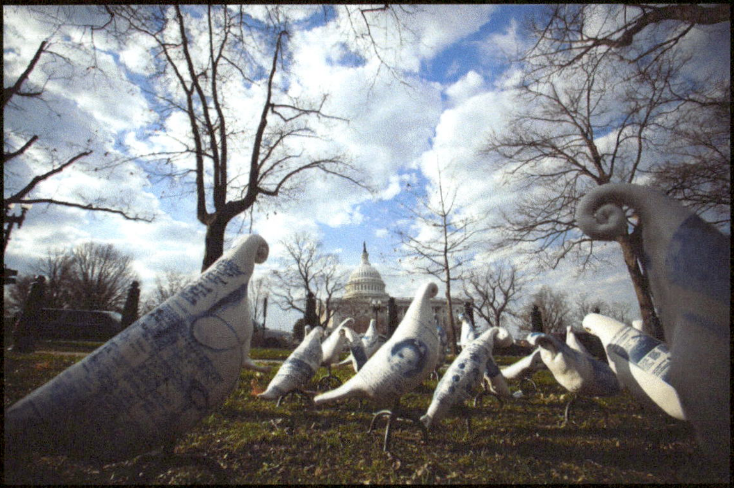

Photo: Genevieve Russell

The landings have an element of unpredictability; the experience is out of the blue and somewhat fleeting, the better to catch the unsuspecting passerby's curiosity. A big part of the project is the interactions with people -- the many hands who help to set up along the way, and all the people we meet on site during the course of the day, listening and conversing.

With the strong gesture of birds, but carrying the reflections of human culture, the birds at times function as a quiet mirror.

-Christy Hengst

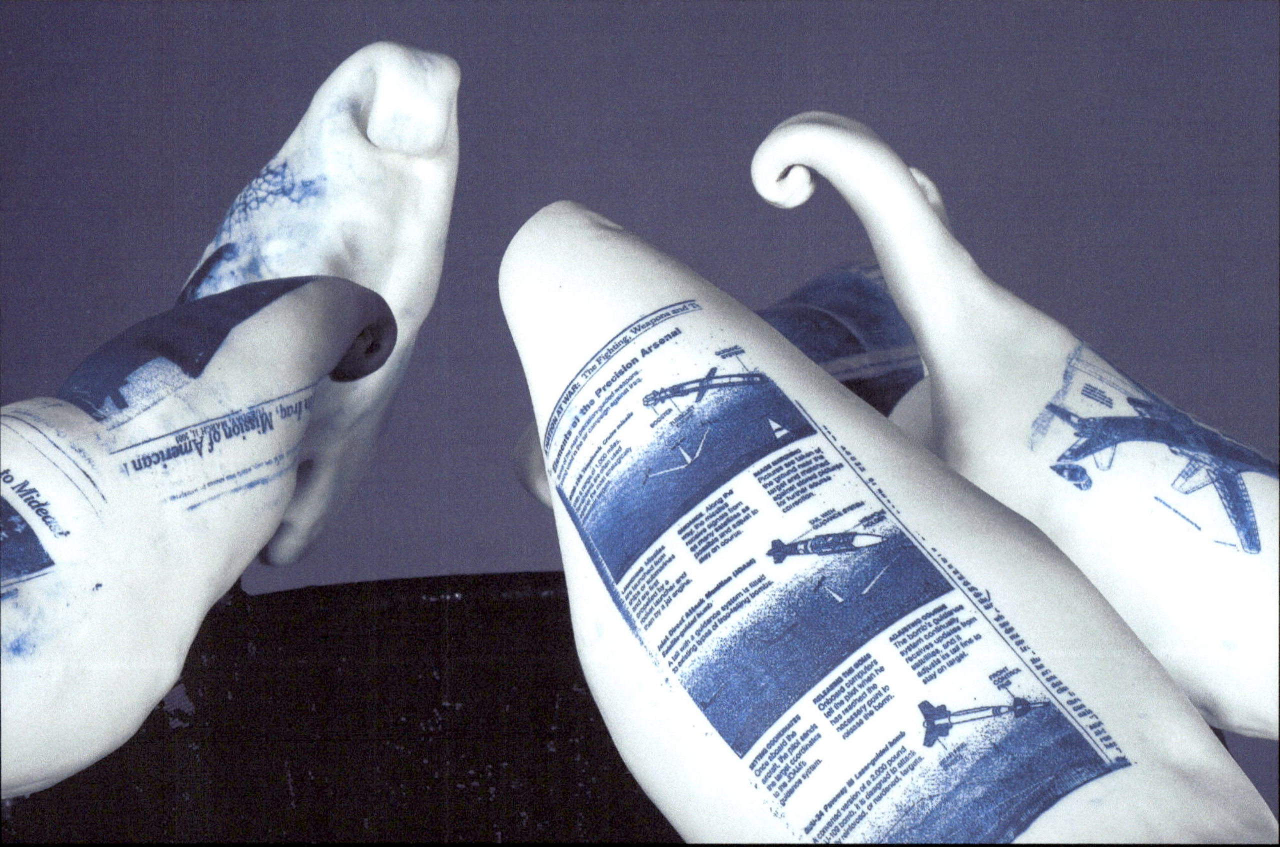

Above and facing page photos: Dan Barsotti

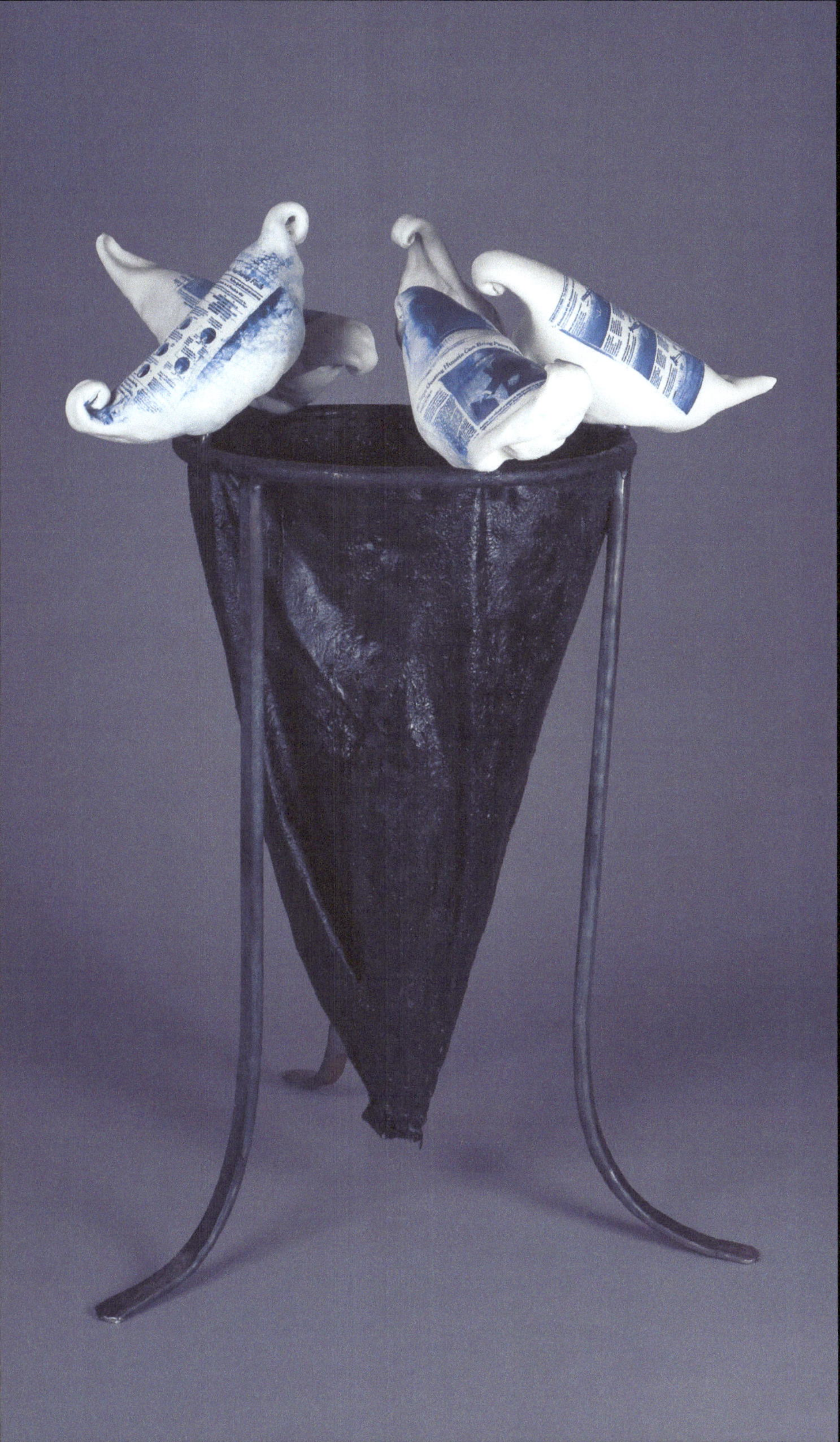

The way the birds started was actually as seed pods; I was just discovering that I could print onto the porcelain while it was still wet, and create a three-dimensional piece afterwards from the printed slab. The pregnant shapes that I thought of as pods started to look surprisingly like birds.

At first I was still oriented towards making pieces that would be shown in an indoor space -- this group (left), with articles and images of the lead-up to the invasion of Iraq, is looking down into a black hole/ feed sack, covered in wax.

But soon it occurred to me that I would really like to see the birds outside, in a park. My first idea of where I wanted to try this out, in the new Santa Fe Railyard Park, was initially turned down. So I thought of other places, lots of other places.

Thus the open road unfolded before us...

Preparing and smoothing a slab of porcelain that will later be formed into a bird.

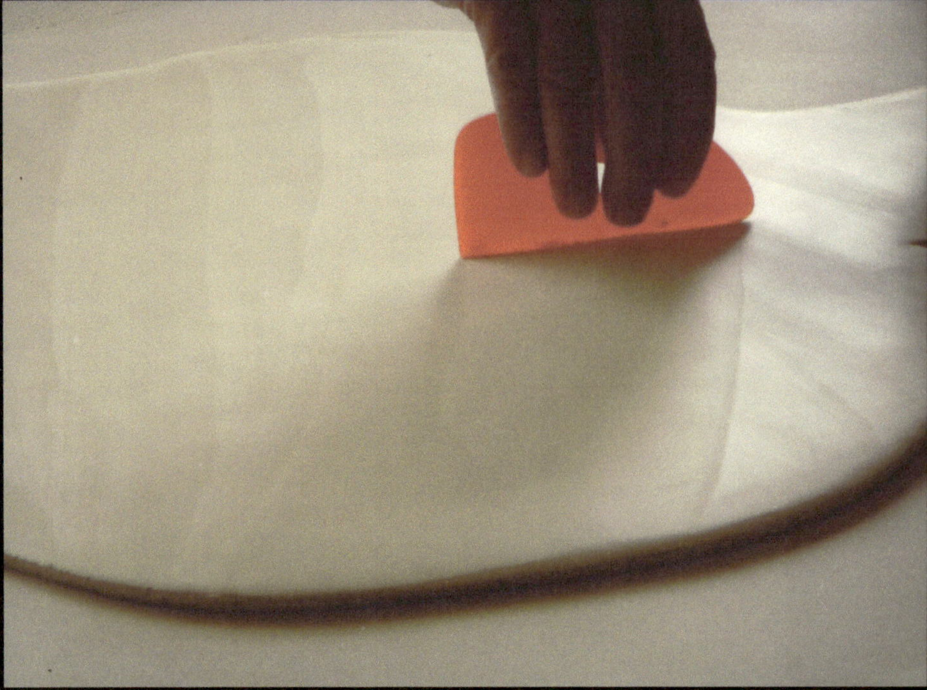

Freehand brushwork onto the slab.

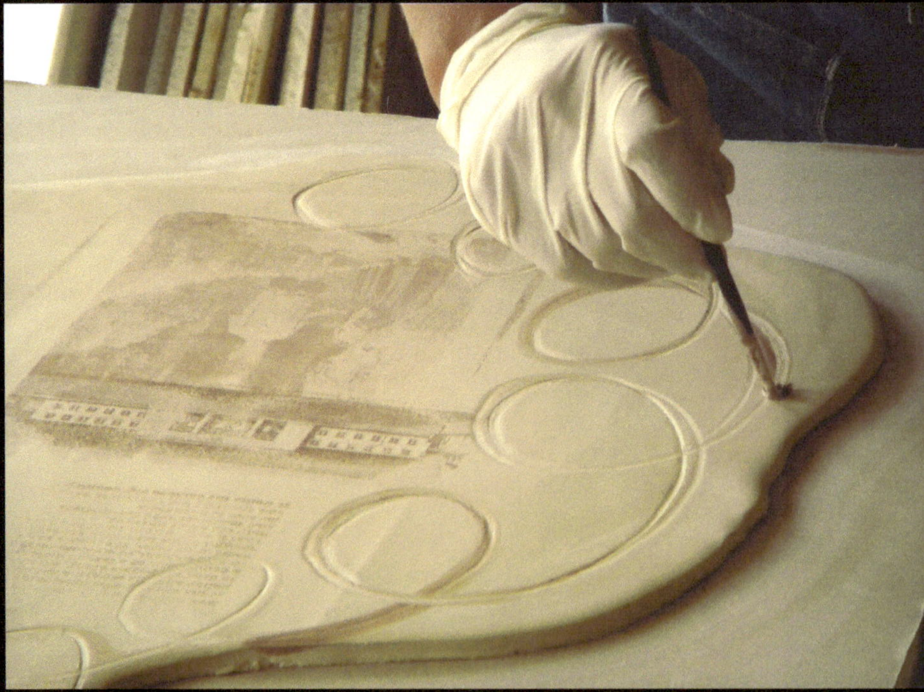

This and facing page photos: Dagmar Diebels

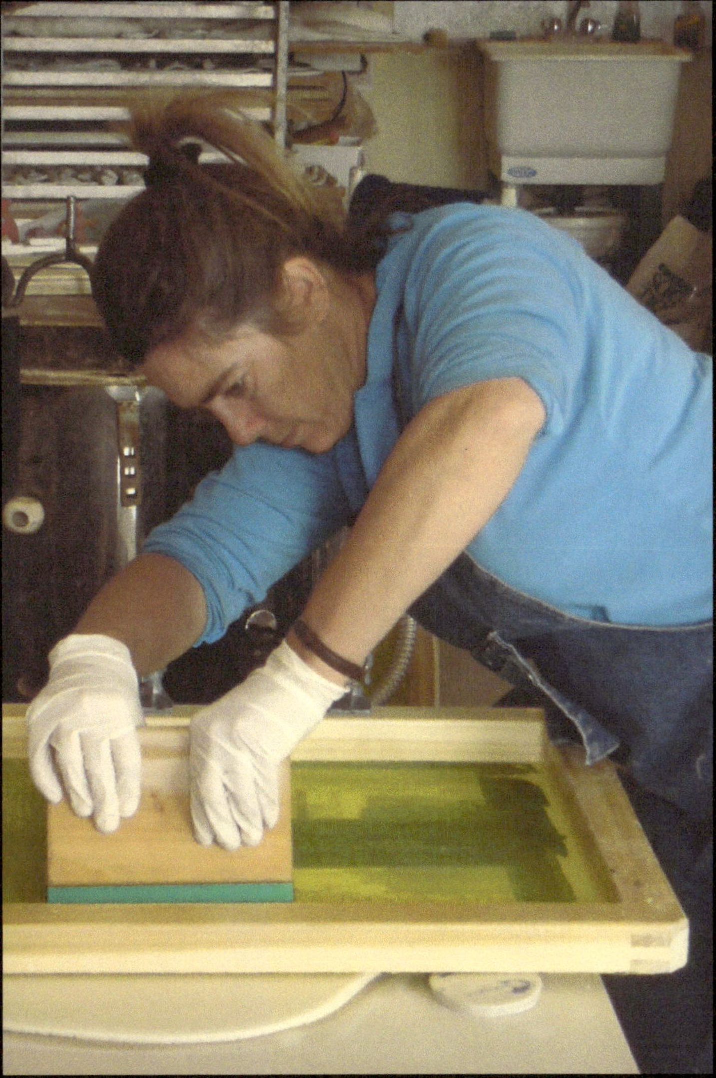

Silkscreen printing onto the slab with cobalt, while the clay is still wet and flexible, so that it can be shaped afterwards.

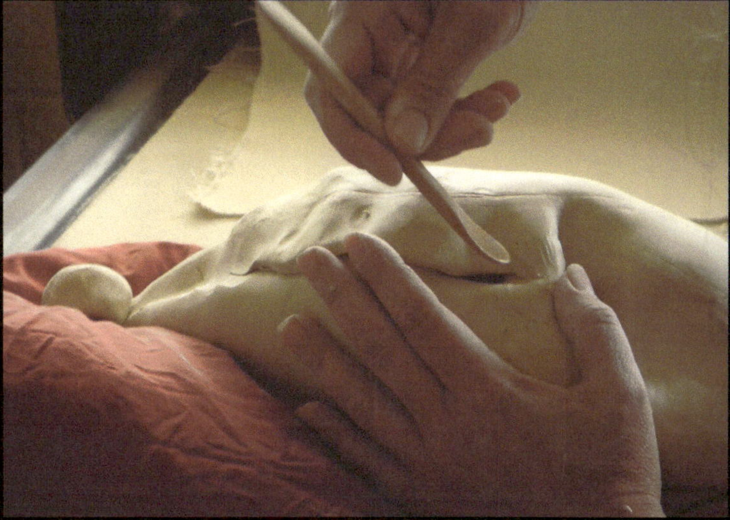

Forming the bird around crumpled newspaper, that will burn out in the firing.

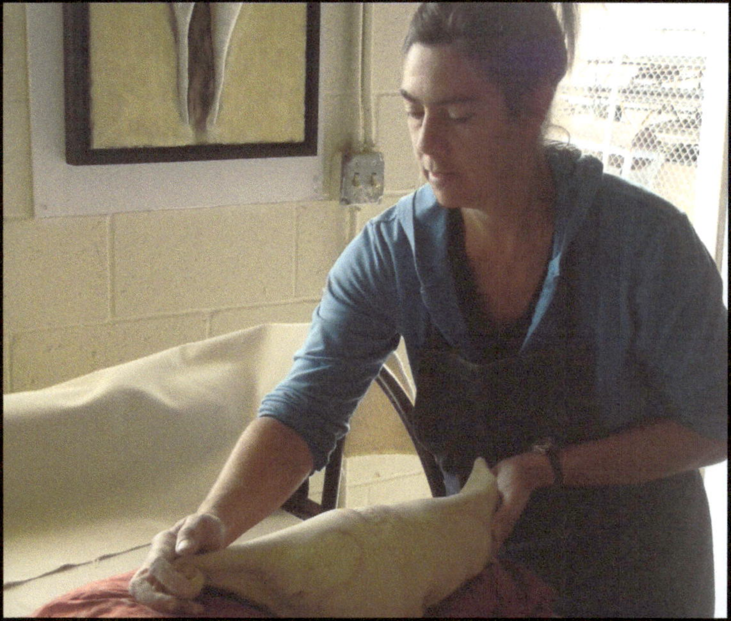

The final shape and attitude of each bird is different, as is the fusion of content on its back.

IT'S WAR

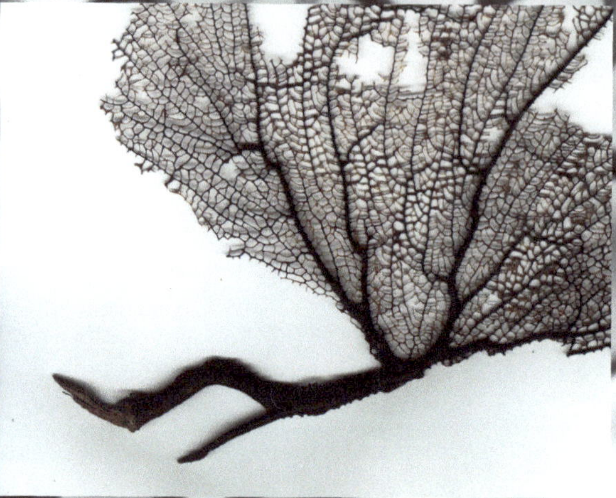

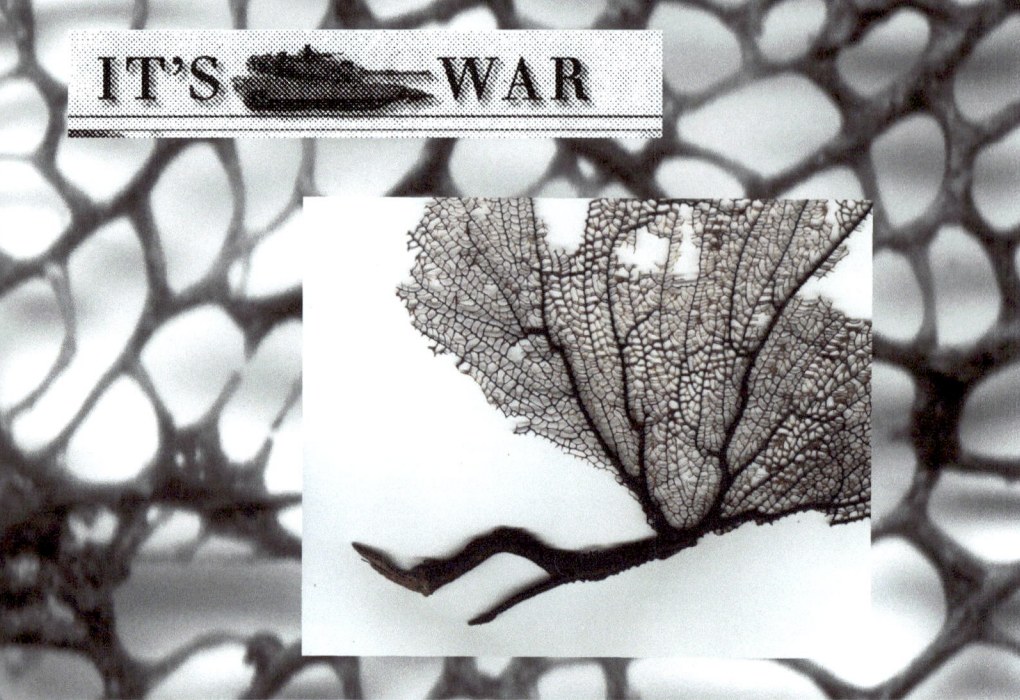

which had seen its better days, having been damaged by weapons fire on more than one occasion.

On the ground lay an old "papa-san", tended by an equally old "mama-san" (presumably his wife.) a "baby-san", perhaps a grandchild, was also present. The "papa san" was attempting to hold his intestines inside the large tear the grenade has created in the muscles of his stomach. Wife & grandchild, both bleeding themselves from numerous small shrapnel wounds, were trying their best to assist him, athough it was obvious the three were collectivly suffering from shock.

Even with the language barrier we managed to learn that "Papa-san had been enroute from the bunker to the latrine when we saw the light of his candle. He was so old that his wife and grandchild had been assisting him when the grenade hit.

We proceed to apply a field dressing to his wound, advising the survivors that if he lived through the night he could be carried to our base camp where a Marine medic would tend to his injuries. We further advised, considering the curfew was still in effect that moving before dawn would put them at risk of being shot again as V.C. We then continued on our patrol.

"Why of course the people don't want war. Why should some poor slob on a farm want to risk his life in a war when the best he can get out of it is to come back to his farm in one piece? Naturally the common people don't want war neither in Russia, nor in England, nor for that matter in Germany. That is understood. But, after all, it is the leaders of the country who determine the policy and it is always a simple matter to drag the people along, whether it is a democracy, or a fascist dictatorship, or a parliament, or a communist dictatorship. Voice or no voice, the people can always be brought to the bidding of the leaders. That is easy. All you have to do is tell them they are being attacked, and denounce the peacemakers for lack of patriotism and exposing the country to danger. It works the same in any country."

-- Hermann Goering

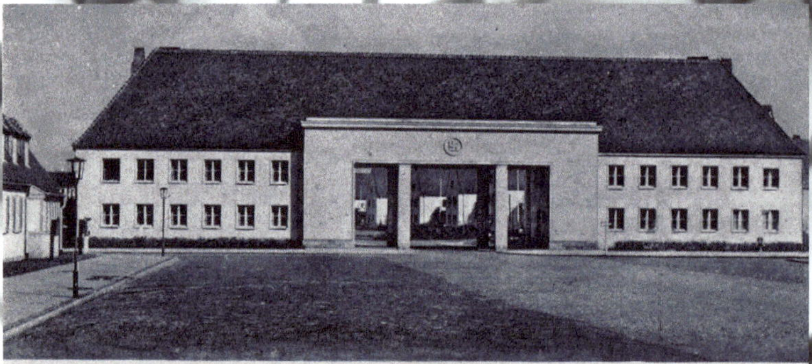

Heeresgutsbezirk Peenemünde. Eingangstor zur Siedlung

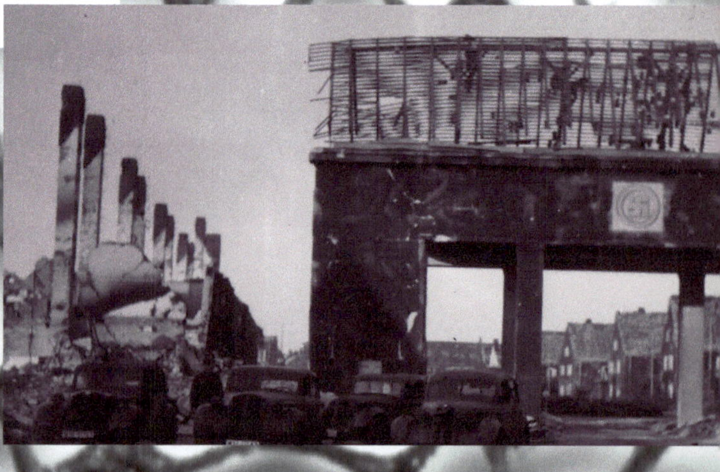

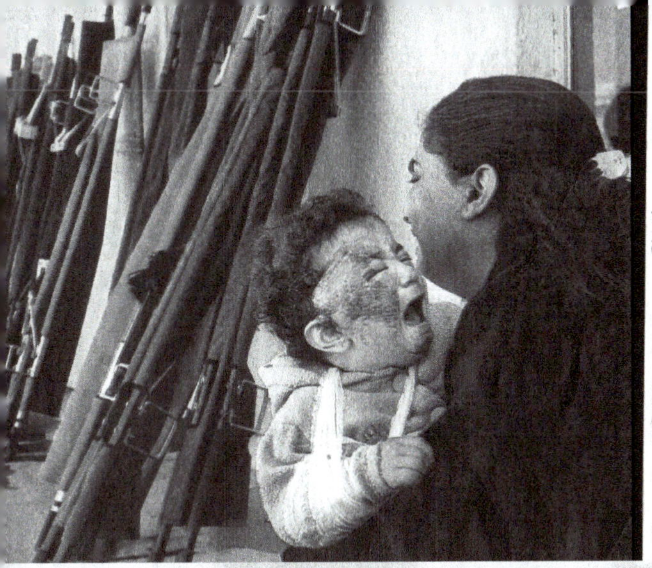

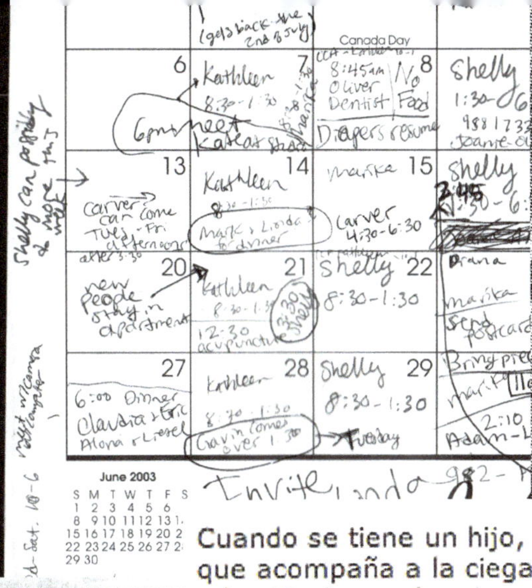

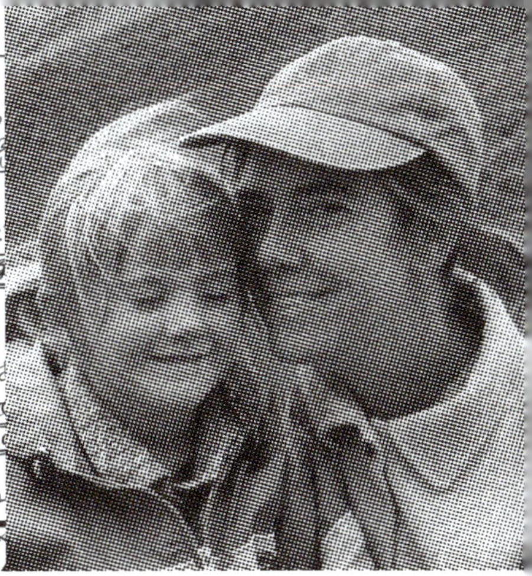

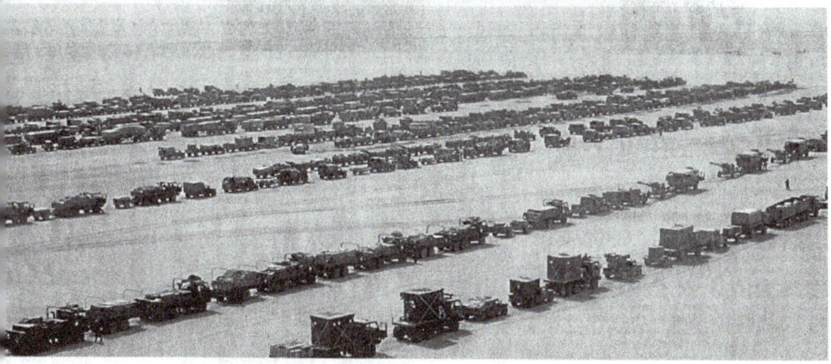

convoy of trucks and armored vehicles of the 101st Airborne Division's Third Brigade Combat Team were lined up in the desert yesterday, looking lik

Good & easy Po

2c. flour (scant) after sifting
2c. sugar
6 eggs
1c. oil
4t. bak. powd.
1t salt
4

Cuando se tiene un hijo, es nuestro el niño
que acompaña a la ciega
y las Meninas y la misma enana
y el Príncipe de Francia y su Princesa
y el que tiene San Antonio en los brazos
y el que tiene la Coromoto en las piernas.
Cuando se tiene un hijo, toda risa nos cala,
todo llanto nos crispa, venga de donde venga.
Cuando se tiene un hijo, se tiene el mundo adentro
y el corazón afuera.
Y cuando se tienen dos hijos
se tienen todos los hijos de la tierra,
los millones de hijos con que las tierras lloran,
con que las madres ríen, con que los mundos sueñan,
los que Paul Fort quería con las manos unidas
para que el mundo fuera la canción de una rueda,
los que el Hombre de Estado, que tiene un lindo niño,
quiere con Dios adentro y las tripas afuera,
los que escaparon de Herodes para caer en Hiroshima
entreabiertos los ojos, como los niños de la guerra,
porque basta para que salga toda la luz de un niño
una rendija china o una mirada japonesa.

Cuando se tienen dos hijos
se tiene todo el miedo del planeta,
todo el miedo a los hombres luminosos
que quieren asesinar la luz y arriar las velas
y ensangrentar las pelotas de goma
y zambullir en llanto ferrocarriles de cuerda.
Cuando se tienen dos hijos
se tiene la alegría y el ¡ay! del mundo en dos cabezas,
toda la angustia y toda la esperanza,
la luz y el llanto, a ver cuál es el que nos llega,
si el modo de llorar del universo
el modo de alumbrar de las estrellas.

SNOWY MORNING

When we were nine or ten and used to play
at dying – hands clasped to the chest,
Goodbye, beautiful world, I love you! –
we didn't believe it could ever really be done.

Say goodbye to *everything*? A gunshot wound
in 'Alias Smith and Jones' could set us thinking –
please *please* don't die – or a feathered mess
that had been a pigeon squashed on the road.

Even Divinity class, that final sponge of vinegar
on a speartip. Goodbye, beautiful vinegar.
Now, under the shag of decades, after so much
contact with things, it takes a morning like this.

Snow has fallen, a light crust. On the white field
green trails zigzag where the horses wandered,
a crazy scribble shows where they fed.
There they are now, two statues stooping.

All the ewes are sitting, thawing their grass.
Puddles crunch like caramel. Little snowfalls
crumble down a hedge. The silver-birch
trembles in its own twigs' shadows.

And under the rusty chestnut I walk
through a rain of crystals. There isn't much to say.
This is a day that decides by itself to be beautiful.
This field is a bride. How are we to say goodbye?

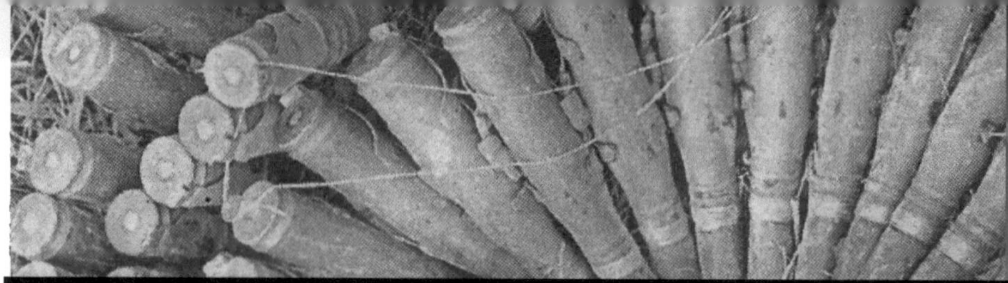

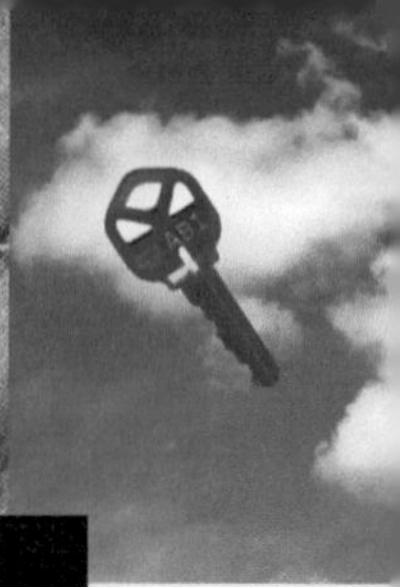

This page, clockwise, starting at upper left: Snowy Morning by Henry Shukman; newspaper photograph of ammunitions pile; key, clouds; plants against fog in Big Sur, CA; excerpt of Werner Hengst's account of the bombing of his town (Peenemünde, Germany) when he was a child; Christy Hengst's children, Oliver and Eliza, playing on the beach in Mexico; layered love letters; sandhill crane.

Previous page, clockwise, starting at upper left: newspaper photo of Iraqi bombing victims, mother and child; daily calendar; mother and child; Los Hijos Infinitos by Andrés Eloy Blanco; grandmother's recipe for Pound Cake; newspaper photo of a convoy waiting in the desert for the invasion of Iraq.

Previous previous page, clockwise, starting at upper left: photo of Betty Hengst (Christy Hengst's mother) as a child; headline from newspaper, 2003; close-up of fan coral, showing skeleton of organisms making up a colony; excerpt of Rule of Law, recounting an experience in Vietnam, by Tim Origer; destroyed building in Peenemünde after bombing; the same building before bombing -- this building housed the scientists who developed the V-1 and V-2 rockets for the Nazis; quote from Hermann Goering, Adolf Hitler's second in command; fan coral.

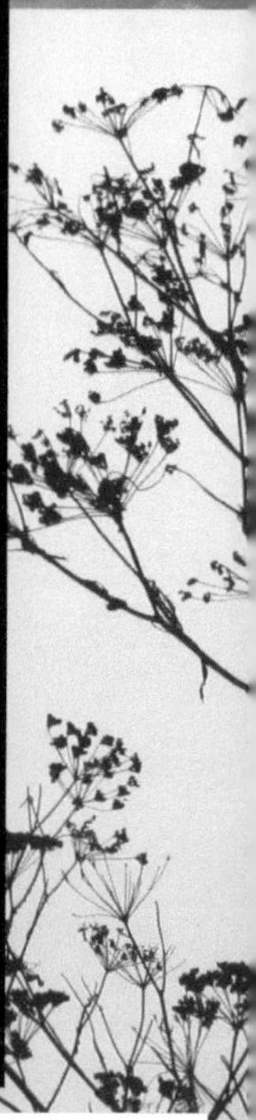

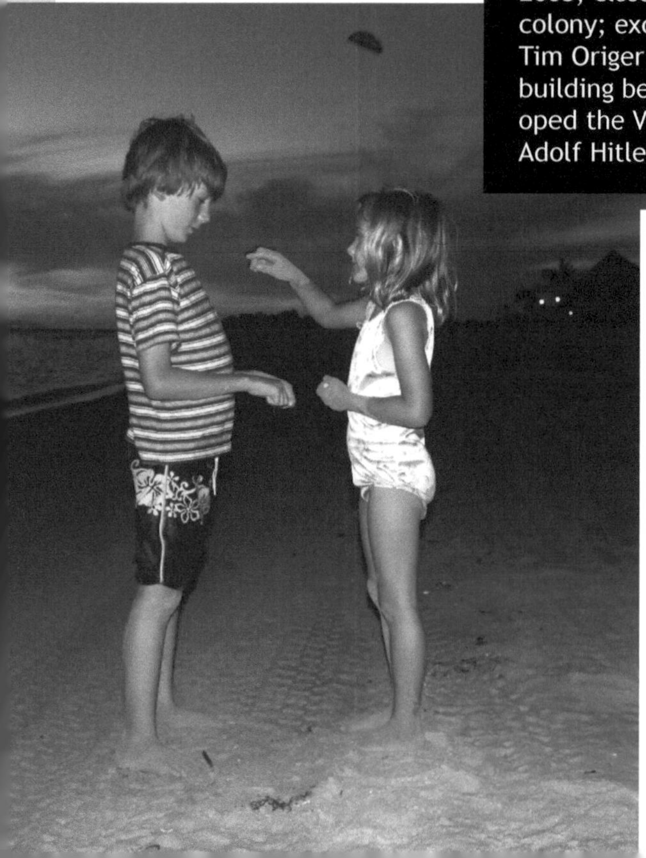

My family and the others who had emerged from the trench stood there for several minutes, stunned by the total destruction of what had been, only an hour before, our homes. Then we started to walk the few blocks to the town square, down by the train station. Next to it was the town hall which also was burning. We shuffled along slowly, with our heads down, trying to avoid the chunks of concrete, the twisted metal and the broken roof tiles that were scattered all over the street. Against the glow of the flames, the others looked like shadows, like the picture I had seen in a book, of dead people rising from their graves on the Day of Judgment. We passed the place where our house had been, and saw only an empty space. It had been completely blown away by a direct hit. Everything was gone, including the new bicycle I had been so proud of. Even the basement had caved in, and smoke was rising from our "bomb-proof" shelter. When Mutti started to cry, I hugged her, and so did my dad, but only with his left arm. His right hand still had a firm grip on the handle of the brown briefcase which, except for the clothes we wore, was our only possession.

In the square, some tables had been set up, manned by soldiers who were writing down the names of those who had survived the bombing. Other soldiers unloaded a big kettle full of hot bouillon from a truck, and soon people were sitting all along the curb with their hands around steaming paper cups. The bouillon reminded me of my mother's chicken soup. It felt warm and comforting. The sky had

landings:

Santa Fe and New Mexico

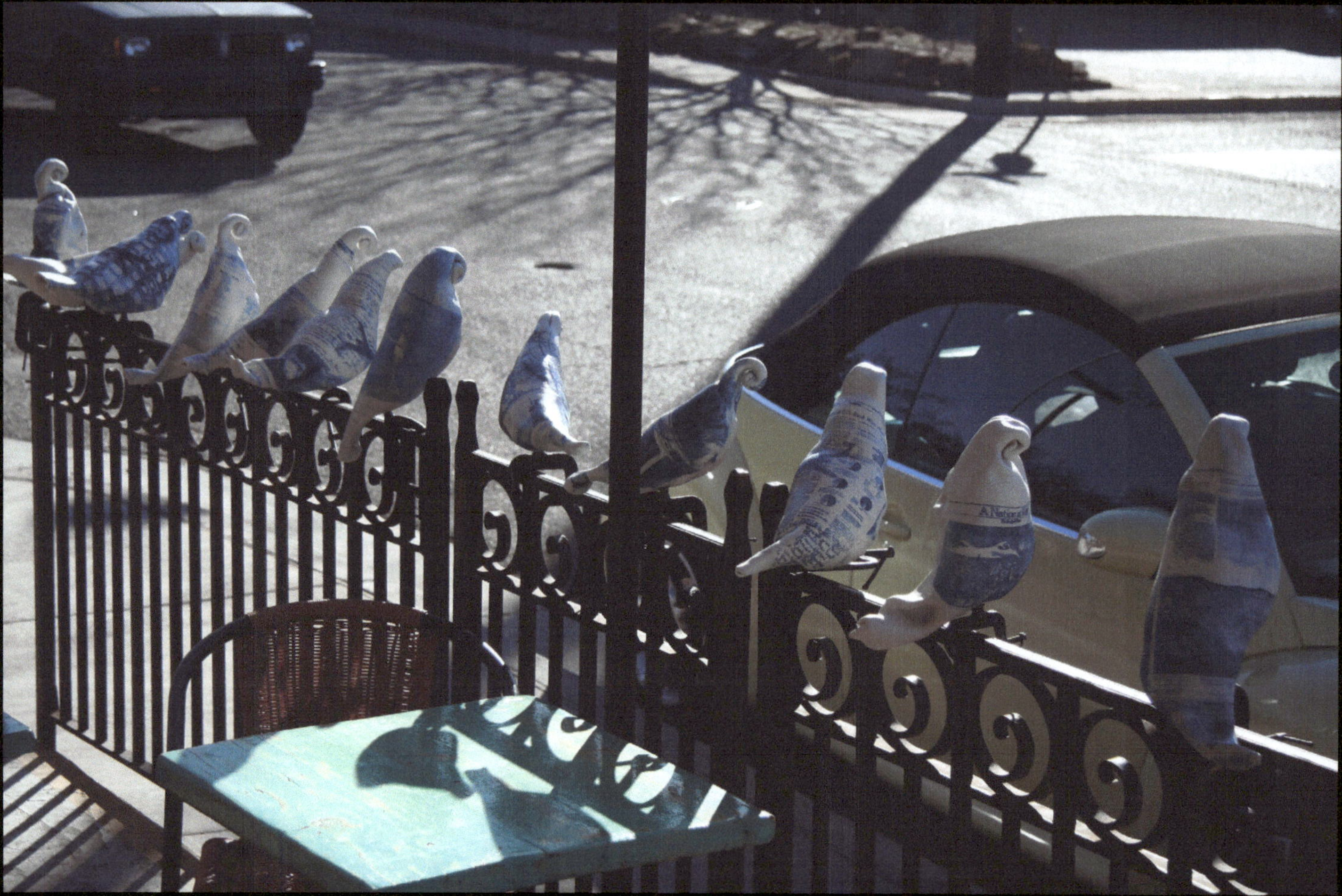

Above and facing page: Tune-Up Cafe, Santa Fe, NM 2/27/2009.

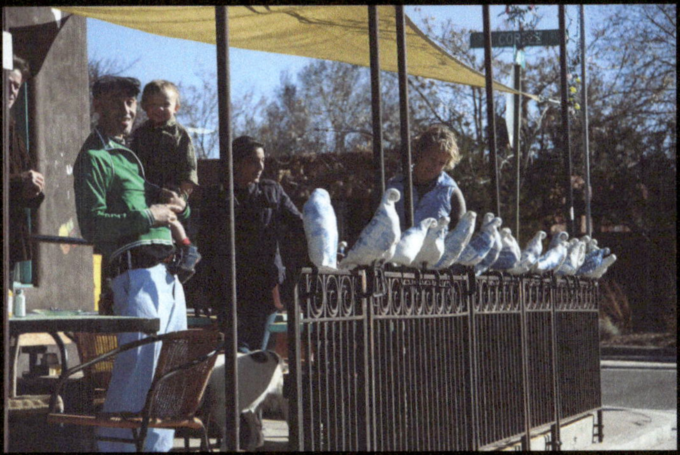

After experimenting around with various formats of placing the birds (e.g., hiding them where only the extremely observant would find them, or mounting them as part of larger sculptures) the idea settled in to have them simply show up as a flock of birds, pecking around on the ground, or alighting on railings.

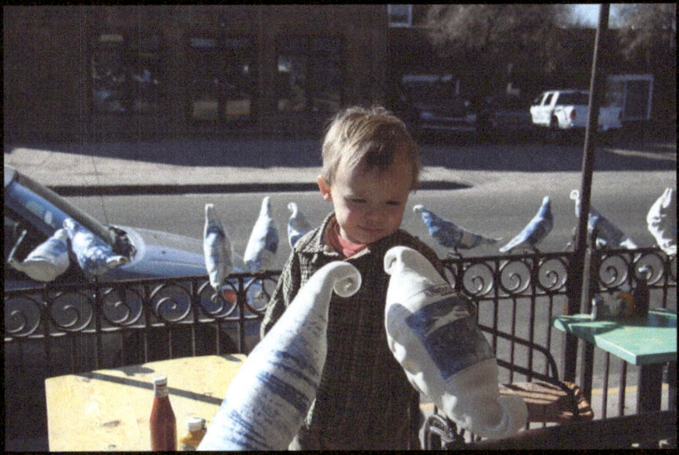

Once I had decided to start having them show up every few days in different locations all around Santa Fe, the Tune-up Cafe was the first scheduled landing. It was exhilarating to plant these surprises early in the morning when no one was around, and then be there the whole day into the night and watch what happened.

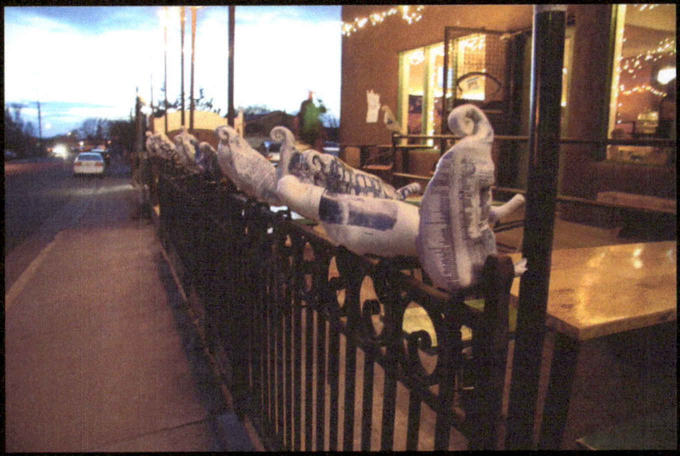

These first landings were pretty anonymous (except for having gotten permission from the host) so, as I kept an eye on my birdies, incognito, I heard all kinds of theories about them...

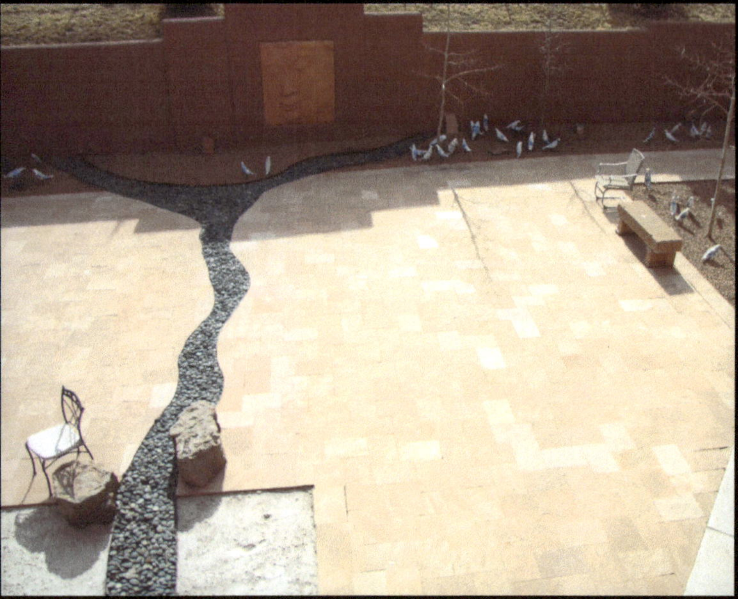

Southwest Acupuncture College, Santa Fe, NM 3/4/2009.

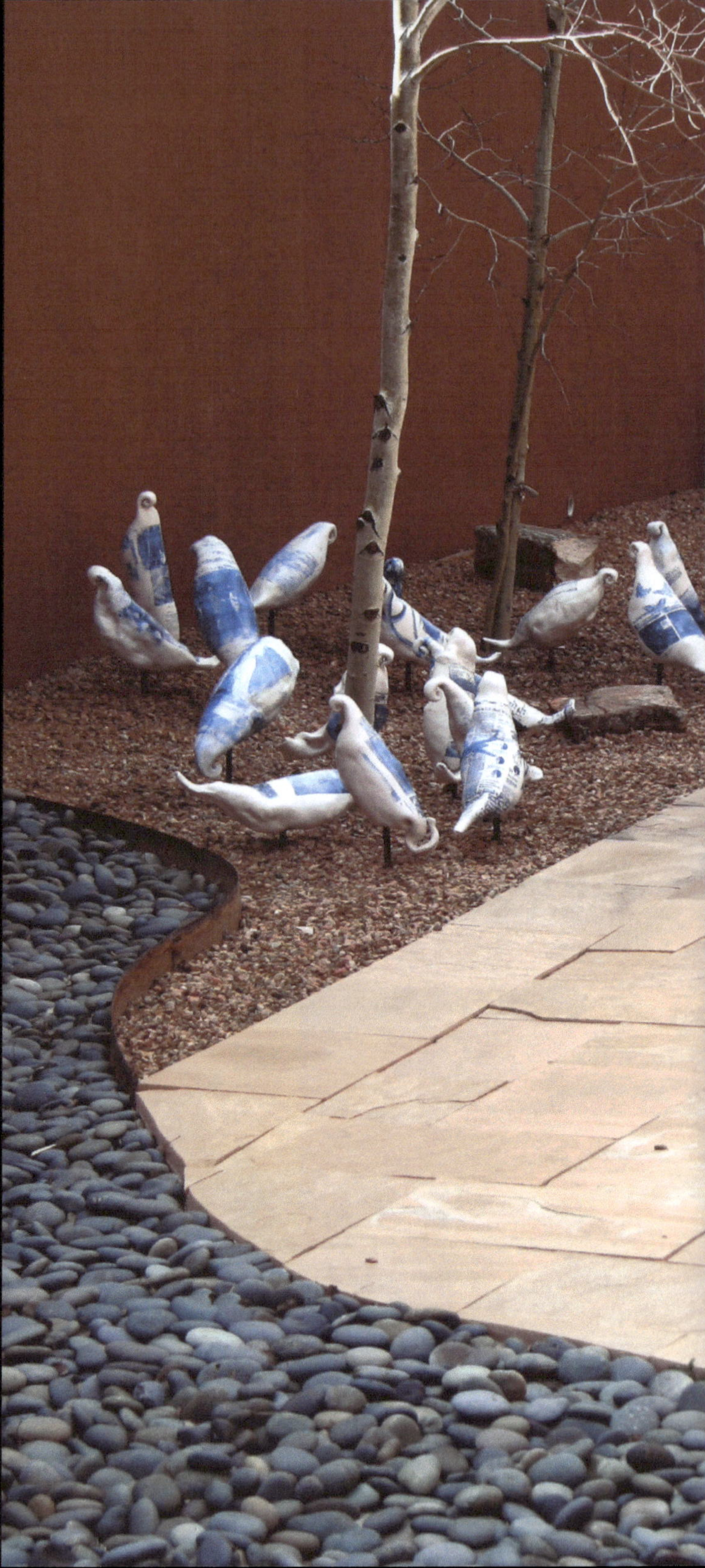

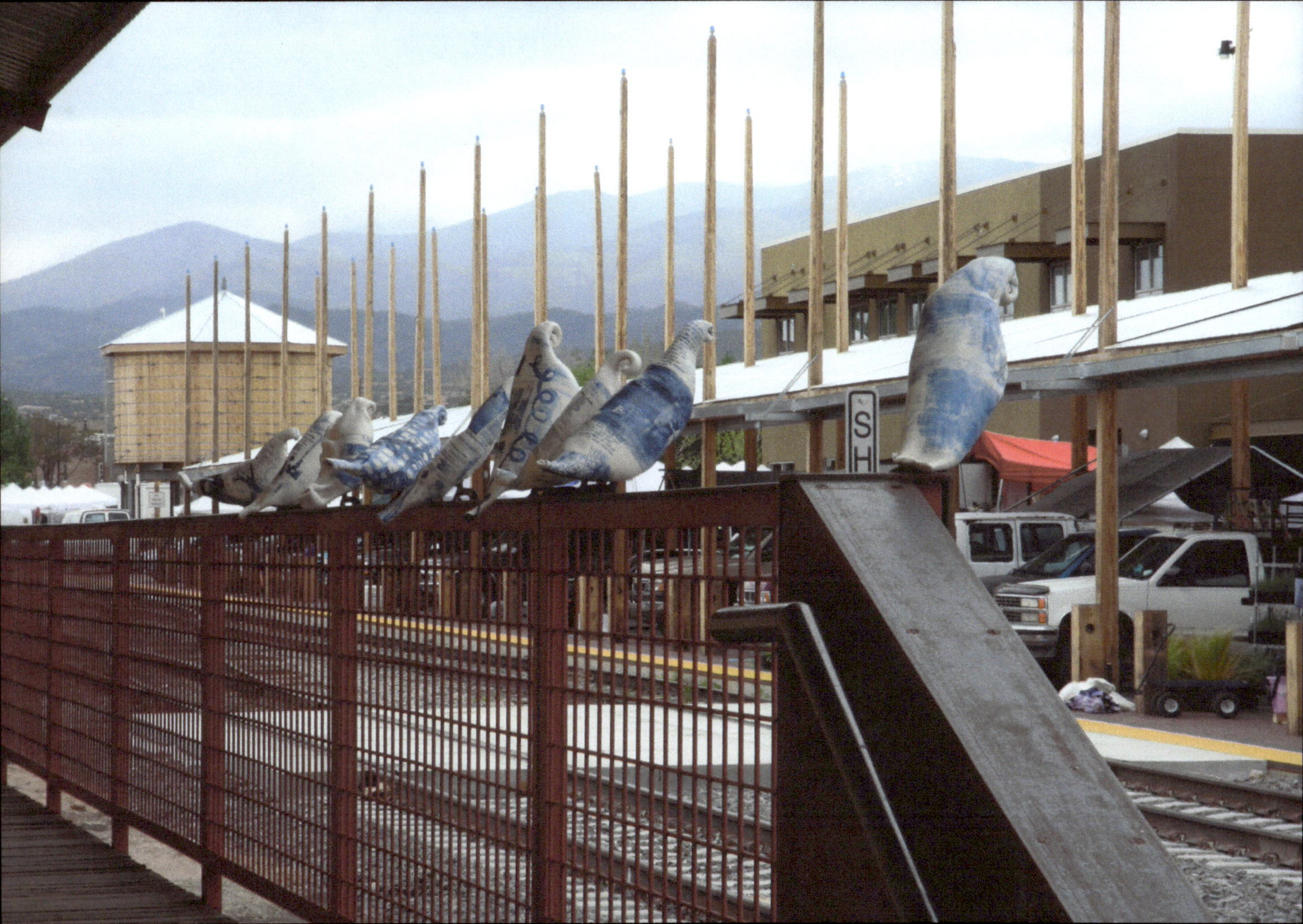

Railyard Performance Center, Santa Fe, NM 5/16/2009.

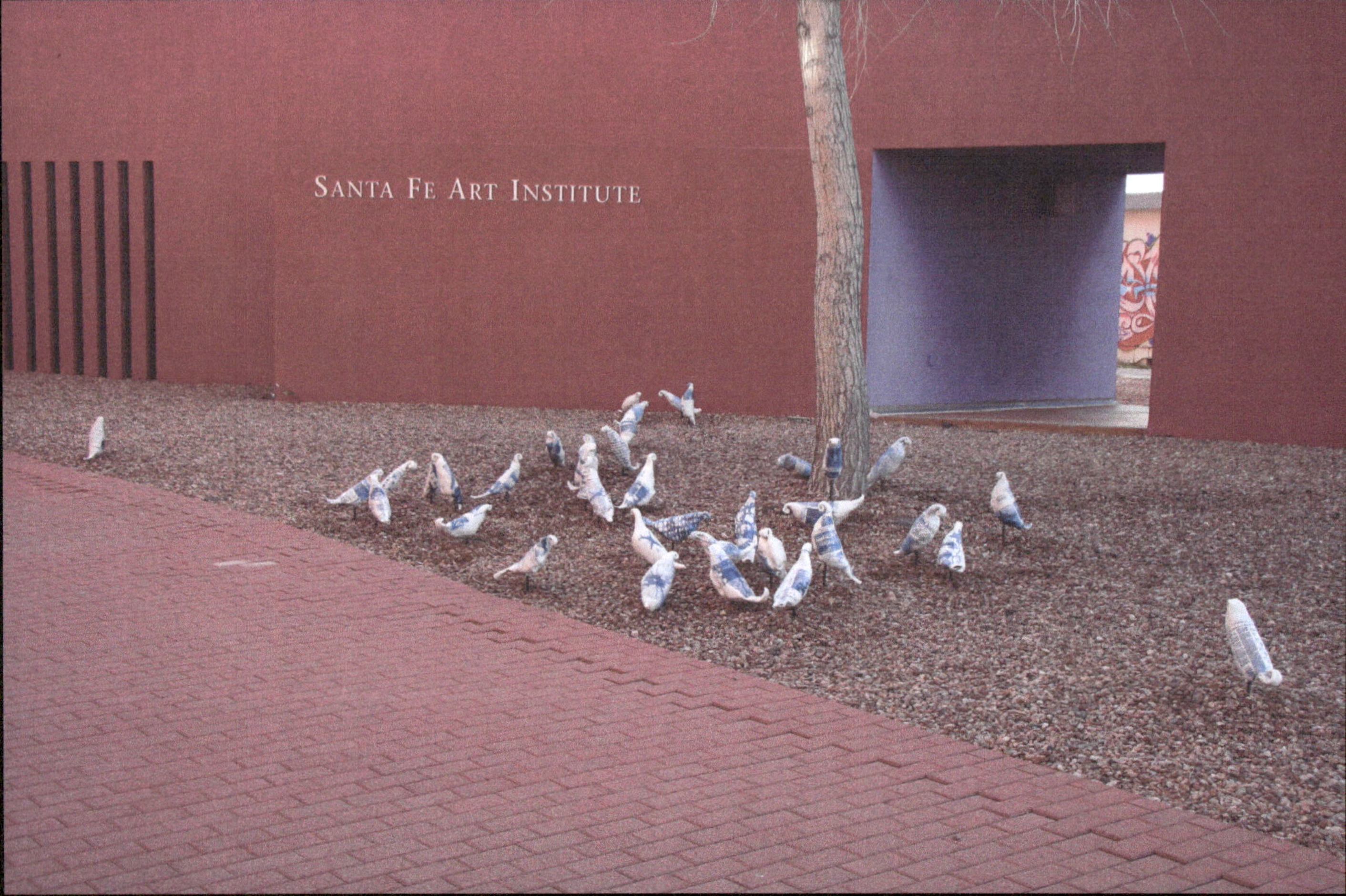

Santa Fe Art Institute, Santa Fe, NM 3/10/2009.

The Santa Fe Art Institute was extremely supportive of this project from the beginning, hosting two landings and a final talk and slide show at the end of the two-year travels.

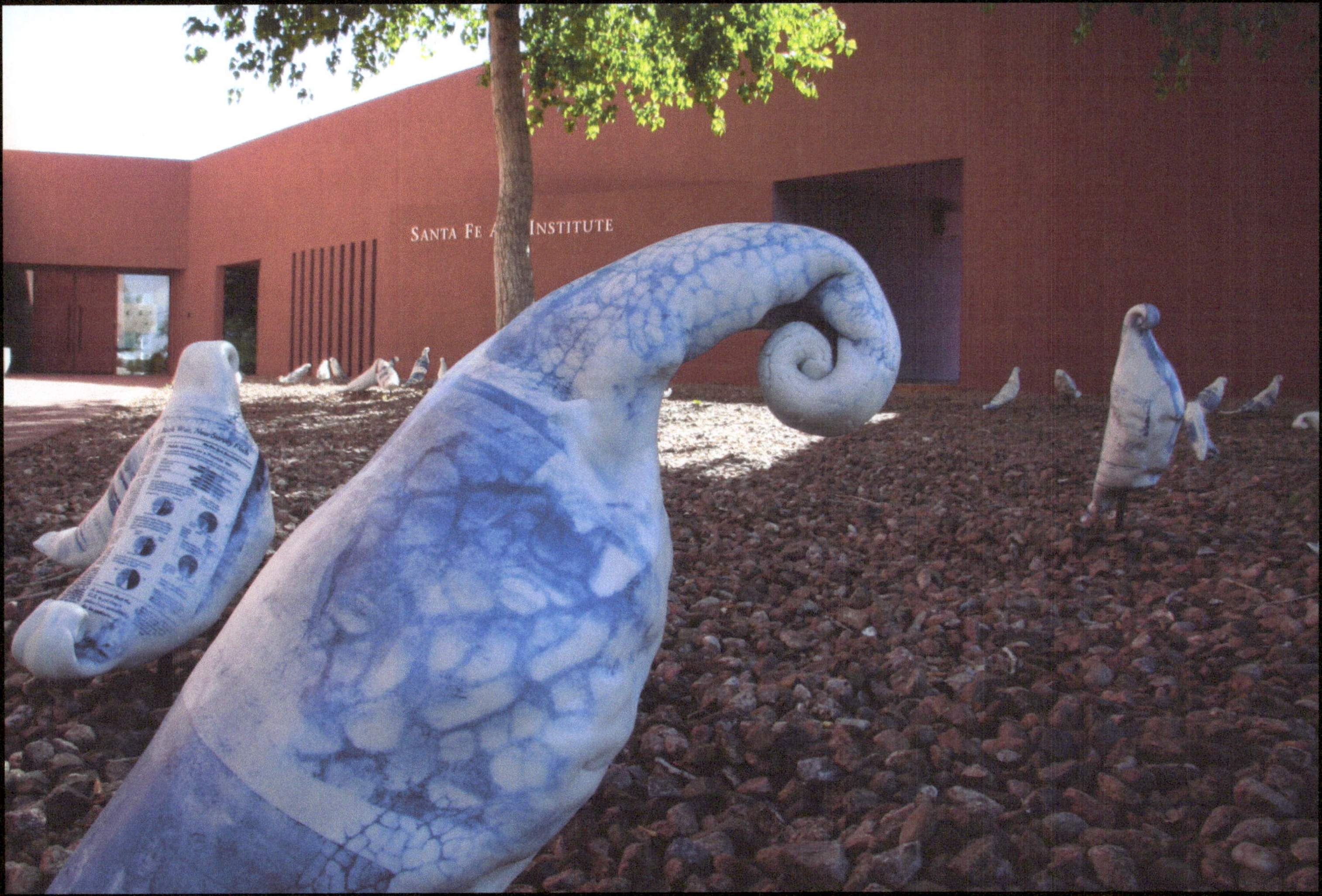

Santa Fe Art Institute, Santa Fe, NM 5/12/2009.

St. Francis statue at City Hall, Santa Fe, NM 3/24/2009.

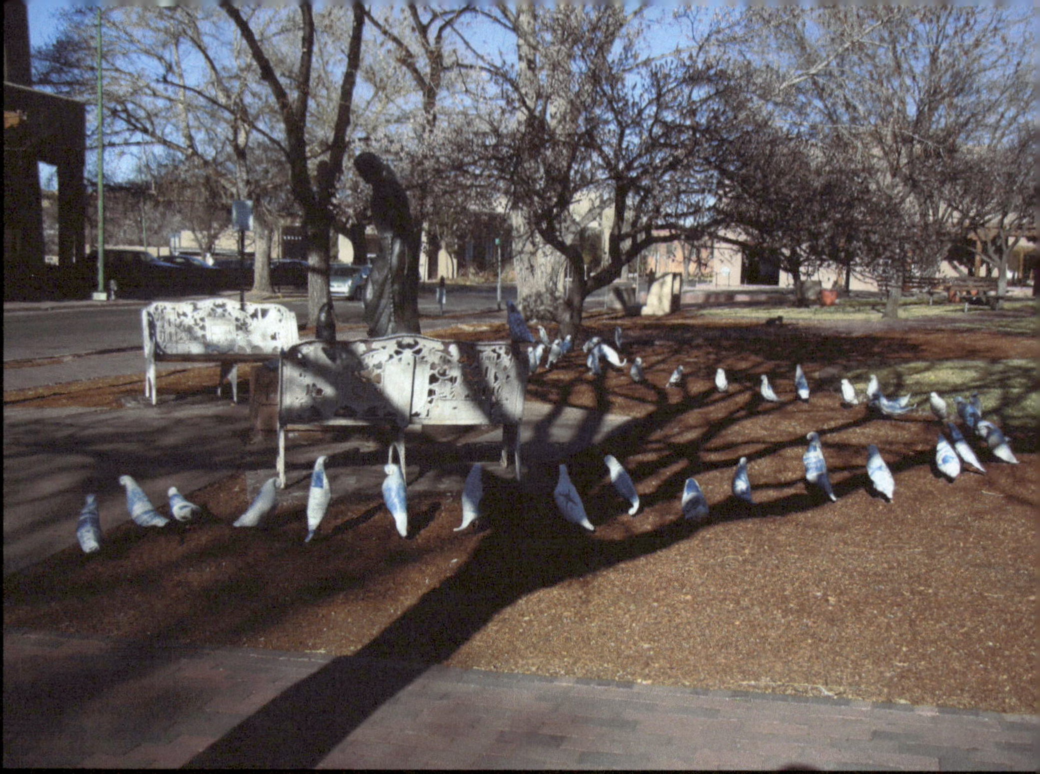

Below: Project assistant, Carol Ware, helping with set-up.

Carol, a fellow artist and also a mother, offered to help with set-up and take-down of the birds. We met early in the morning and again in the evening, juggling schedules and sometimes kids, unwrapping or rewrapping the birds in their protective transporting cloths: old sheets, kids clothes that had become too small, even cloth diapers (clean)!

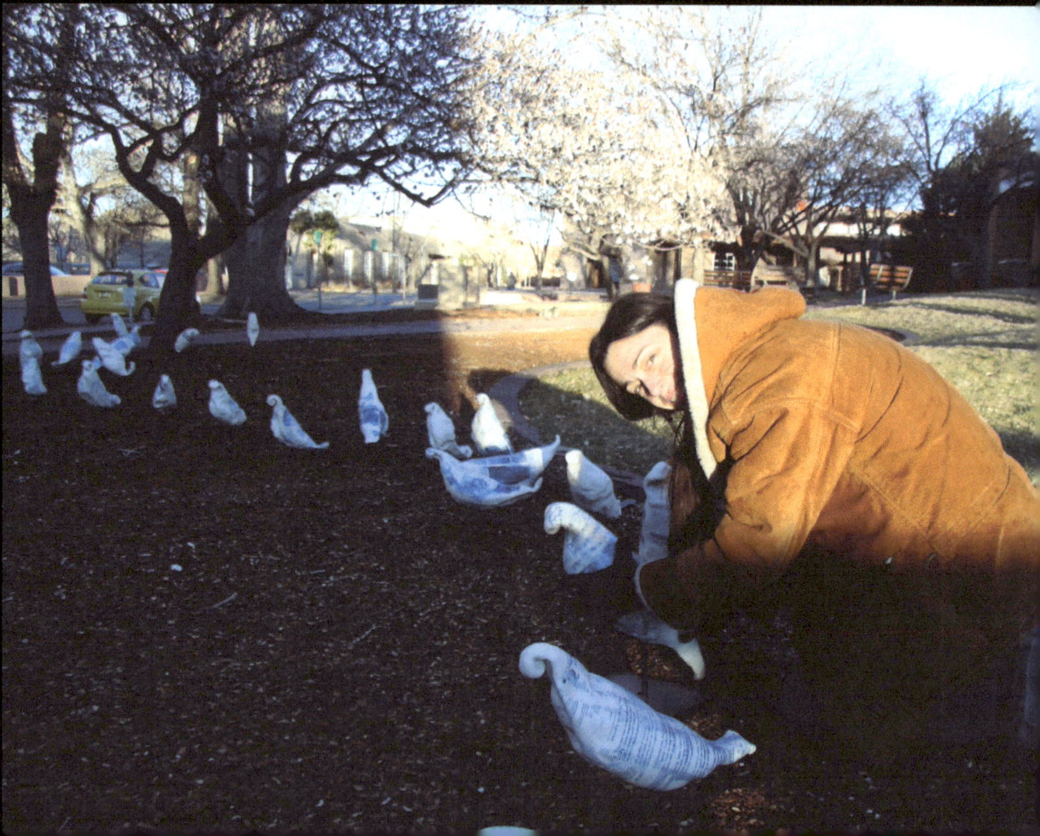

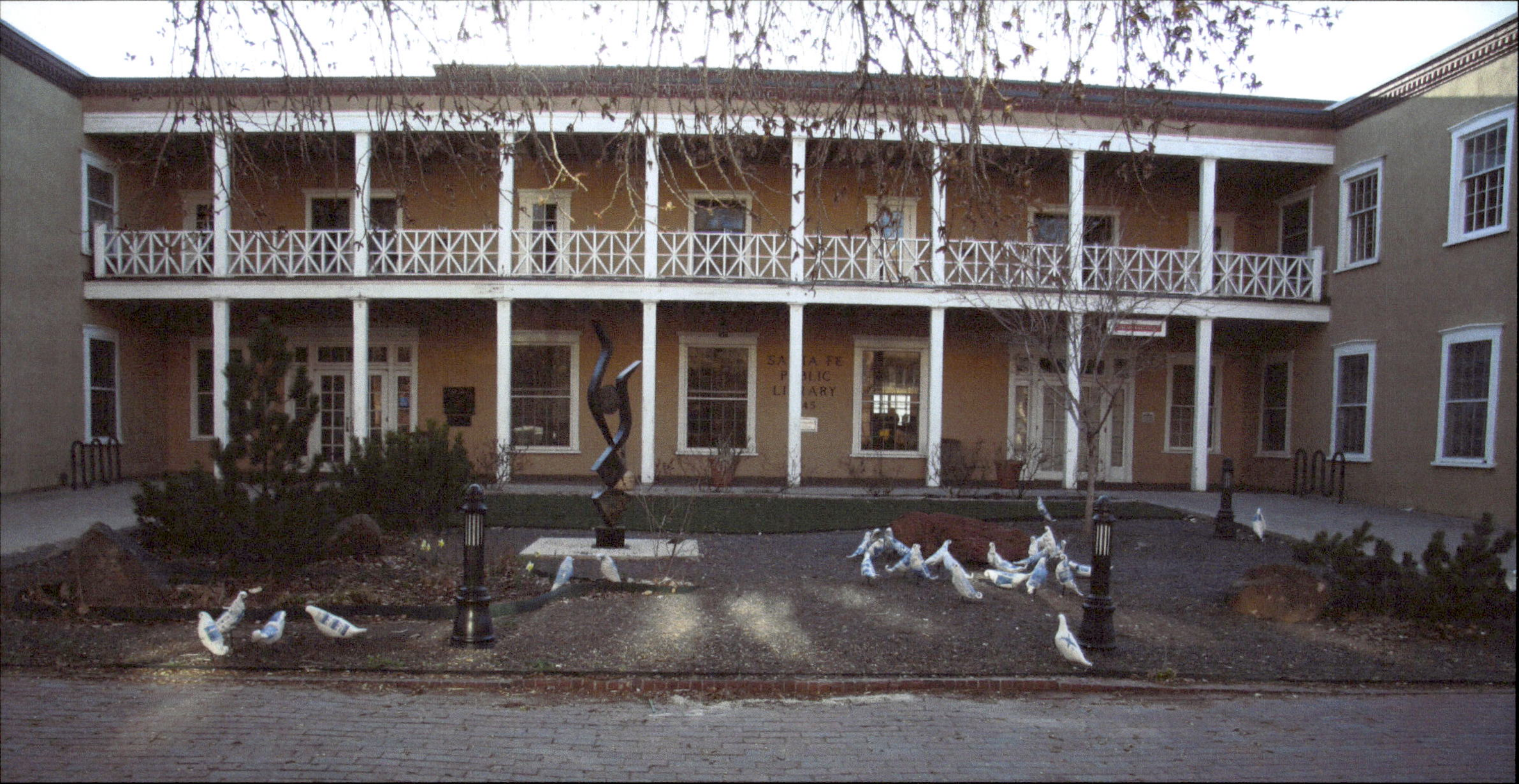

Public Library, main branch, Santa Fe, NM 3/21/2009

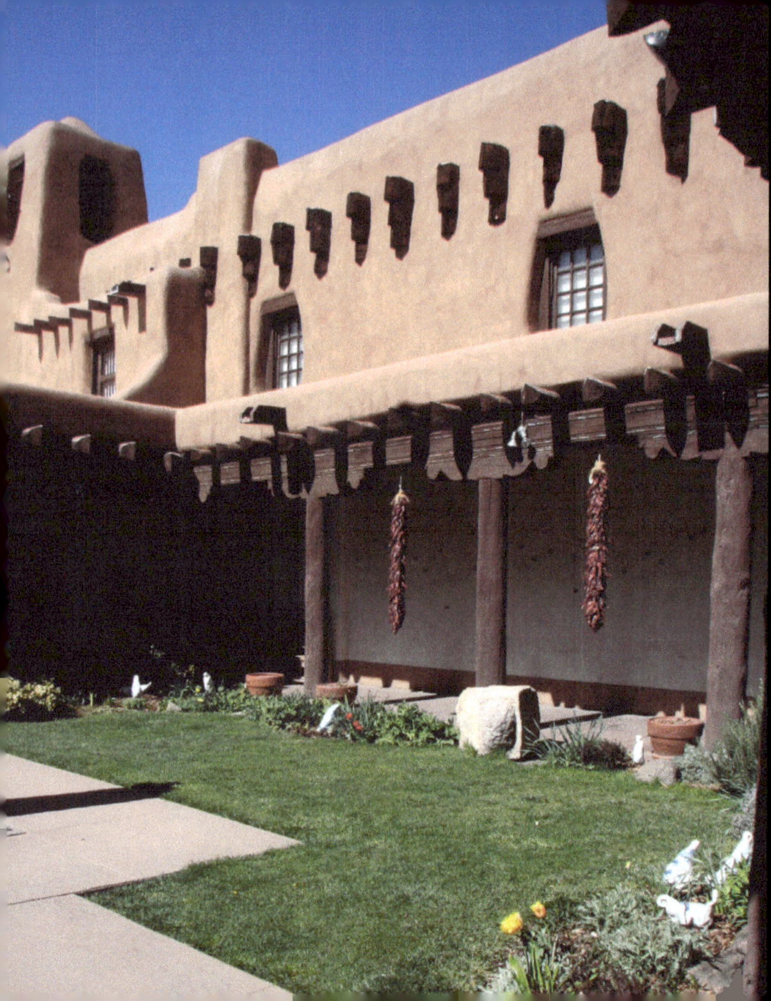
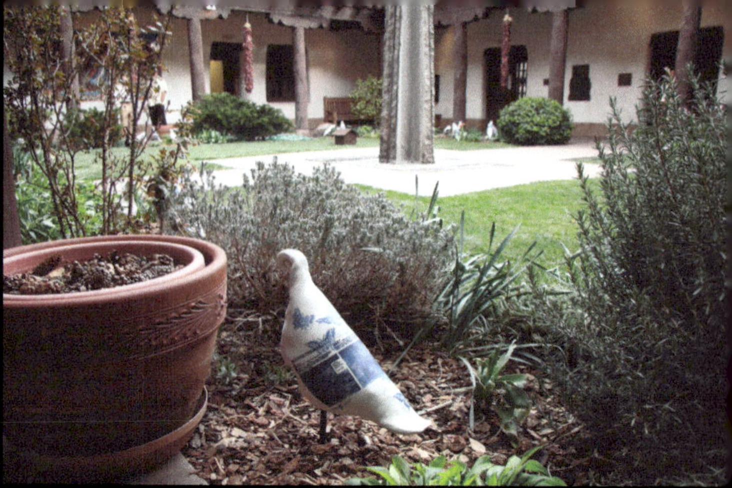
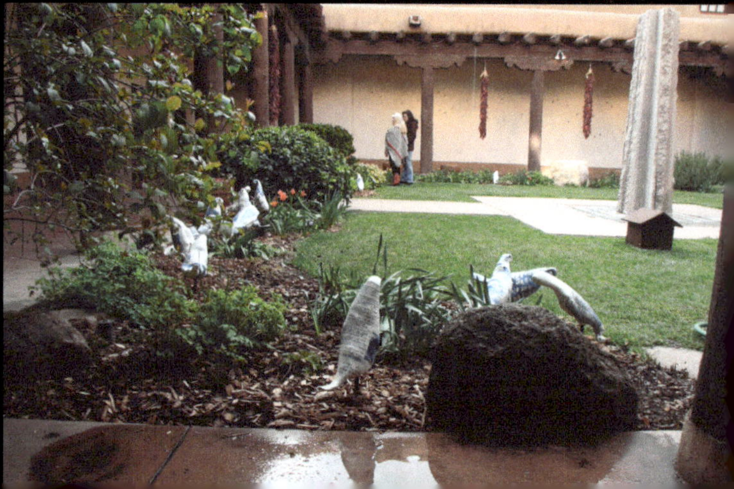

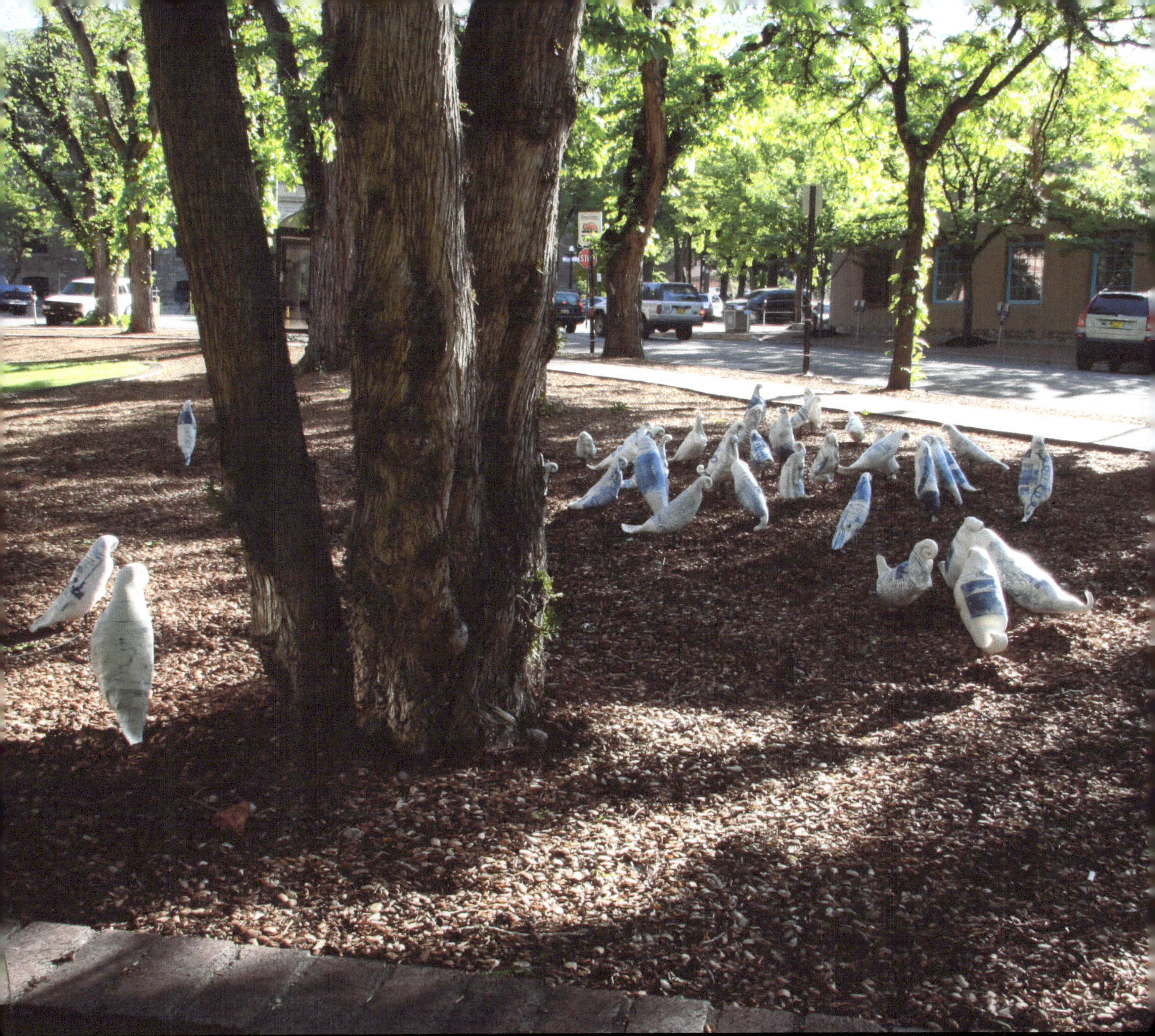

City Hall, main entrance, Santa Fe, NM 5/19/2009

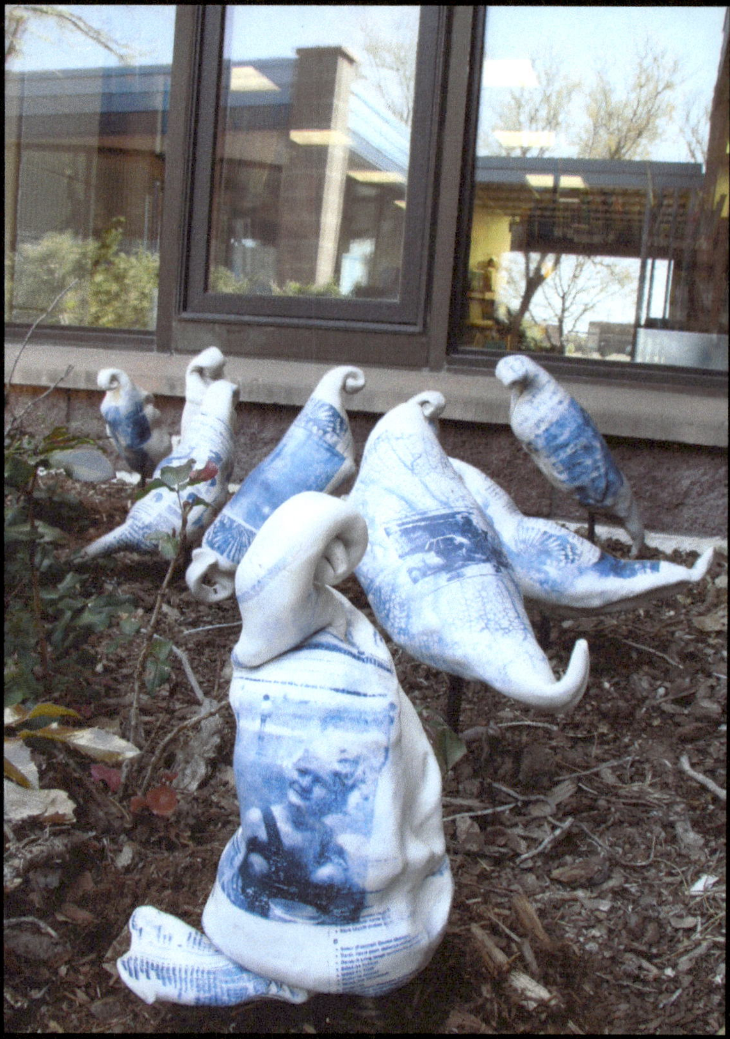

Public Library, LaFarge branch,
Santa Fe, NM 4/30/2009.

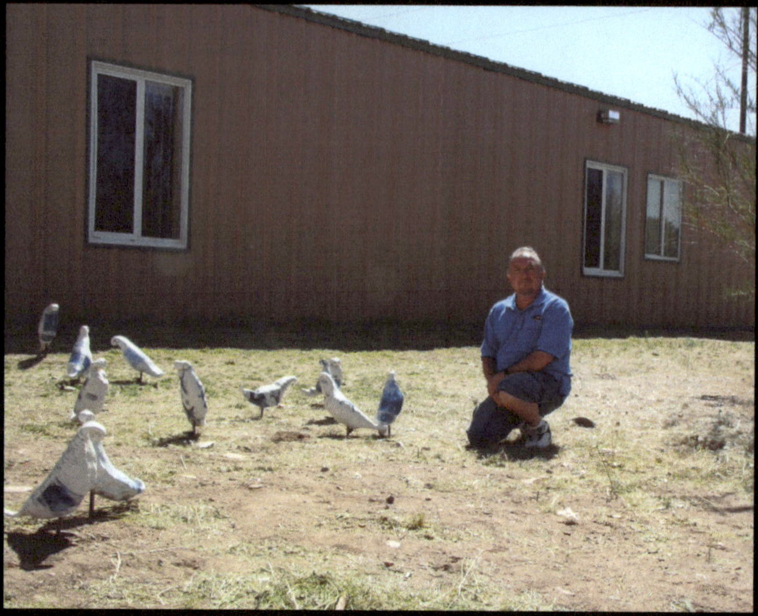

Santa Fe Trails Transit Center,
Santa Fe, NM 5/14/2009.

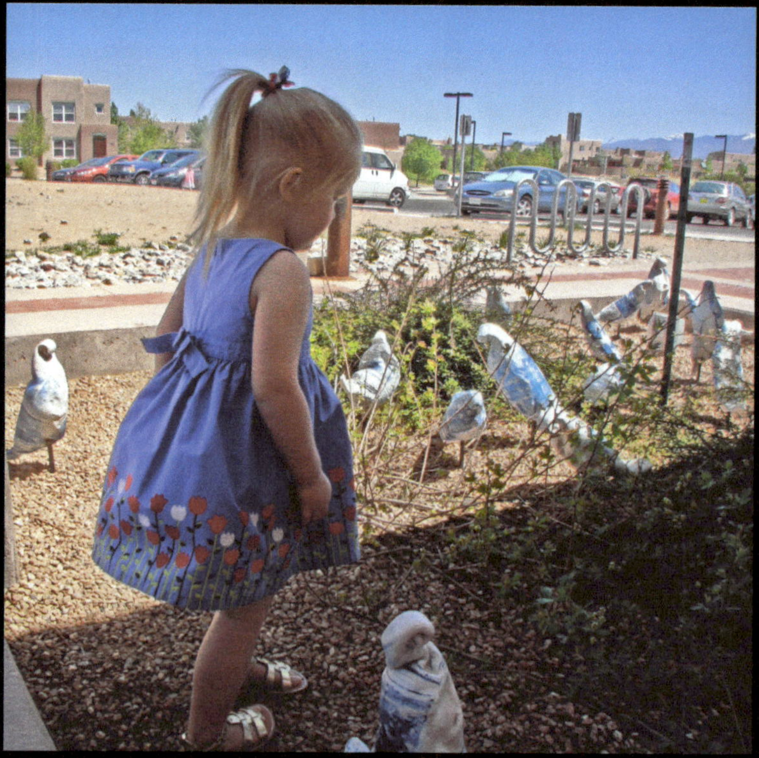

Public Library, Southside branch,
Santa Fe, NM 5/6/2009.

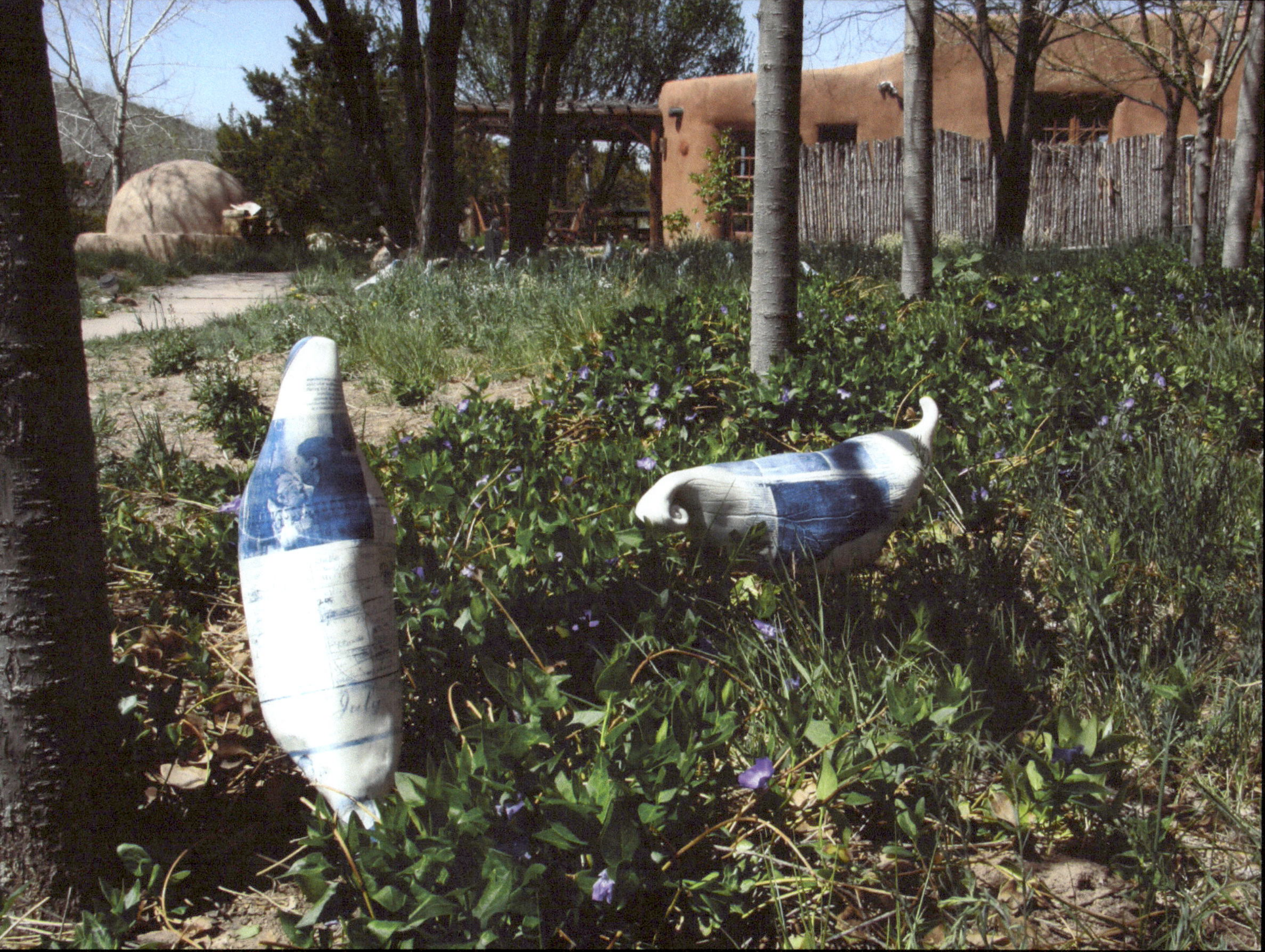

Upaya Zen Center, Santa Fe, NM 4/29/2009.

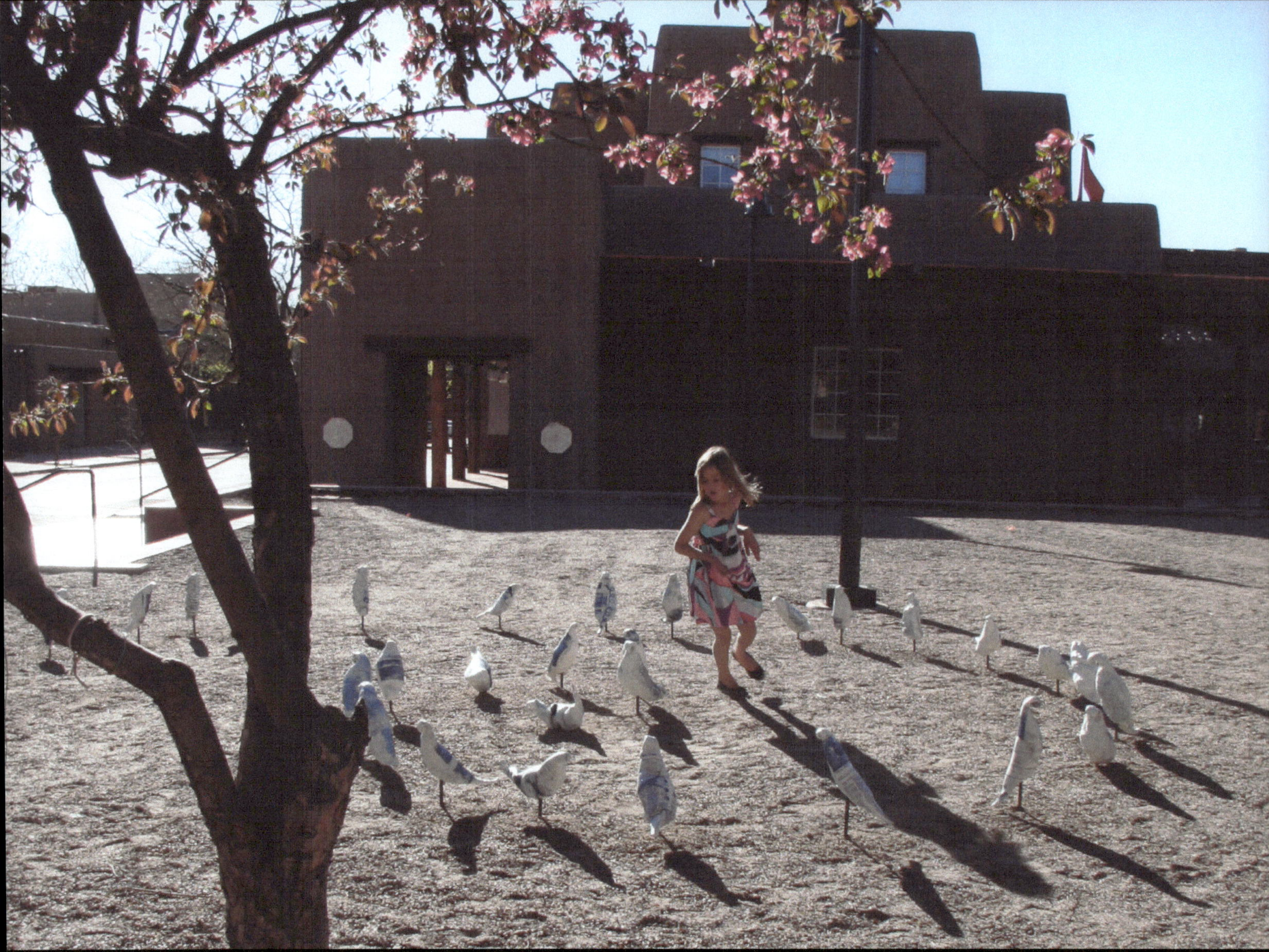

Santa Fe Convention Center, Santa Fe, NM 4/21/2009.

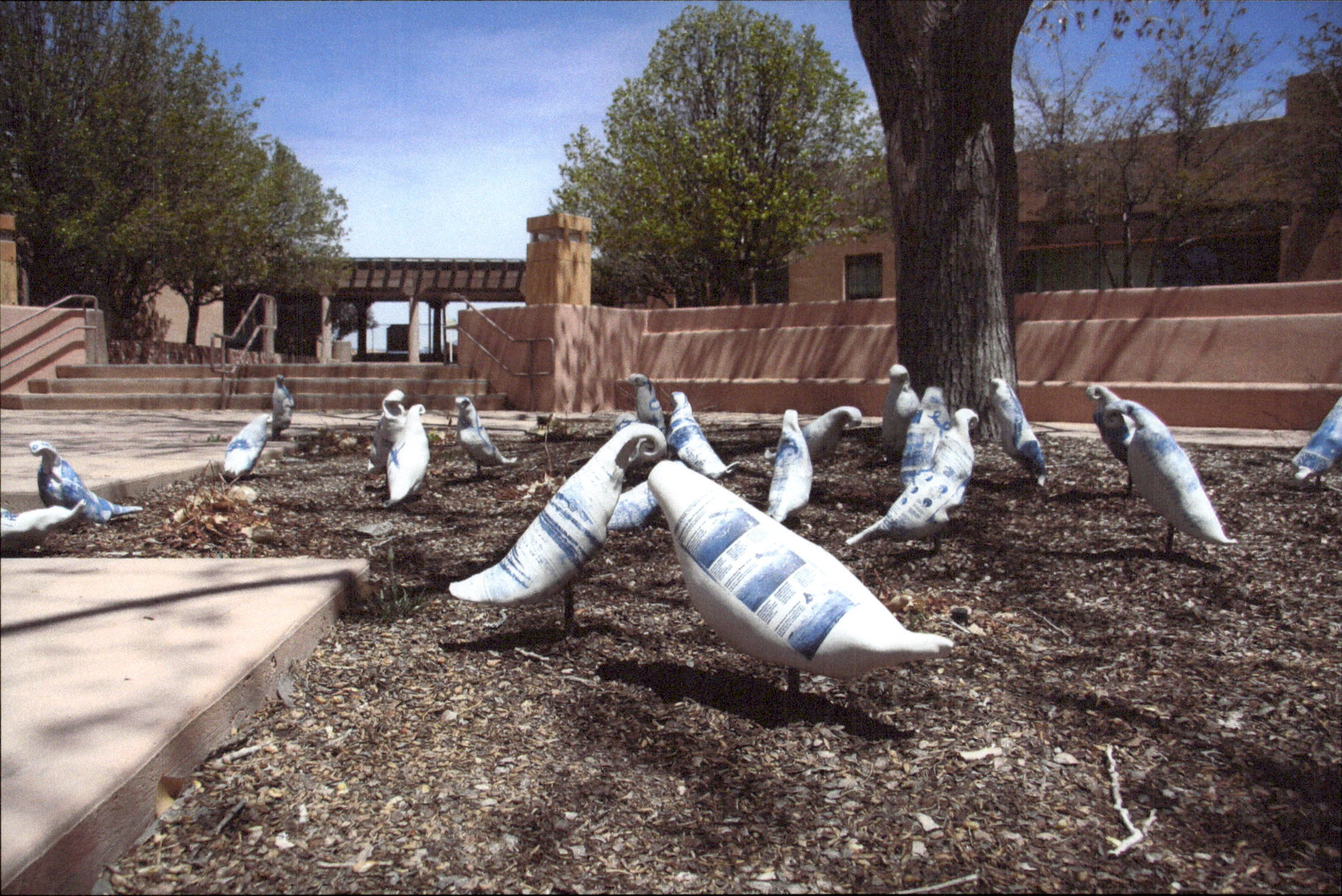

Santa Fe Community College, Santa Fe, NM 4/24/2009.

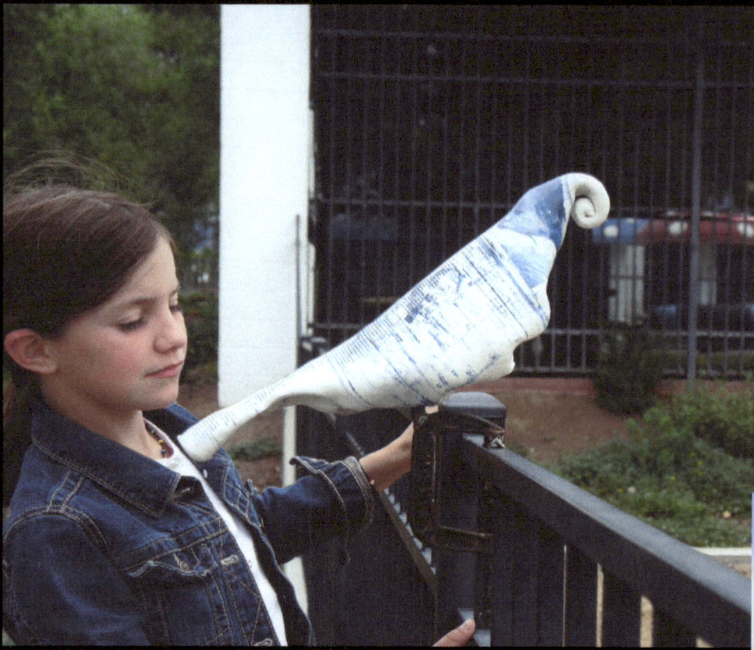

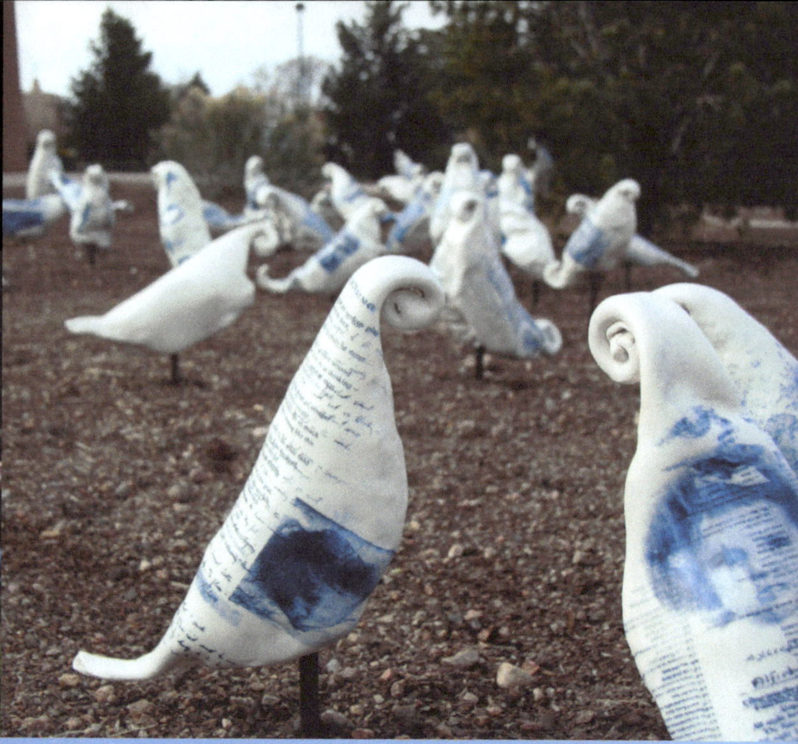

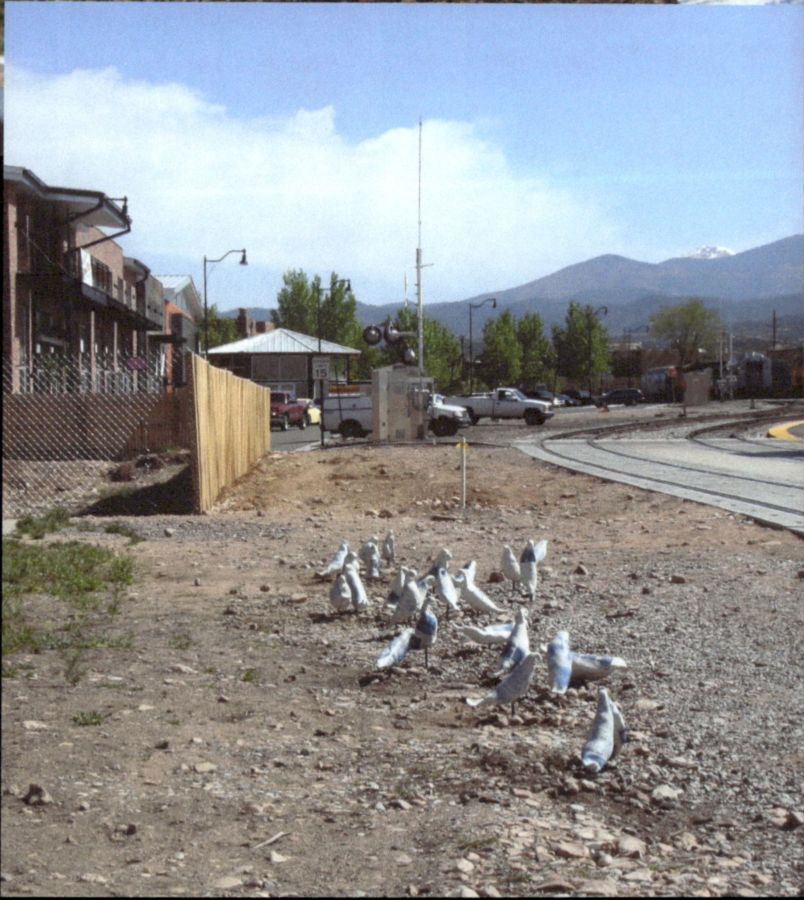

Above: Bicentennial Park, Santa Fe, NM 5/23/2009.
Top right: Santa Fe Prep, Santa Fe, NM 4/14/2009.
Bottom Right: Santa Fe Clay, Santa Fe, NM 5/5/2009.

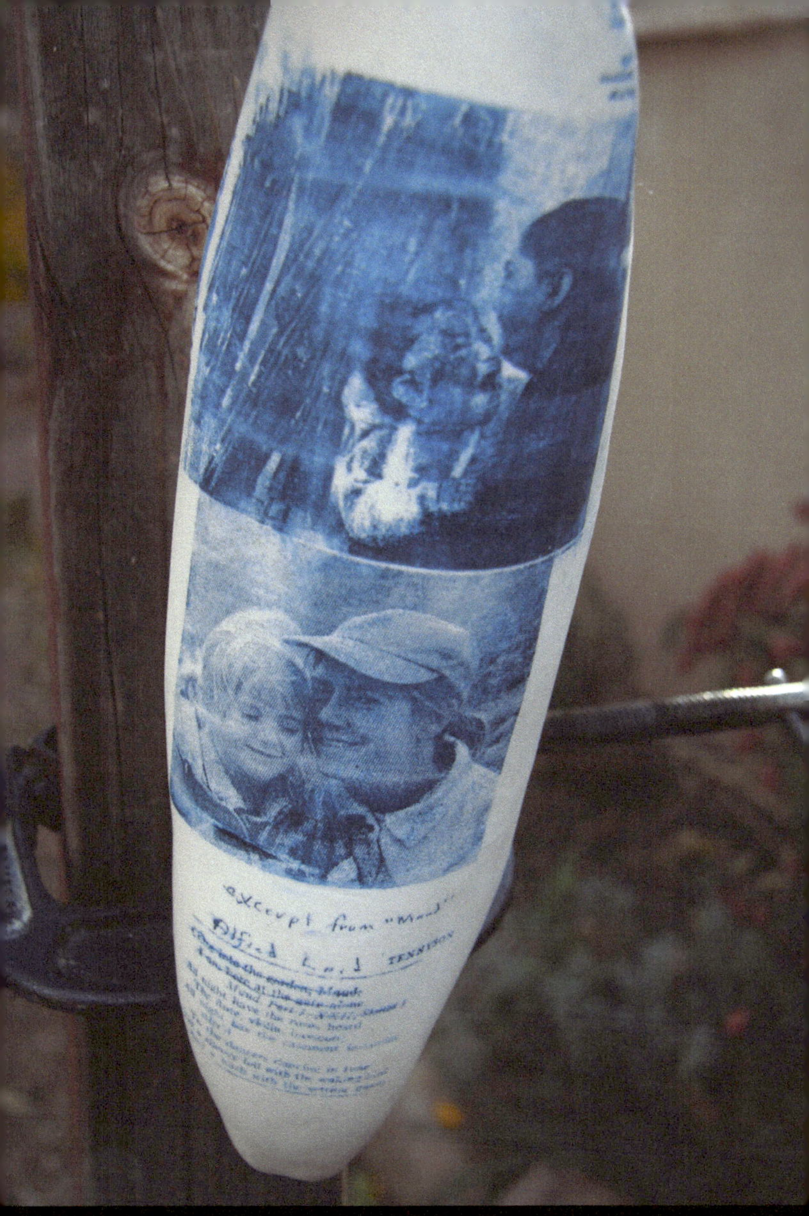

The Teahouse, Santa Fe, NM 11/8/2008

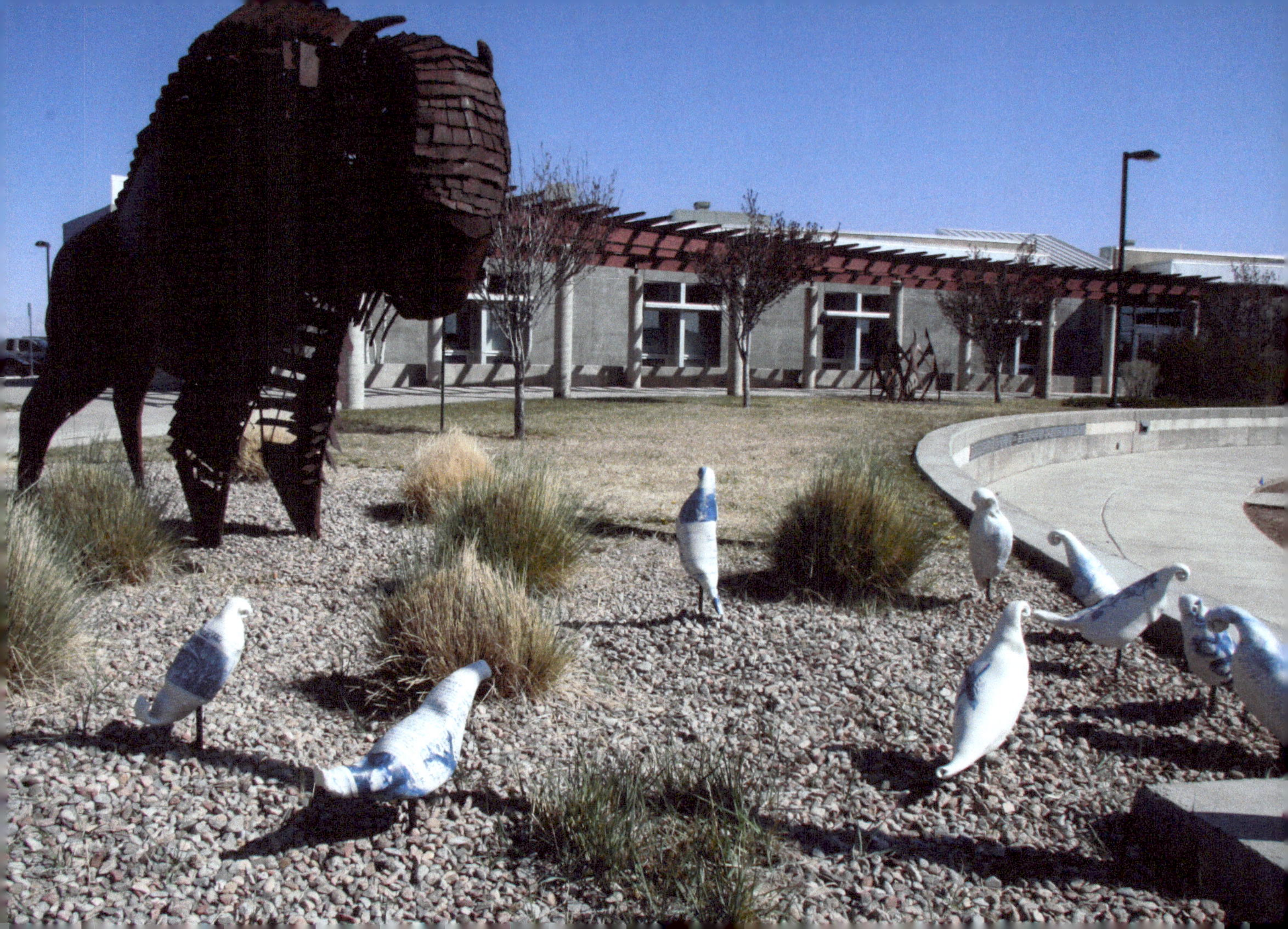

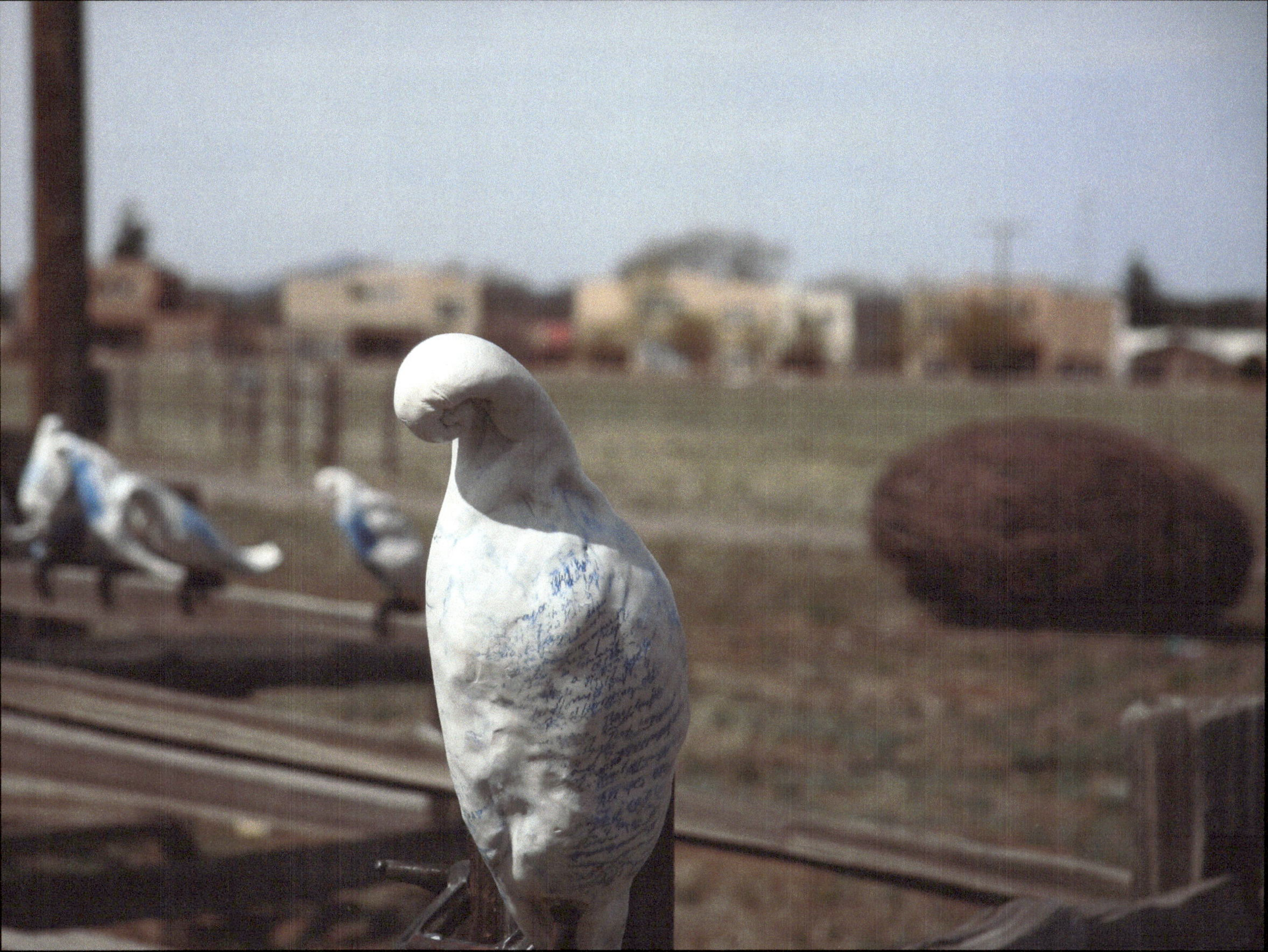

Frenchy's Field, Santa Fe, NM 3/29/2009.

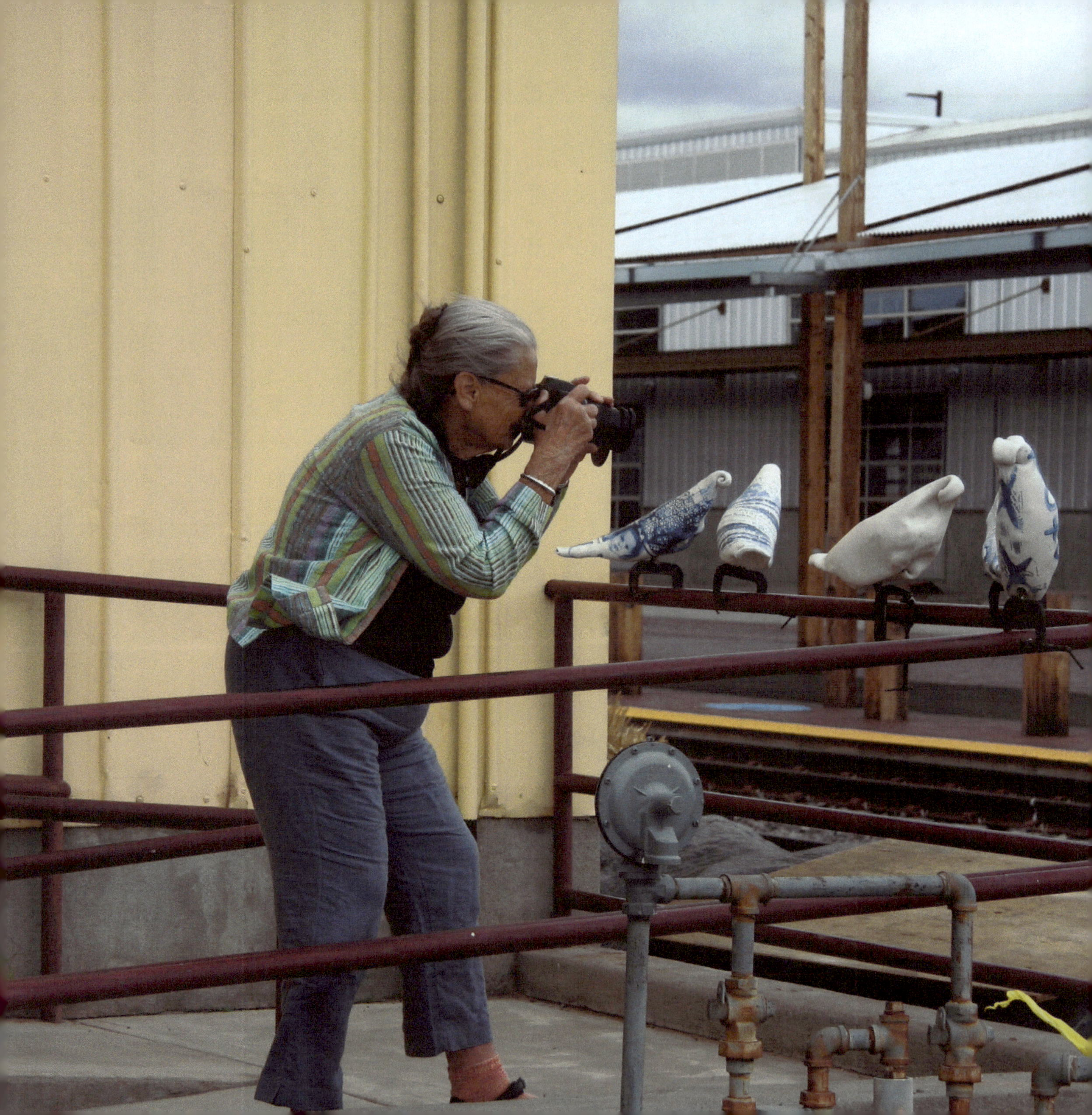

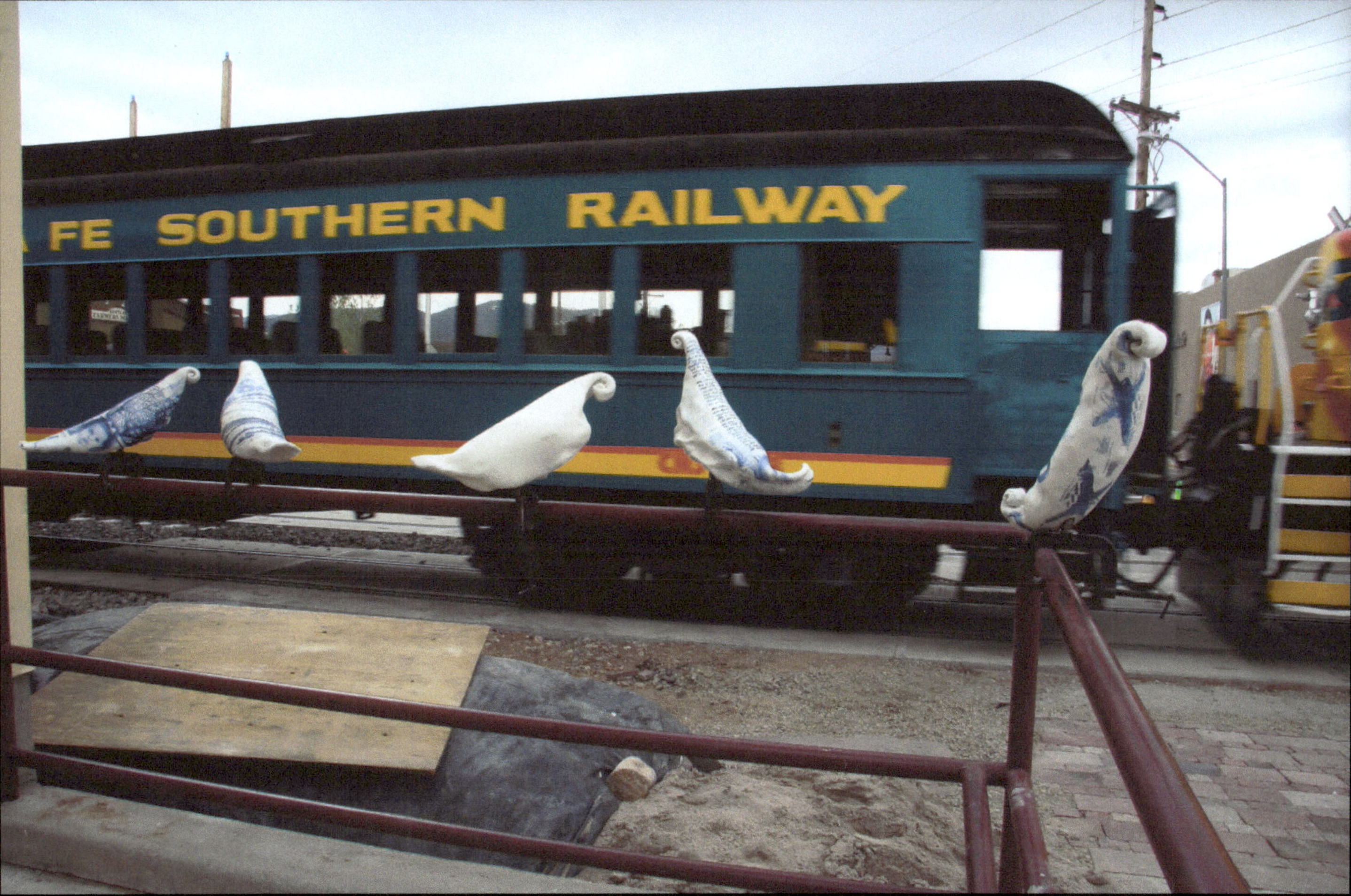

Above and facing page: Box Gallery, Santa Fe, NM 5/16/2009.

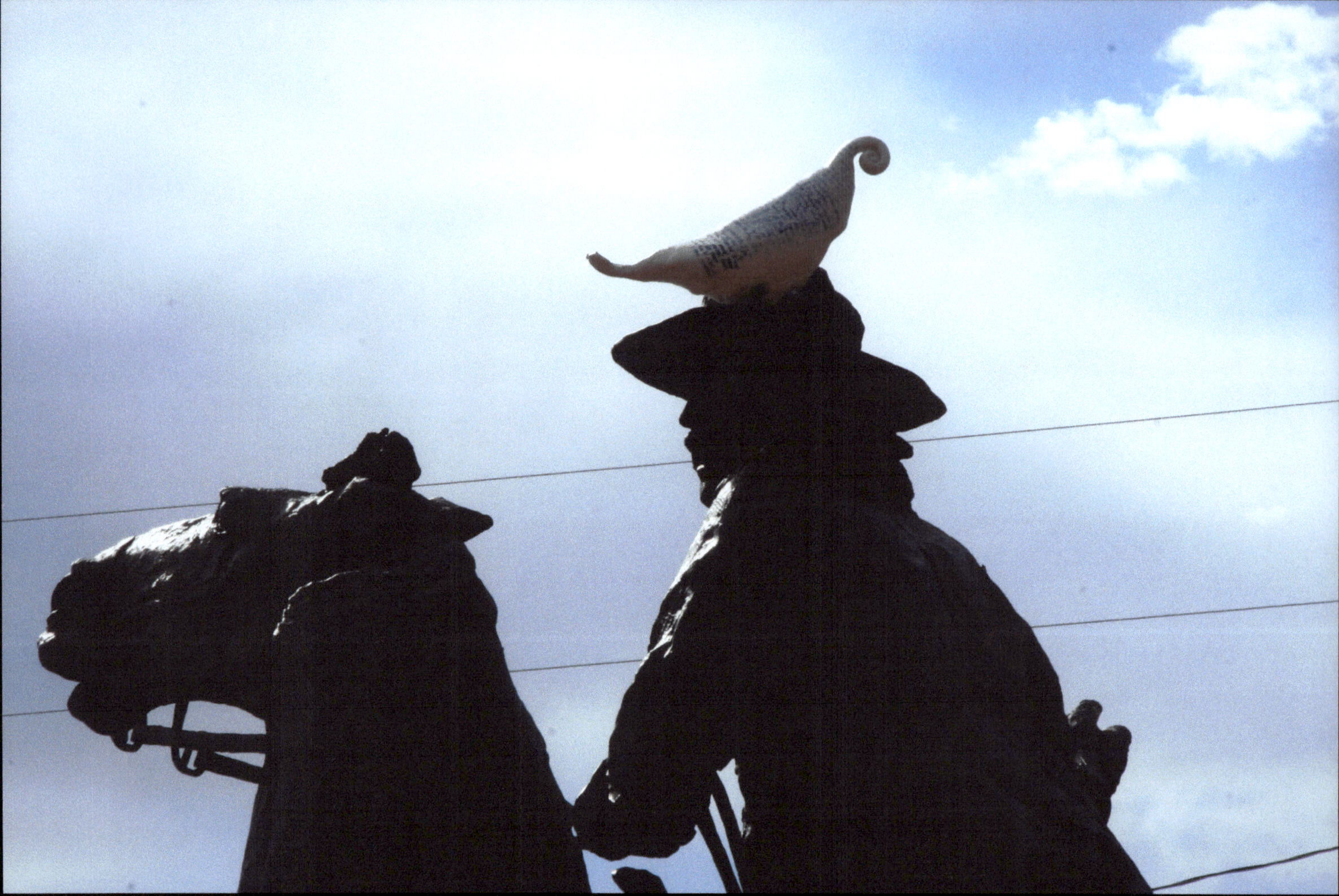

Journey's End, Museum Hill, Santa Fe, NM 5/24/2009.

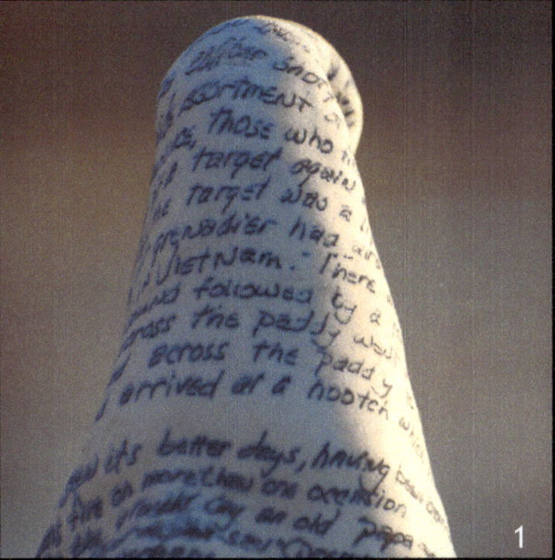
those who
target
target was a
grenadier had
Vietnam." There
followed by a
across the paddy
across the paddy
arrived at a hootch
its better days, having been
fire on more than one occasion
1

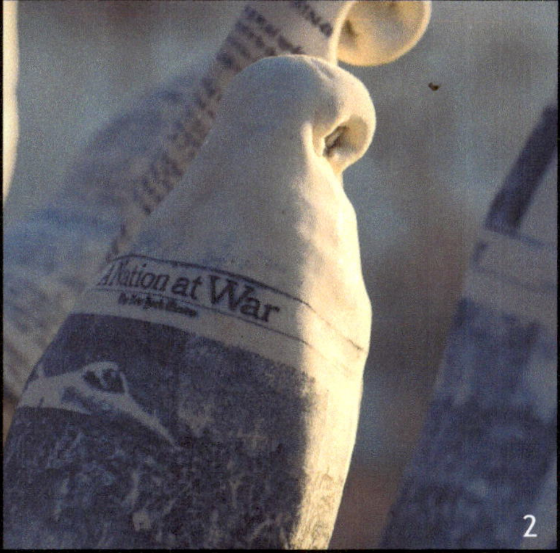
A Nation at War
2

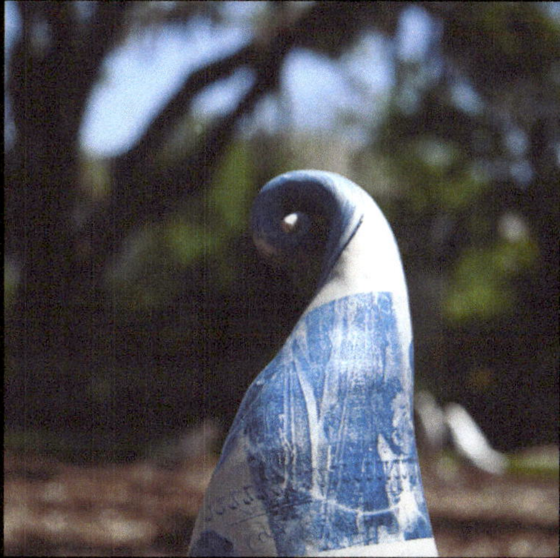

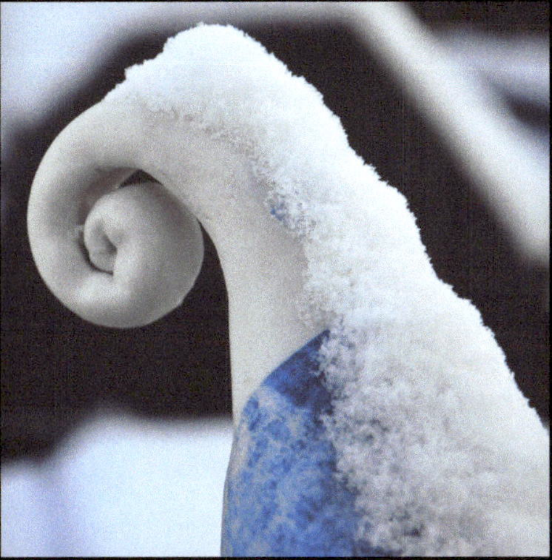

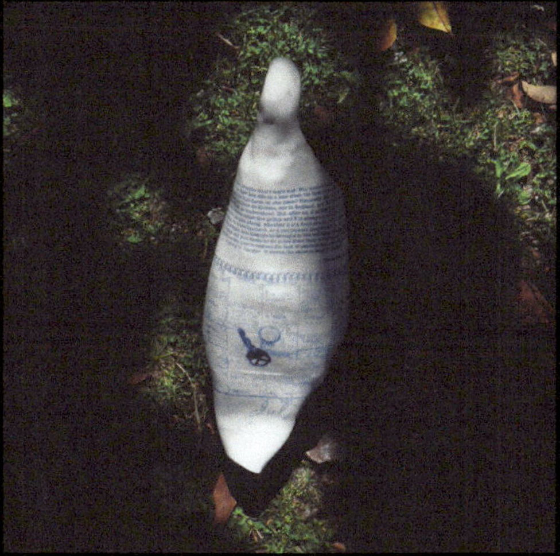

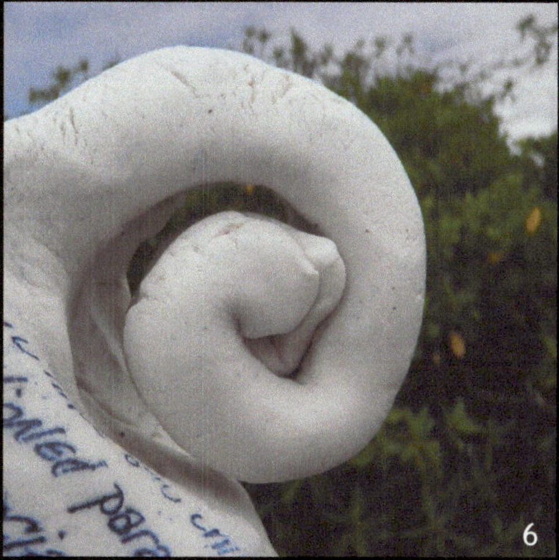
6

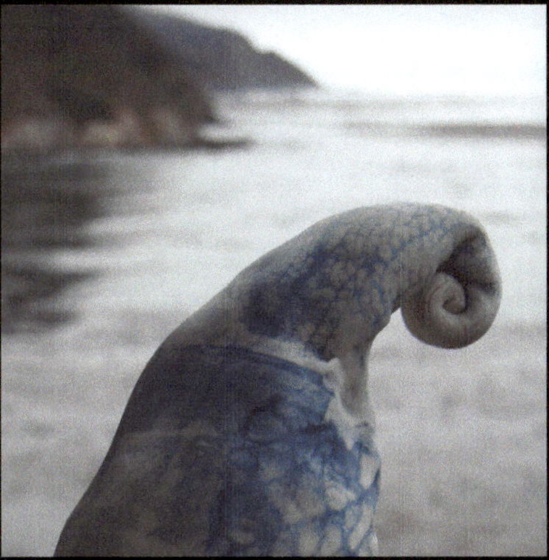

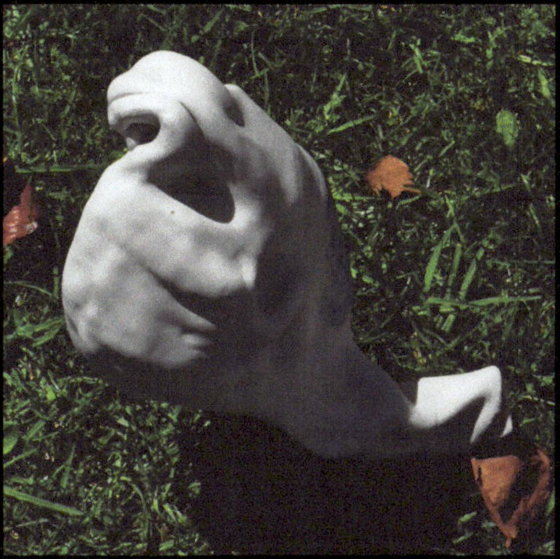

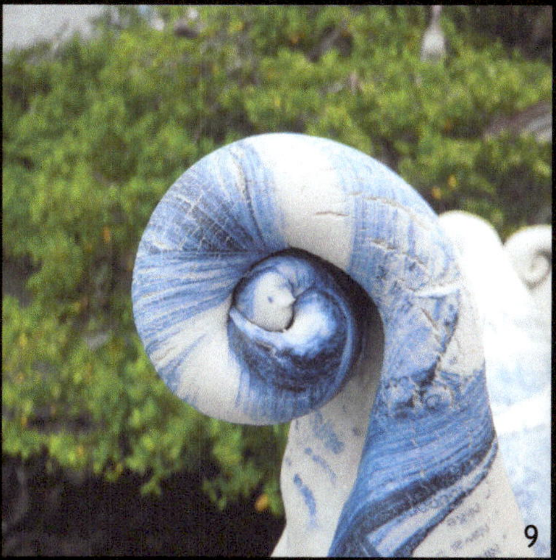
9

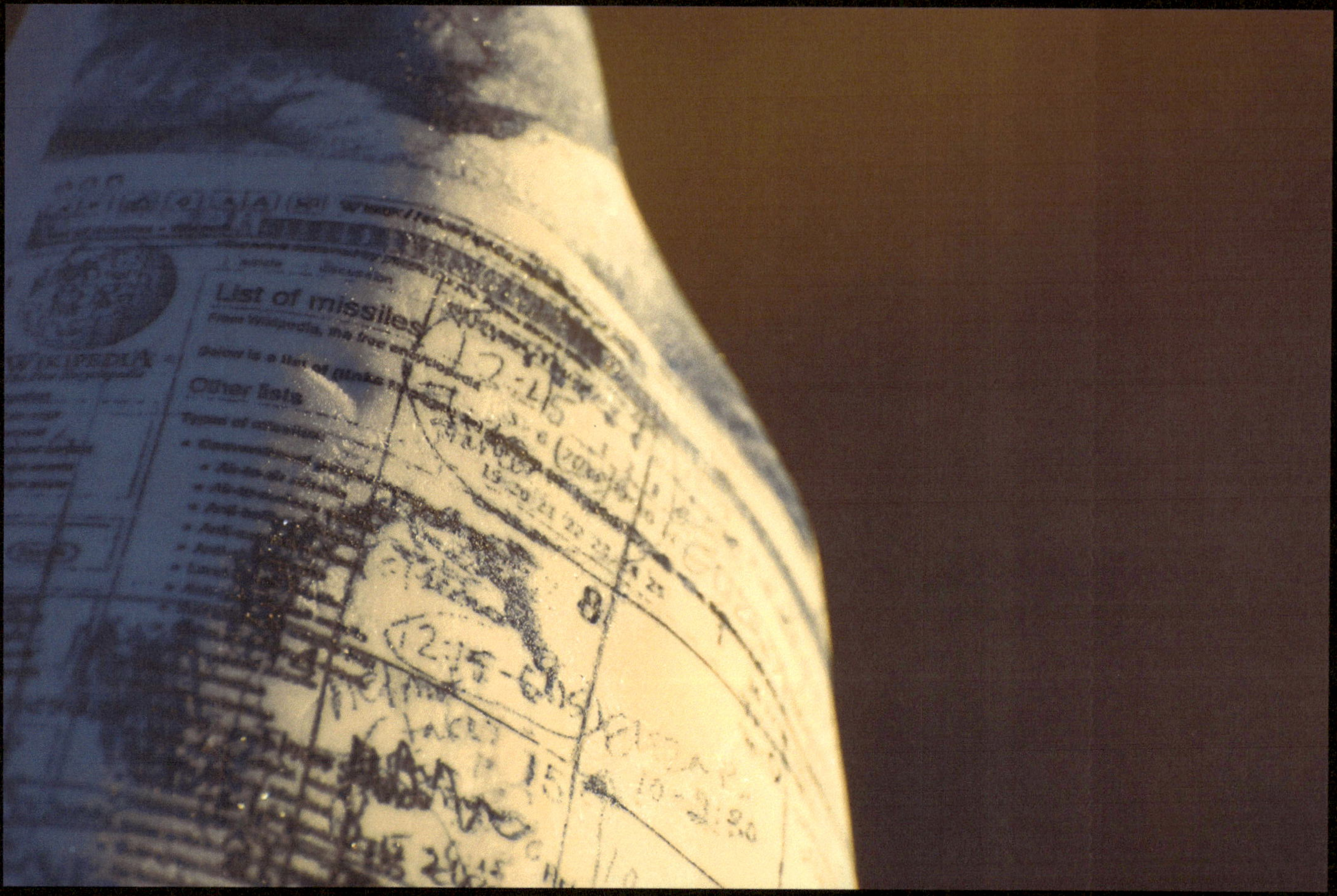
List of missiles
Other lists

Dawn

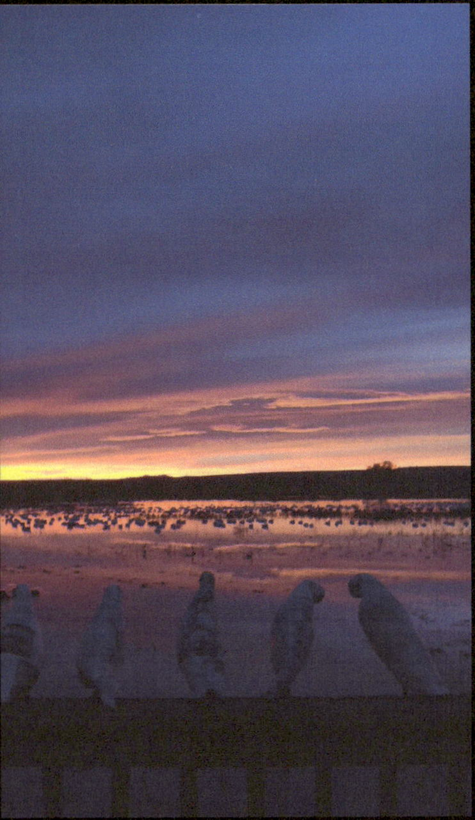

Midday

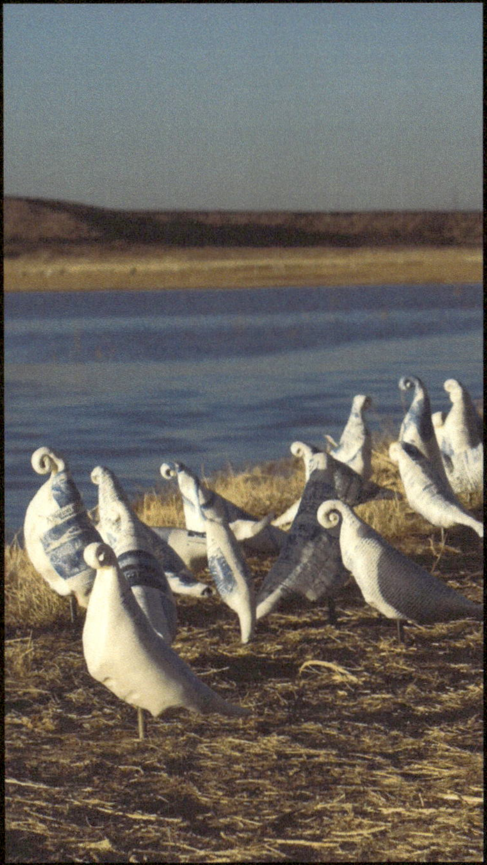

Dusk

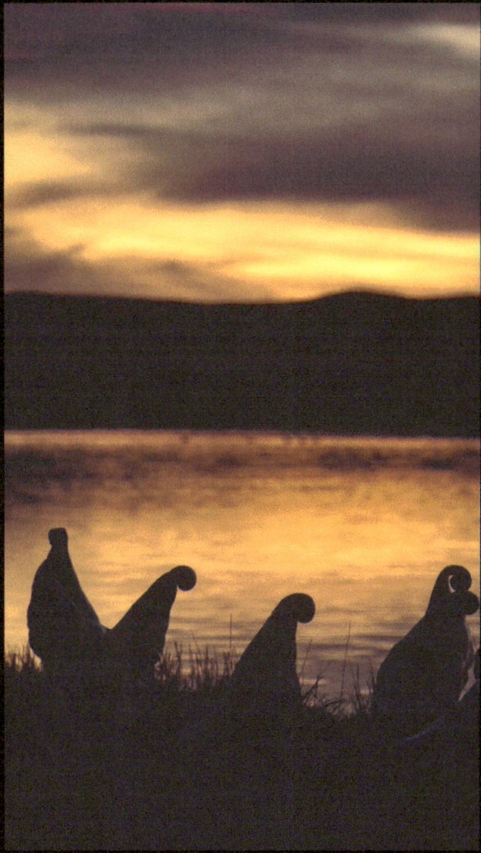

This and facing page: Bosque del Apache Bird Refuge, San Antonio, NM 12/6/2009. Photos: Maria De Las Casas.

For the documentary being made about the bird project, we wanted to also film some real birds. Coming to the Bosque Bird Refuge, and having the porcelain birds near their warm counterparts, was a beautiful experience. On a December morning at 4am, we were out with the dawn frost, to be ready for the “mass ascension” when thousands of Sandhill Cranes and Snow Geese lift off from the water simultaneously.

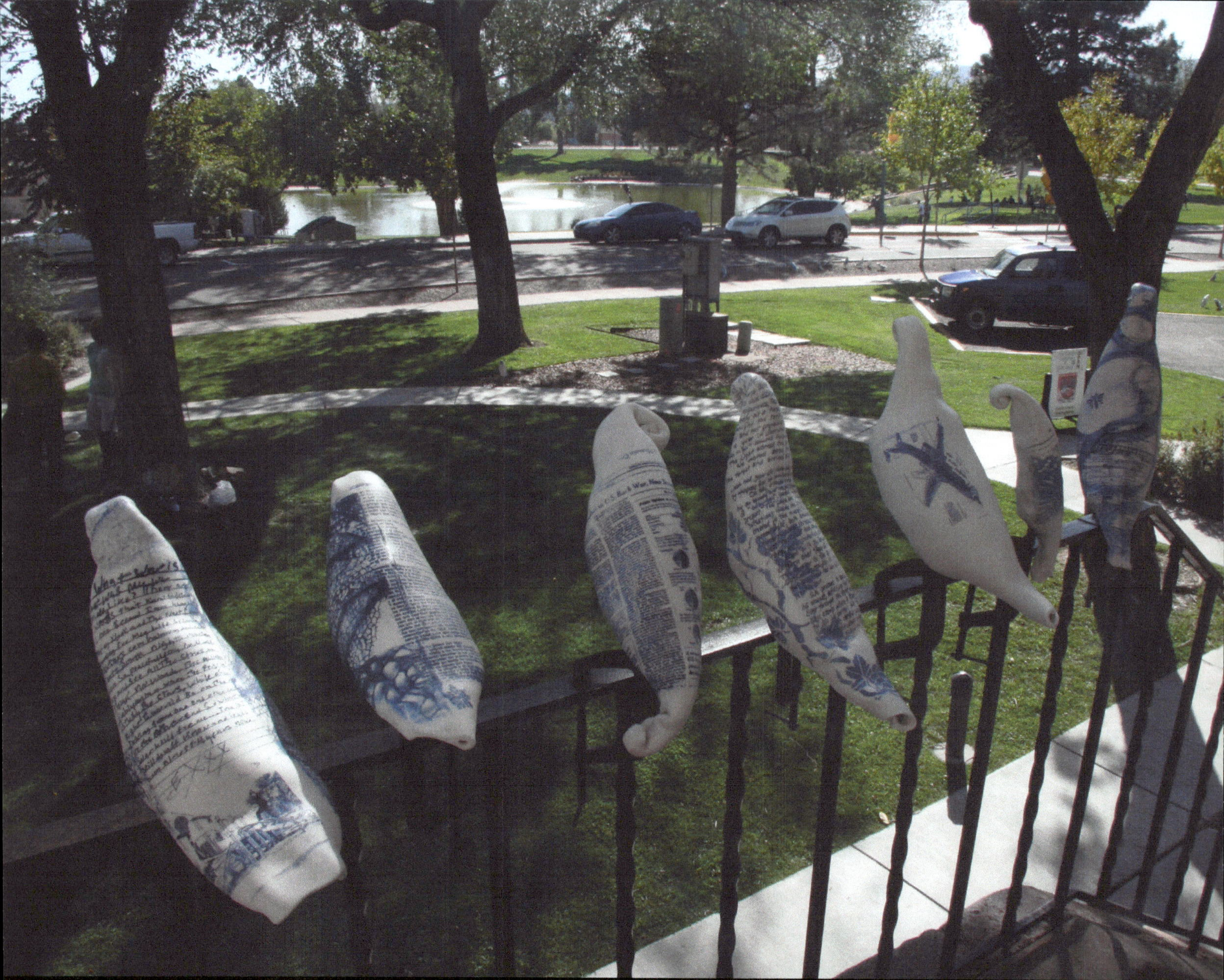

Above: Fuller Lodge, Los Alamos, NM 9/26/2009.
Facing page: Ashley Pond, Los Alamos, NM 9/27/2009.

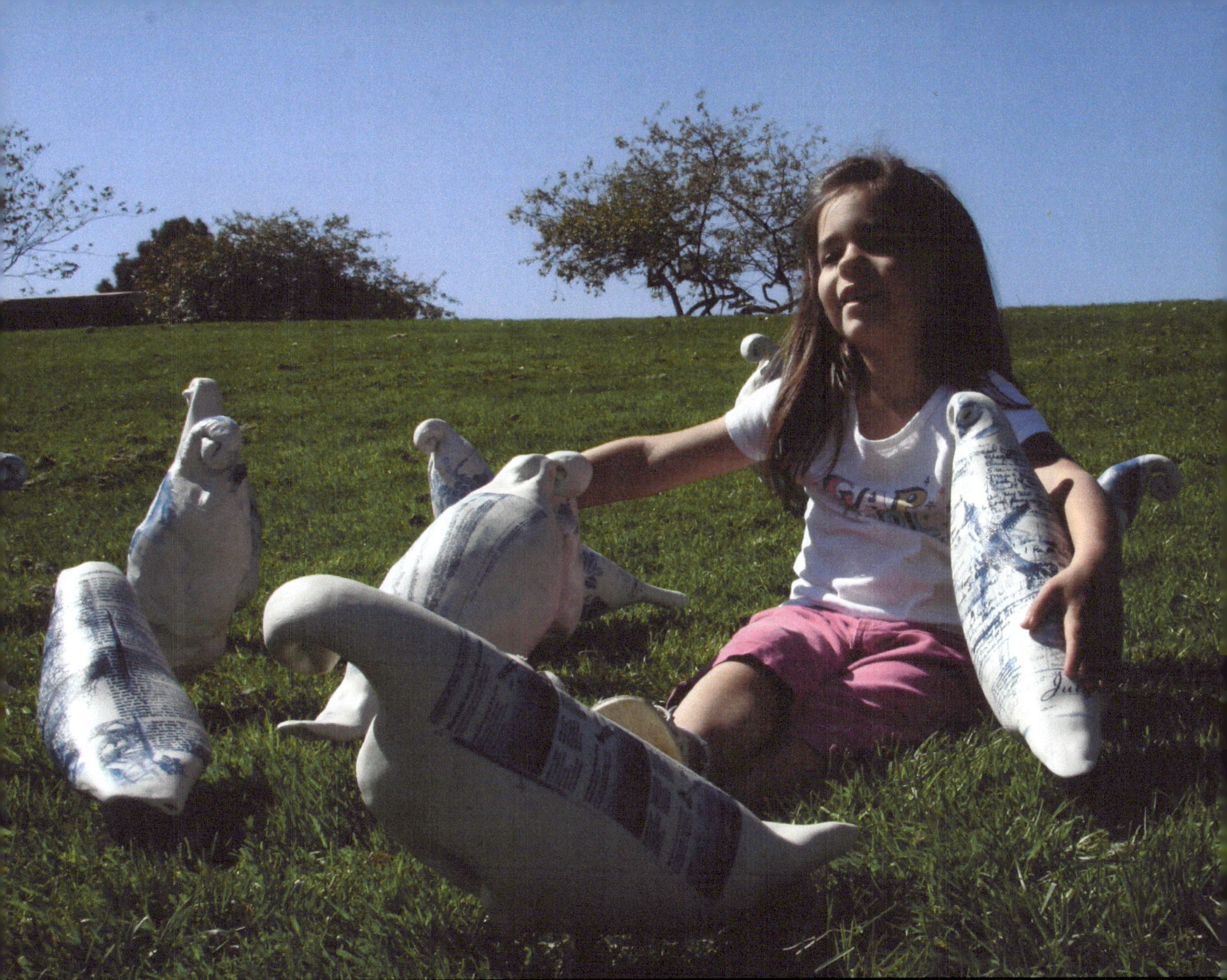

Photo: Genevieve Russell

Los Alamos, New Mexico is the place where the first Atom Bomb was created. The town of Los Alamos has a small-town idyllic identity, while the Labs th[illegible] continue to be primarily devoted to nuclear and other weapons development

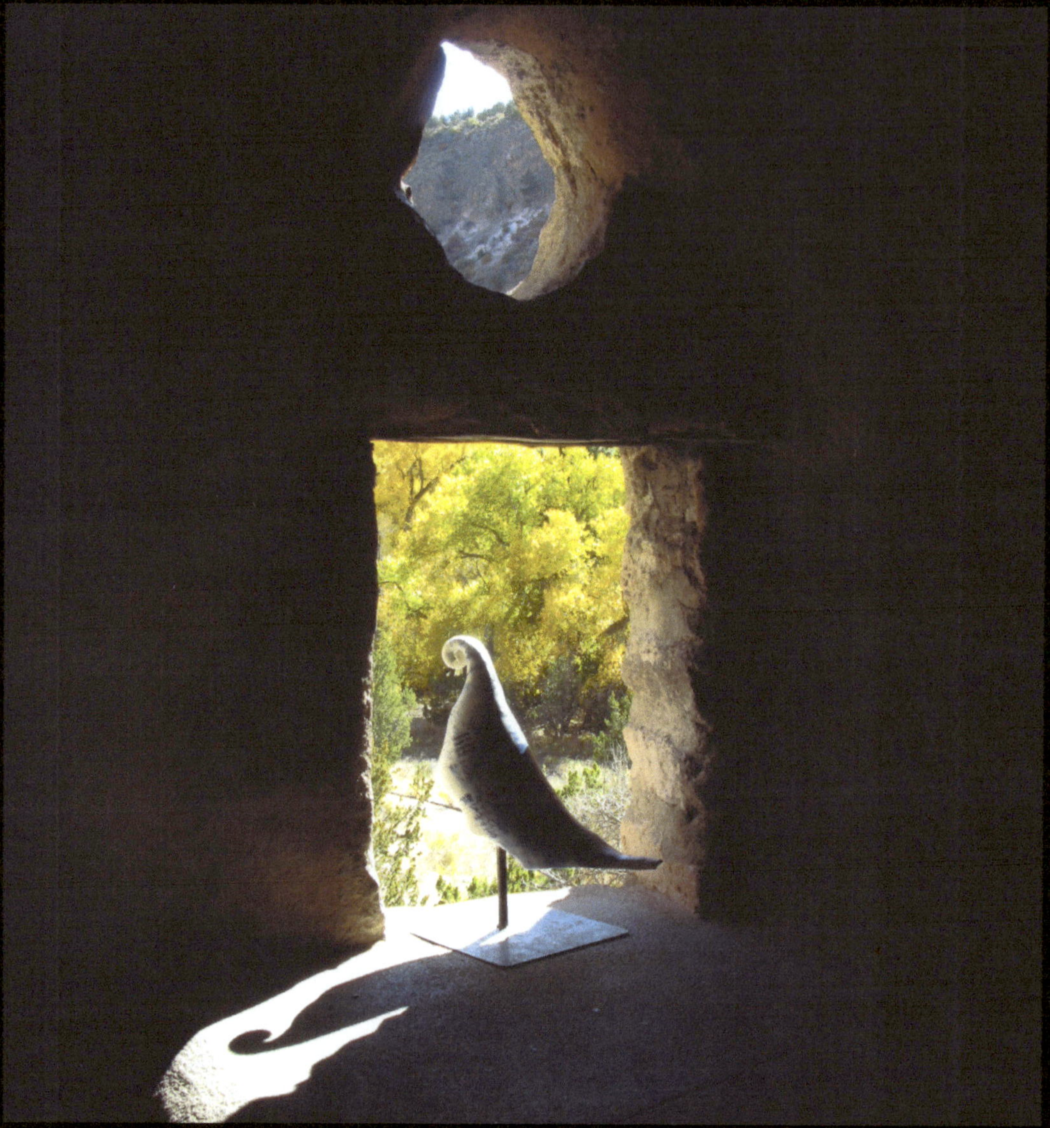

Above, facing and following page: Bandelier National Monument, Los Alamos, NM 10/16/2009.

Bandelier is only about a thirty minute drive from Los Alamos Laboratories but has a very different feeling. It is home to Ancestral Pueblo cliff dwellings.

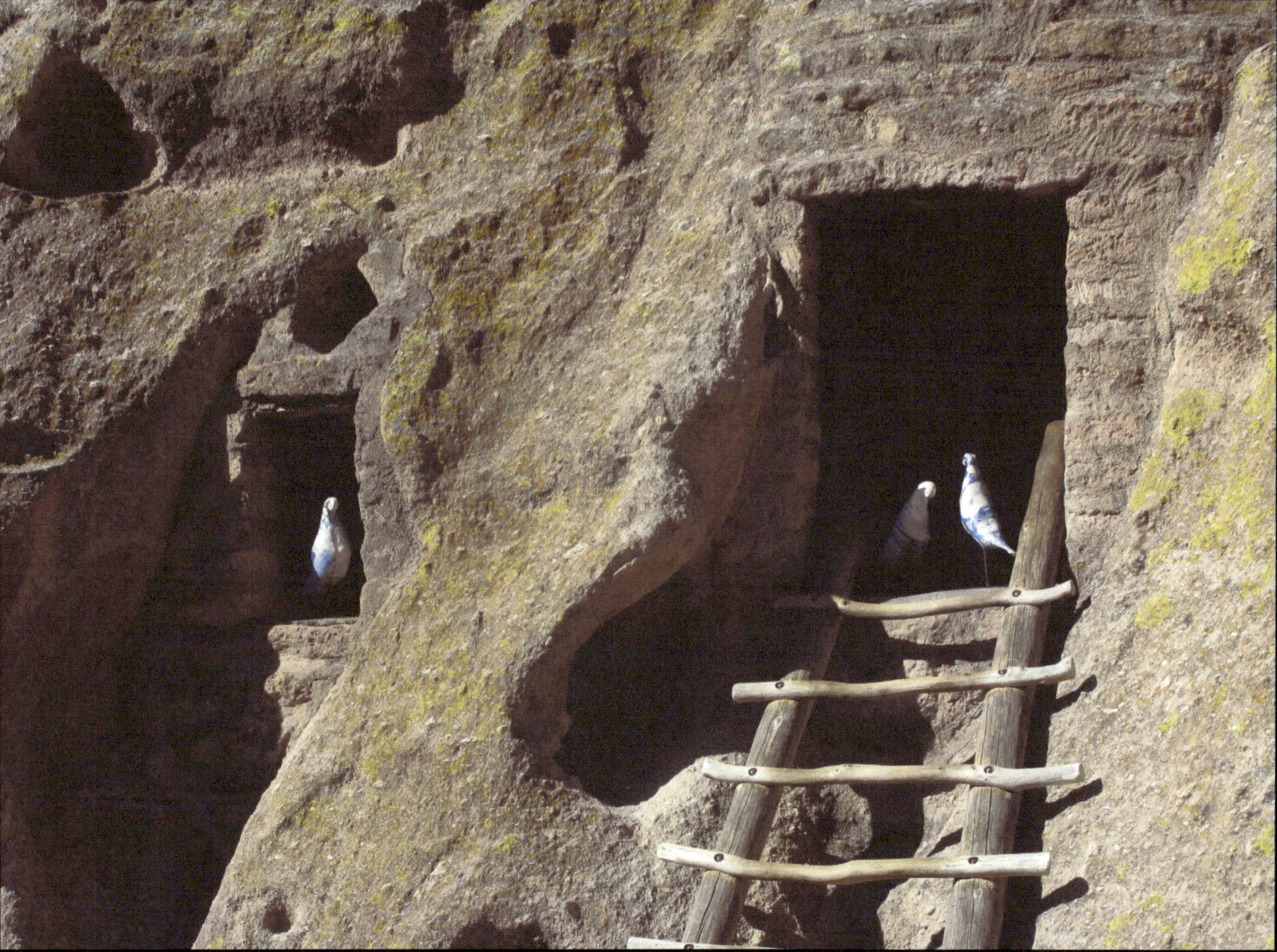

Photo: Dagmar Diebels

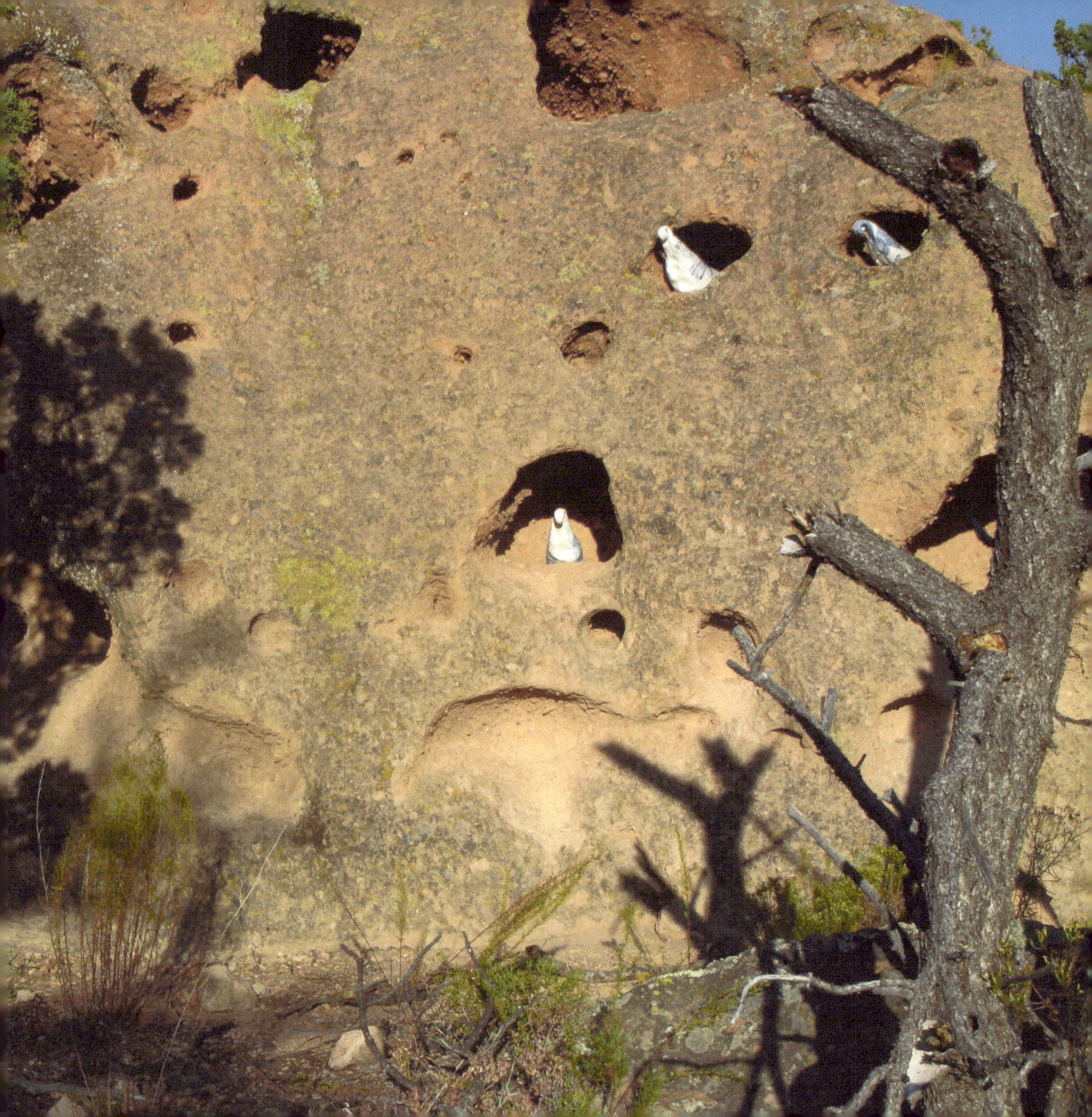

Other places in the US:

California
New Orleans
Washington D.C.
New York
Massachusetts
Vermont

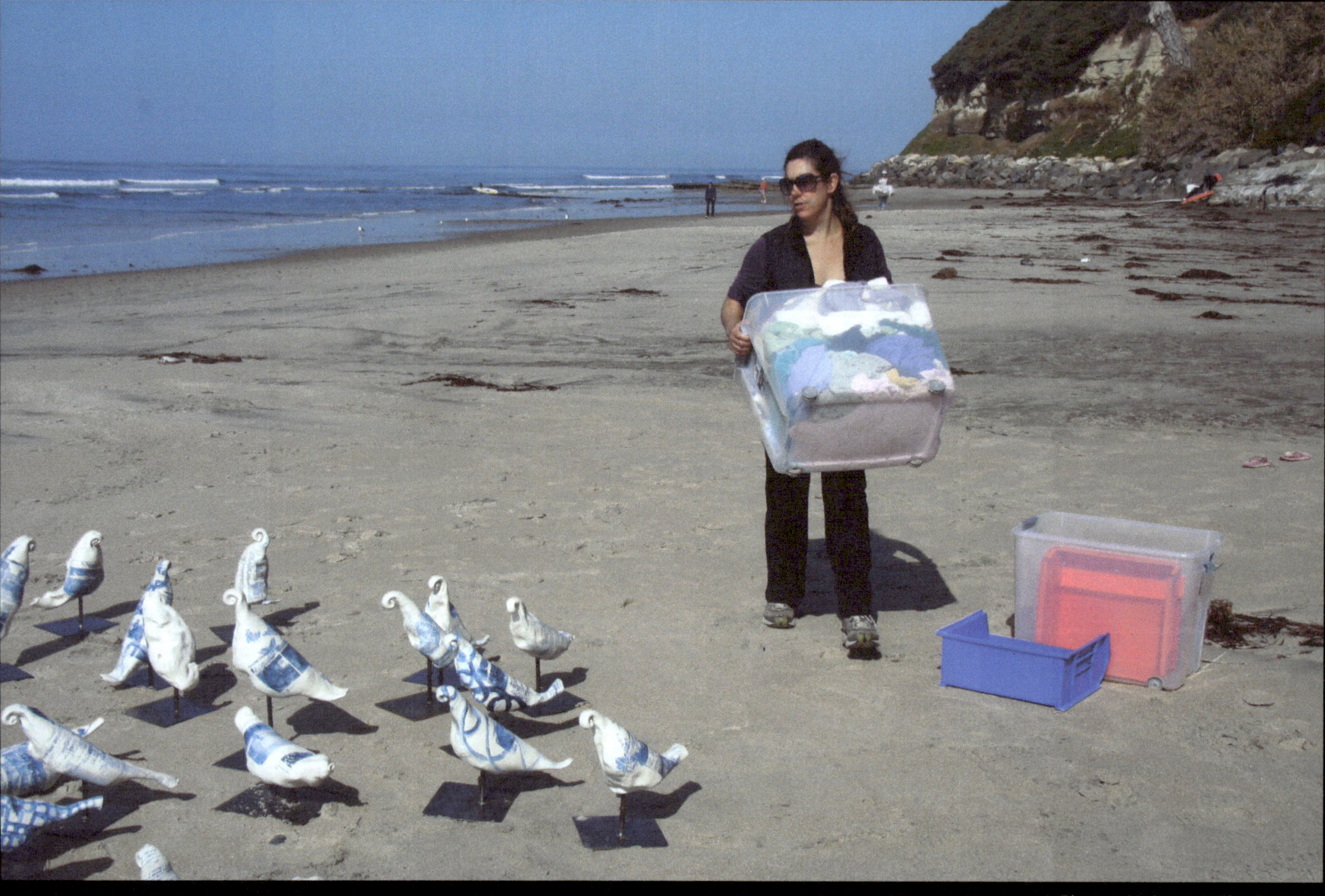

Photo: Helmut Hillenkamp

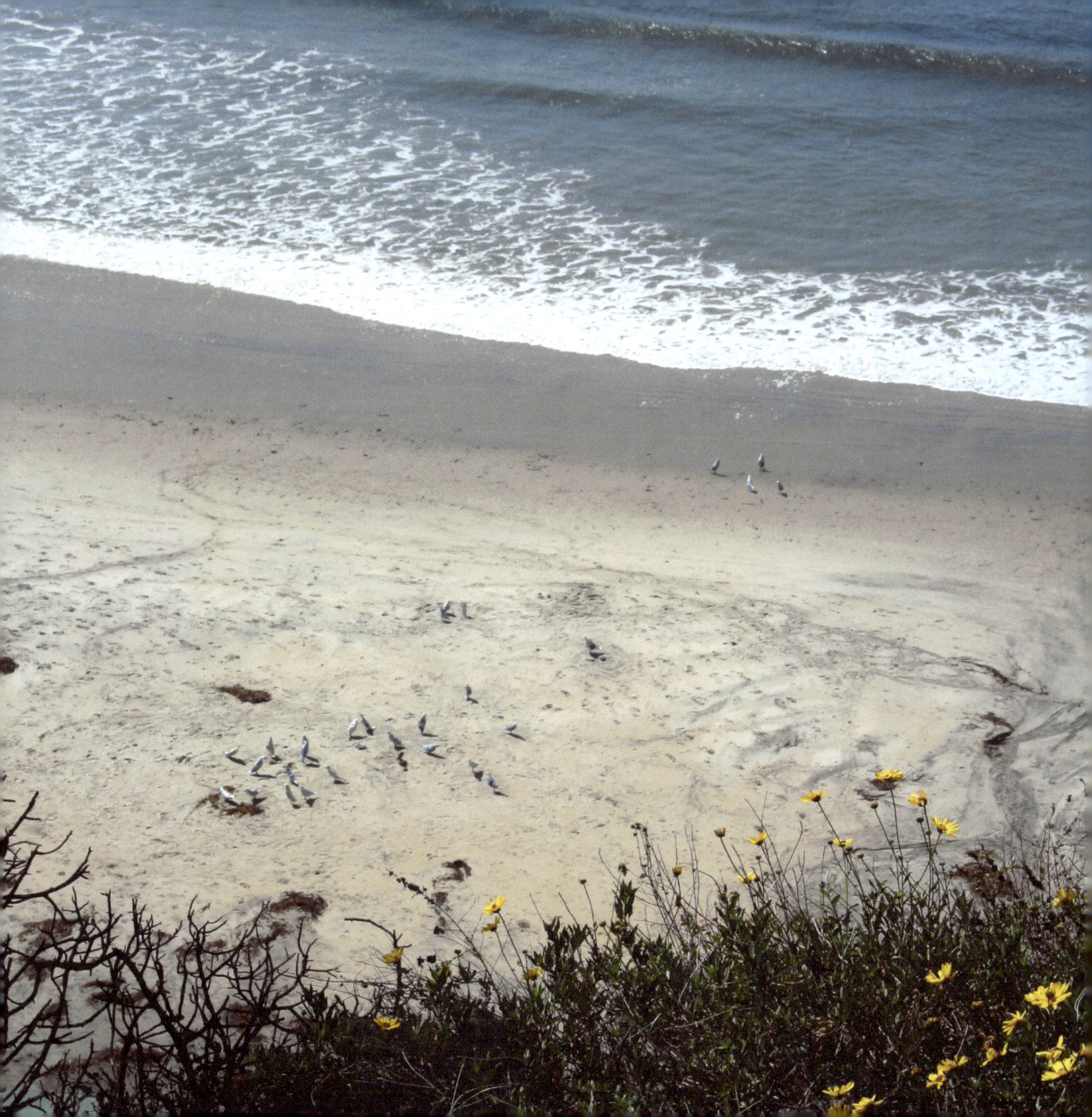

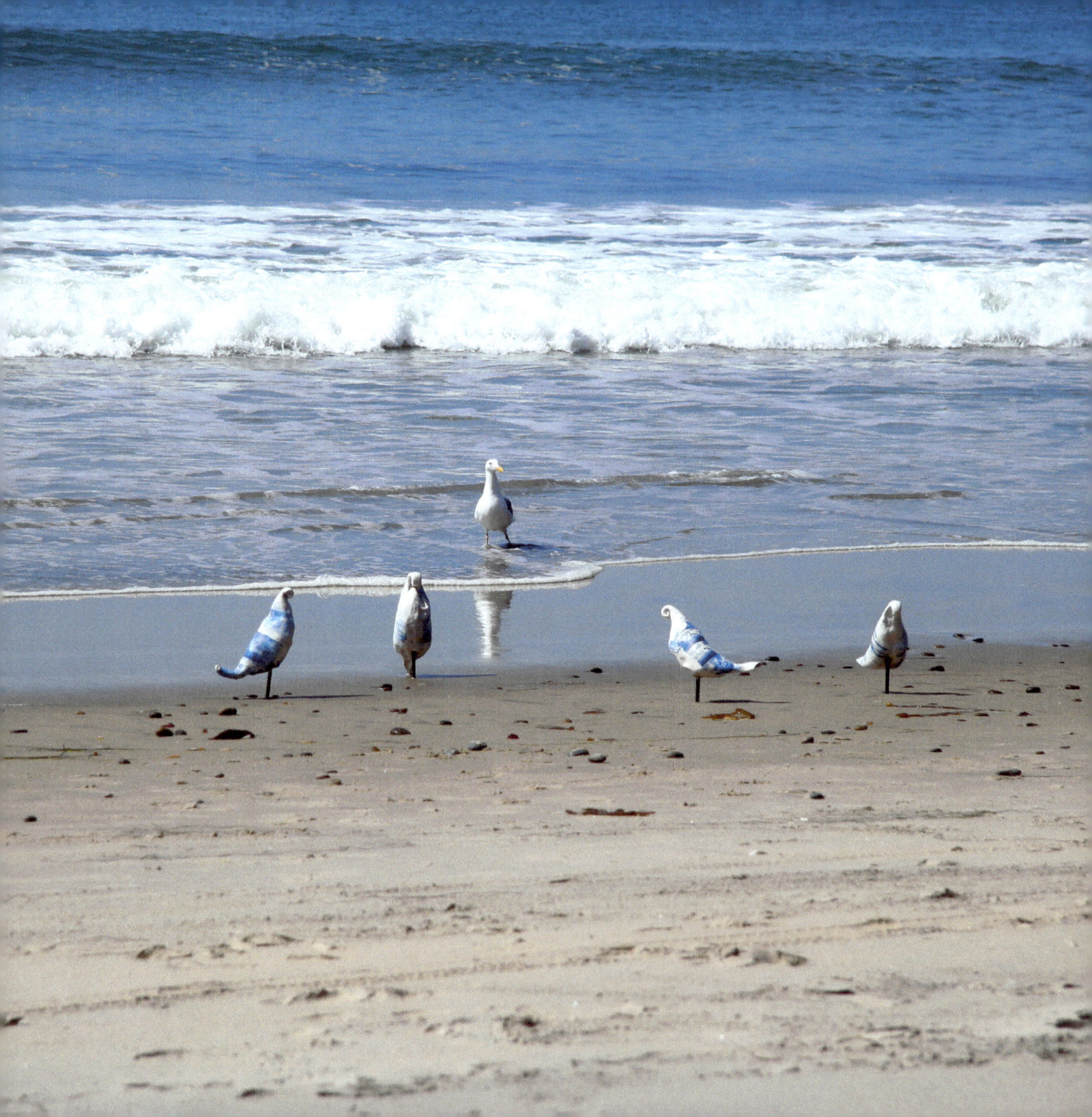

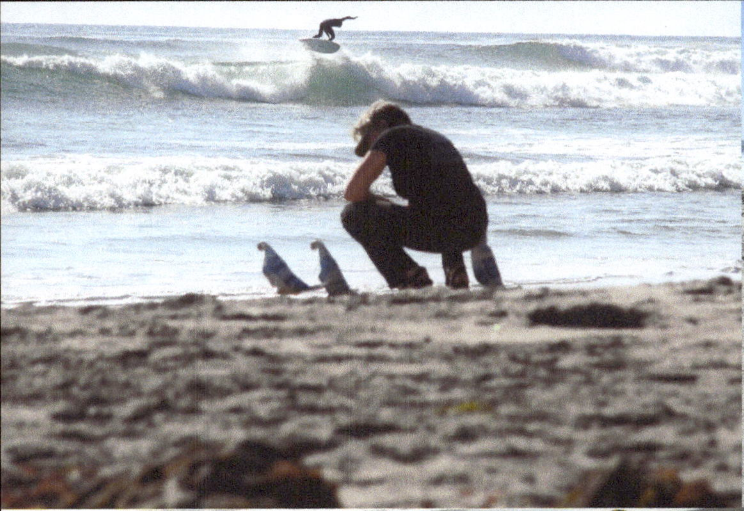
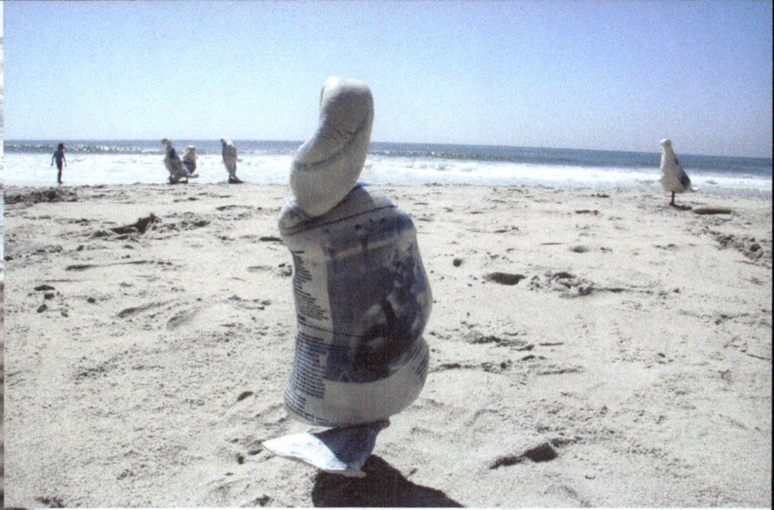
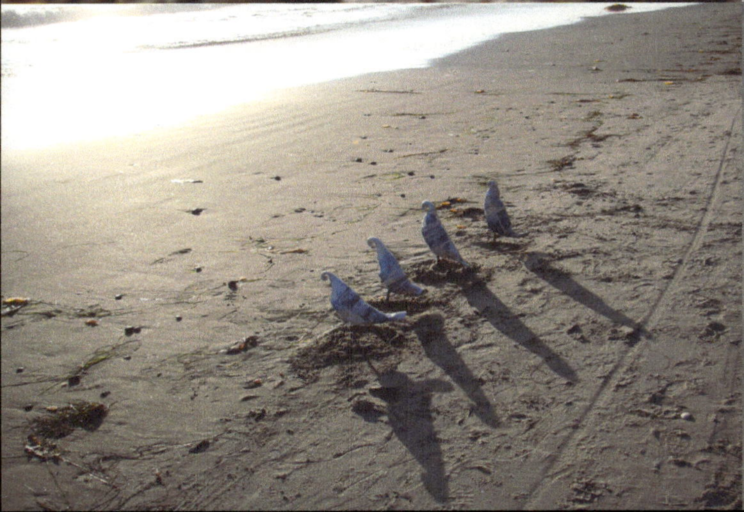
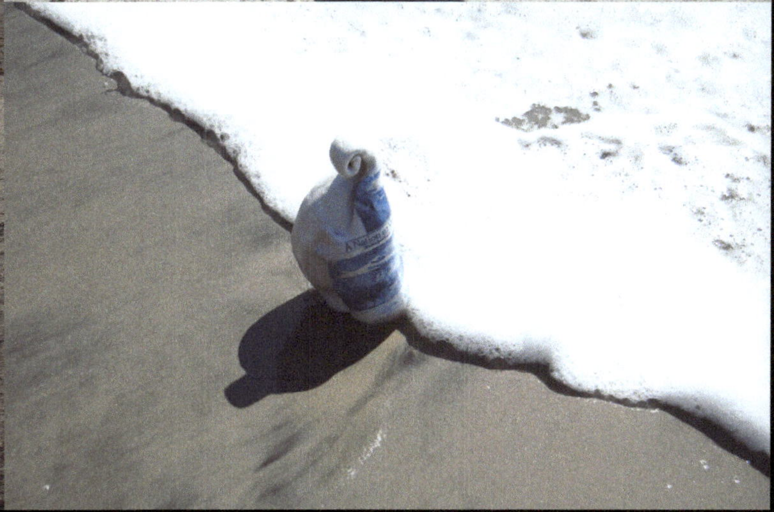

One of the strong motivations for the format of this project has been the gratification of getting to see the pieces I make in all kinds of settings; watching the waves wash up around a porcelain bird is one of those moments.

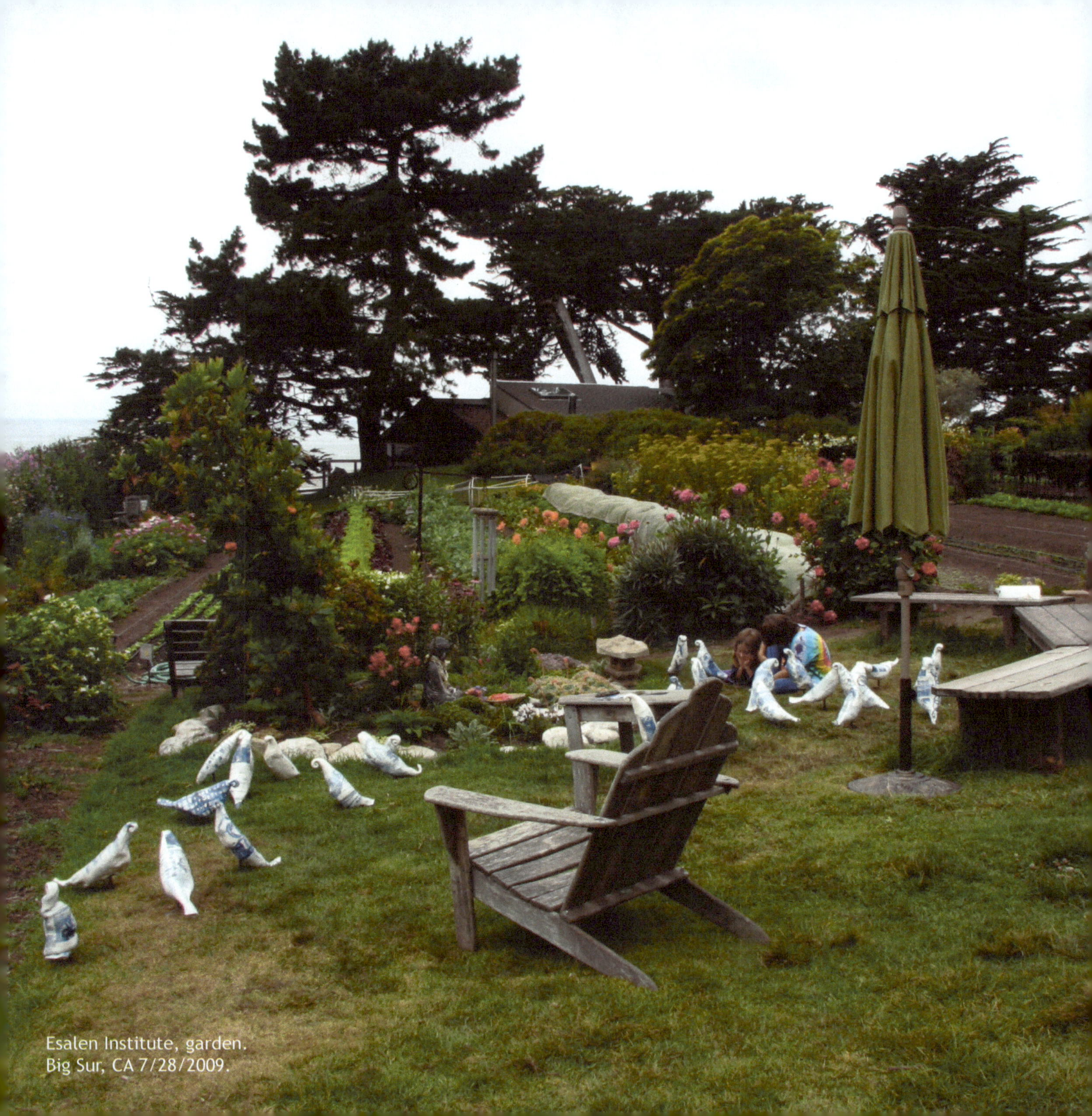

Esalen Institute, garden.
Big Sur, CA 7/28/2009.

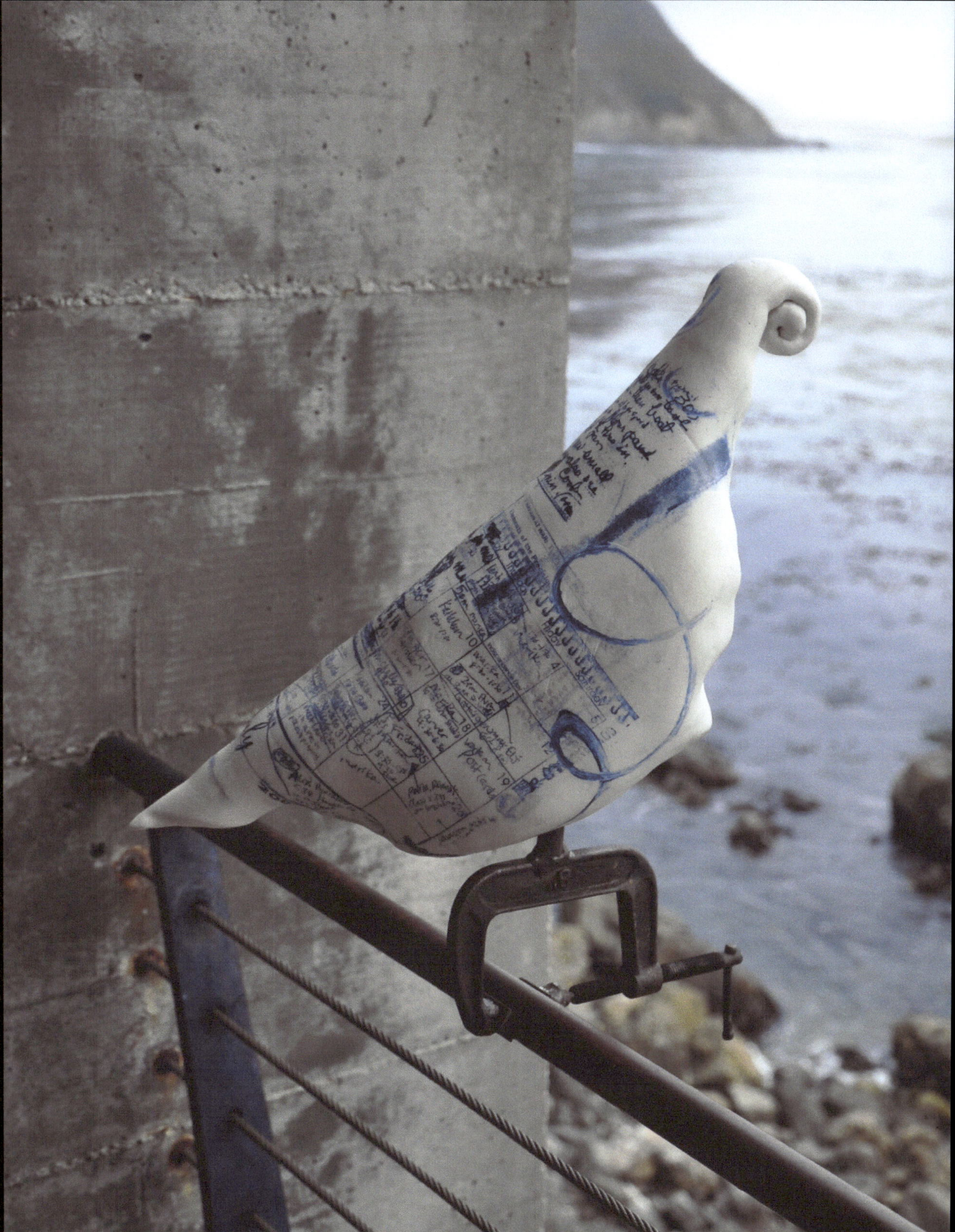

Esalen Institute,
baths.
Big Sur, CA
7/31/2009.

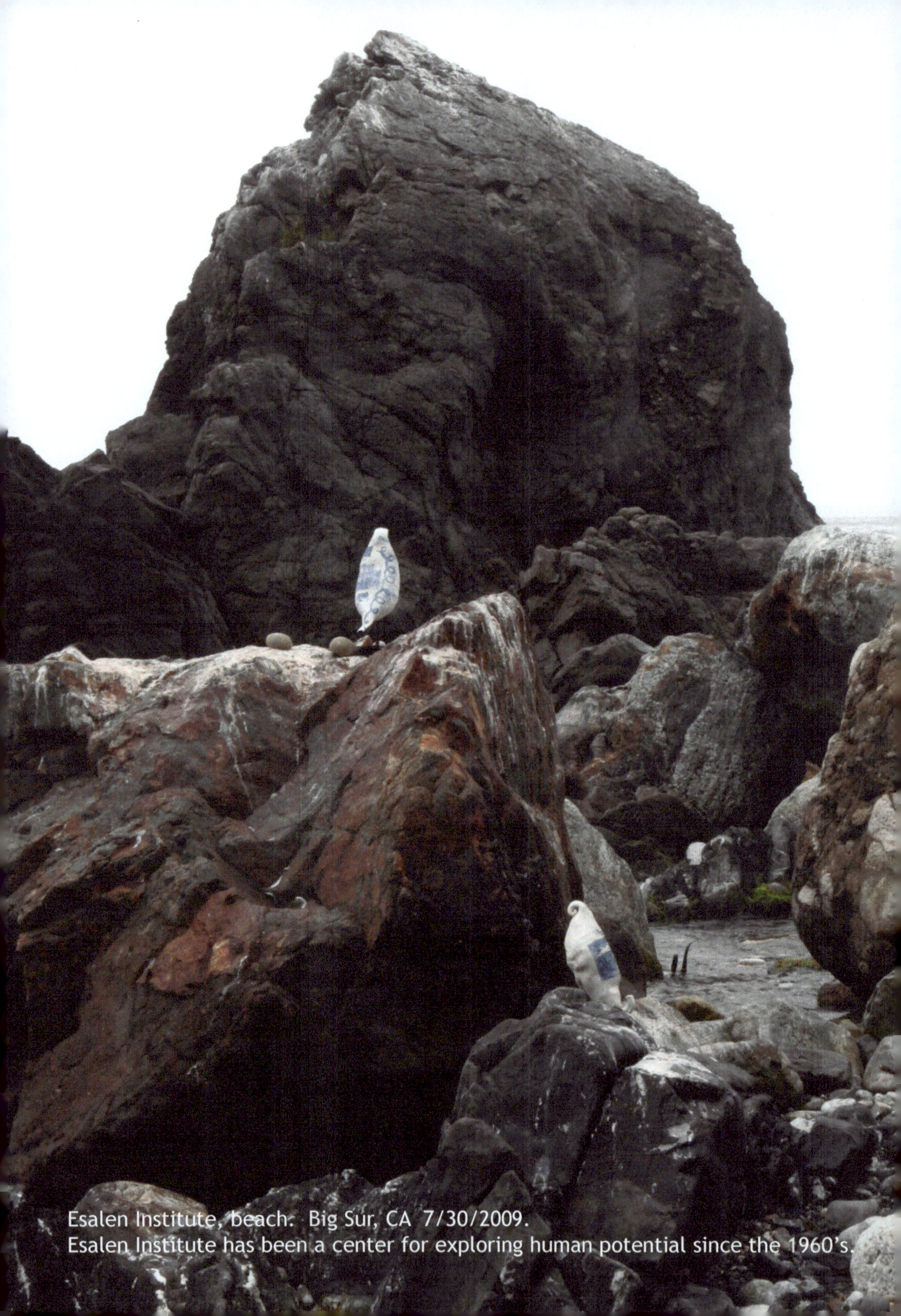

Esalen Institute, beach. Big Sur, CA 7/30/2009.
Esalen Institute has been a center for exploring human potential since the 1960's.

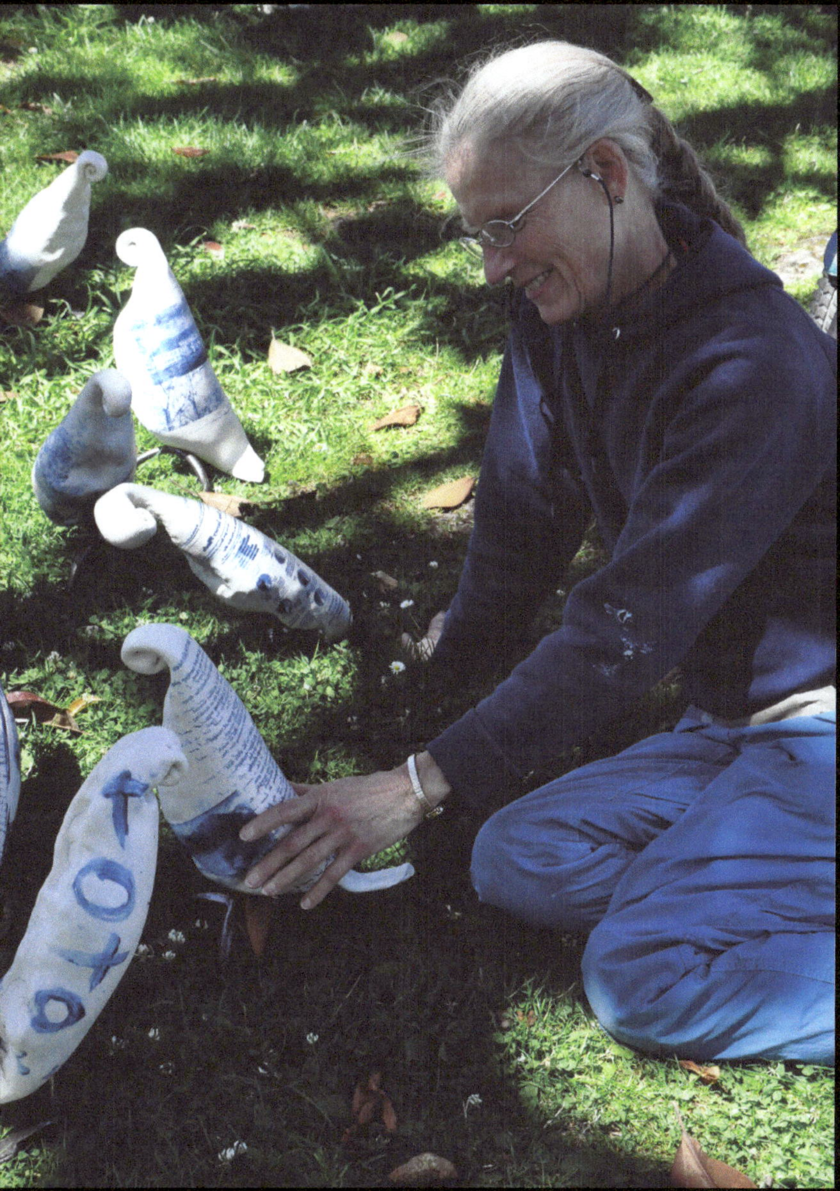

Civic Center Park, Berkeley, CA 8/28/2010.

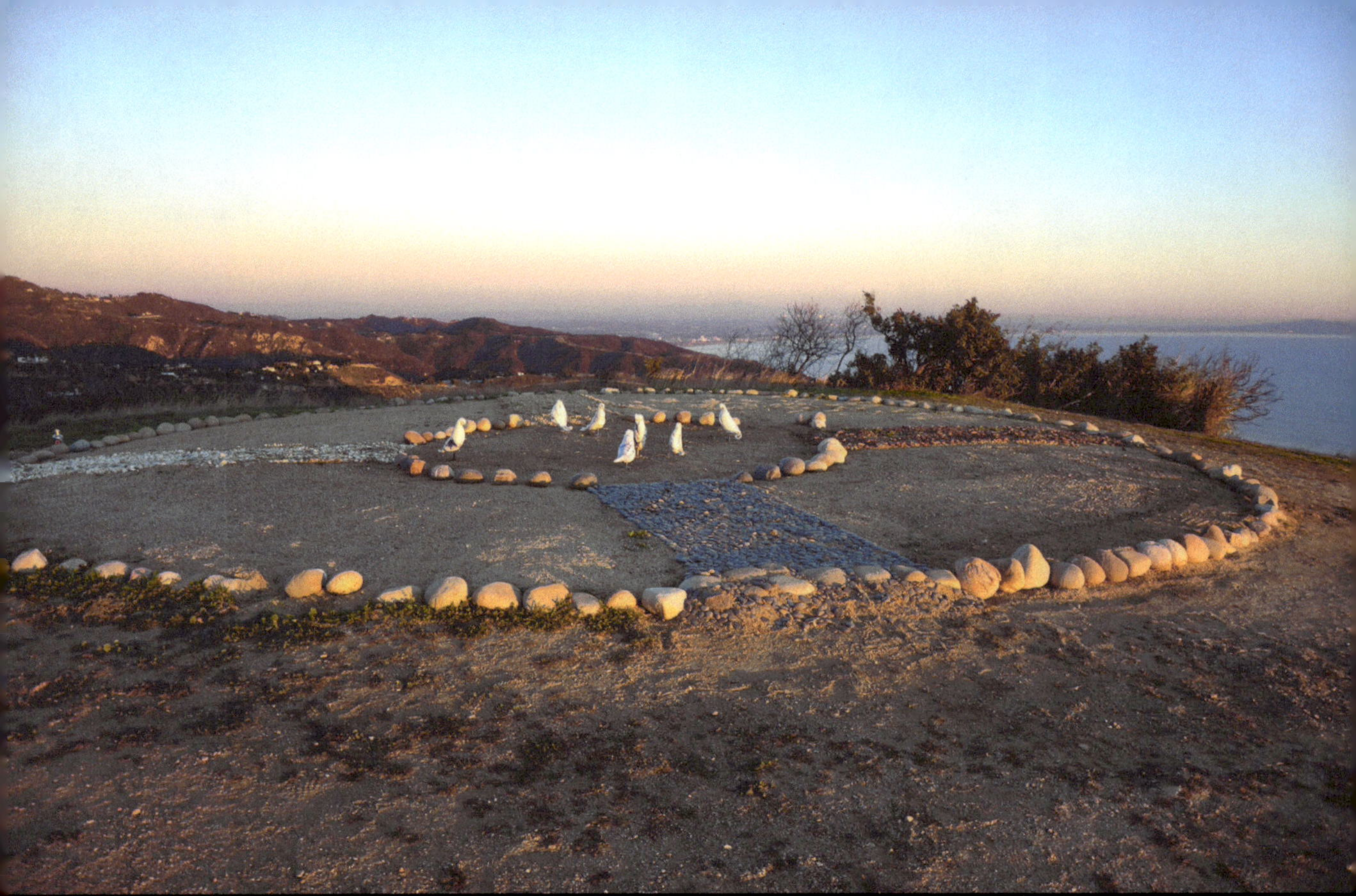

Above and facing page: Malibu, CA 11/26/2009.
A medicine wheel used as a gathering place

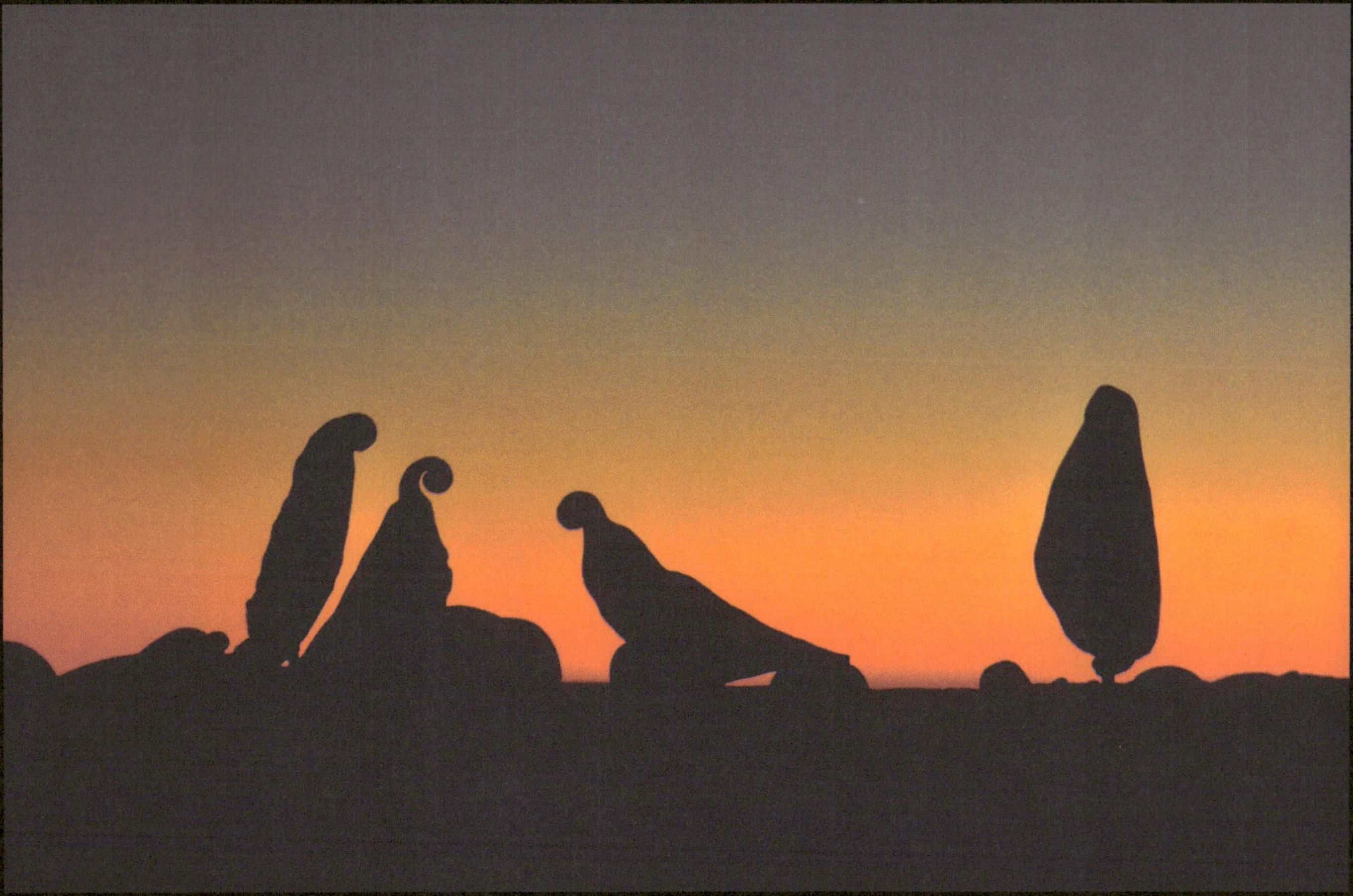

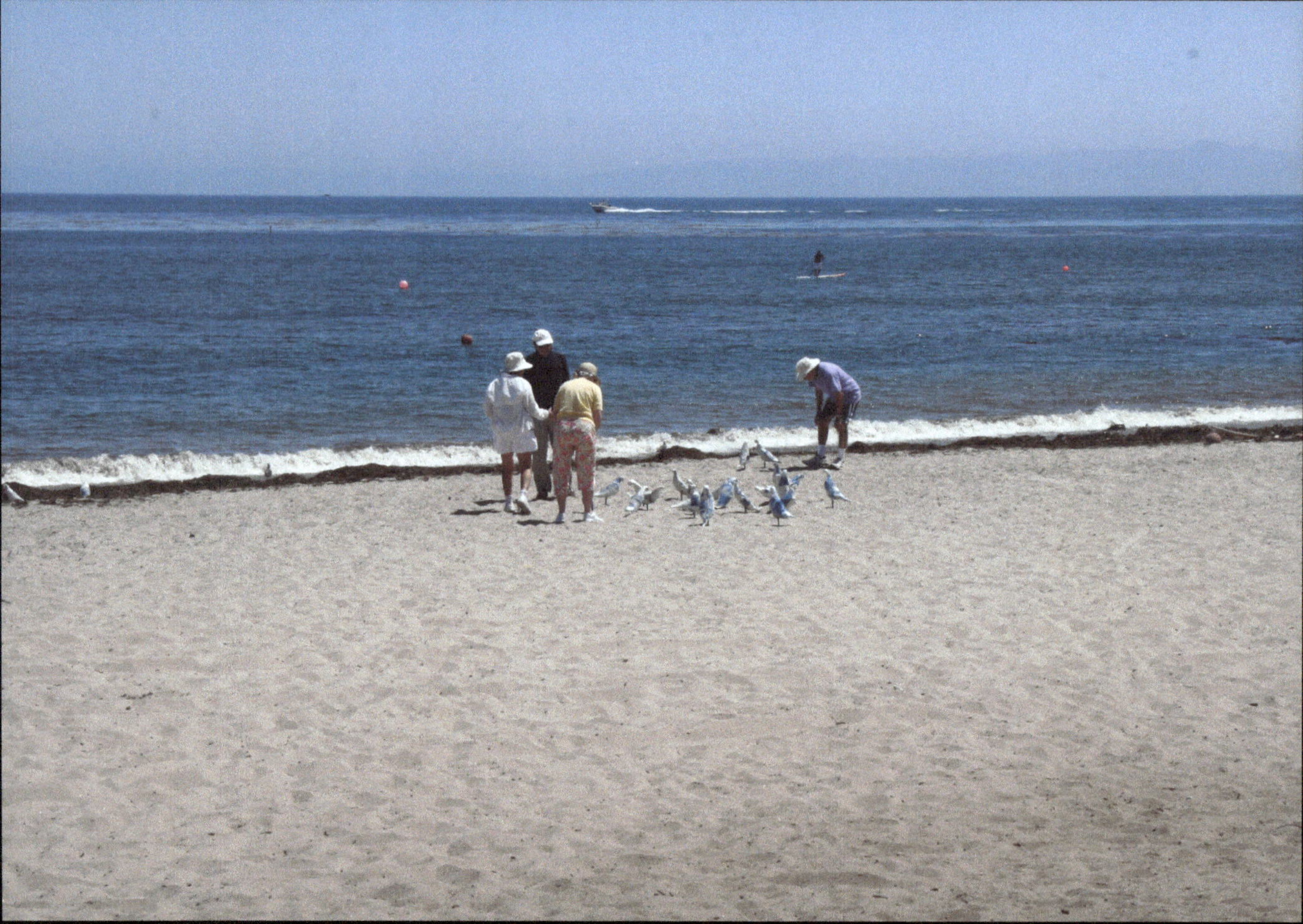

Above and facing page: Leadbetter Beach, Santa Barbara, CA 7/22/2009.

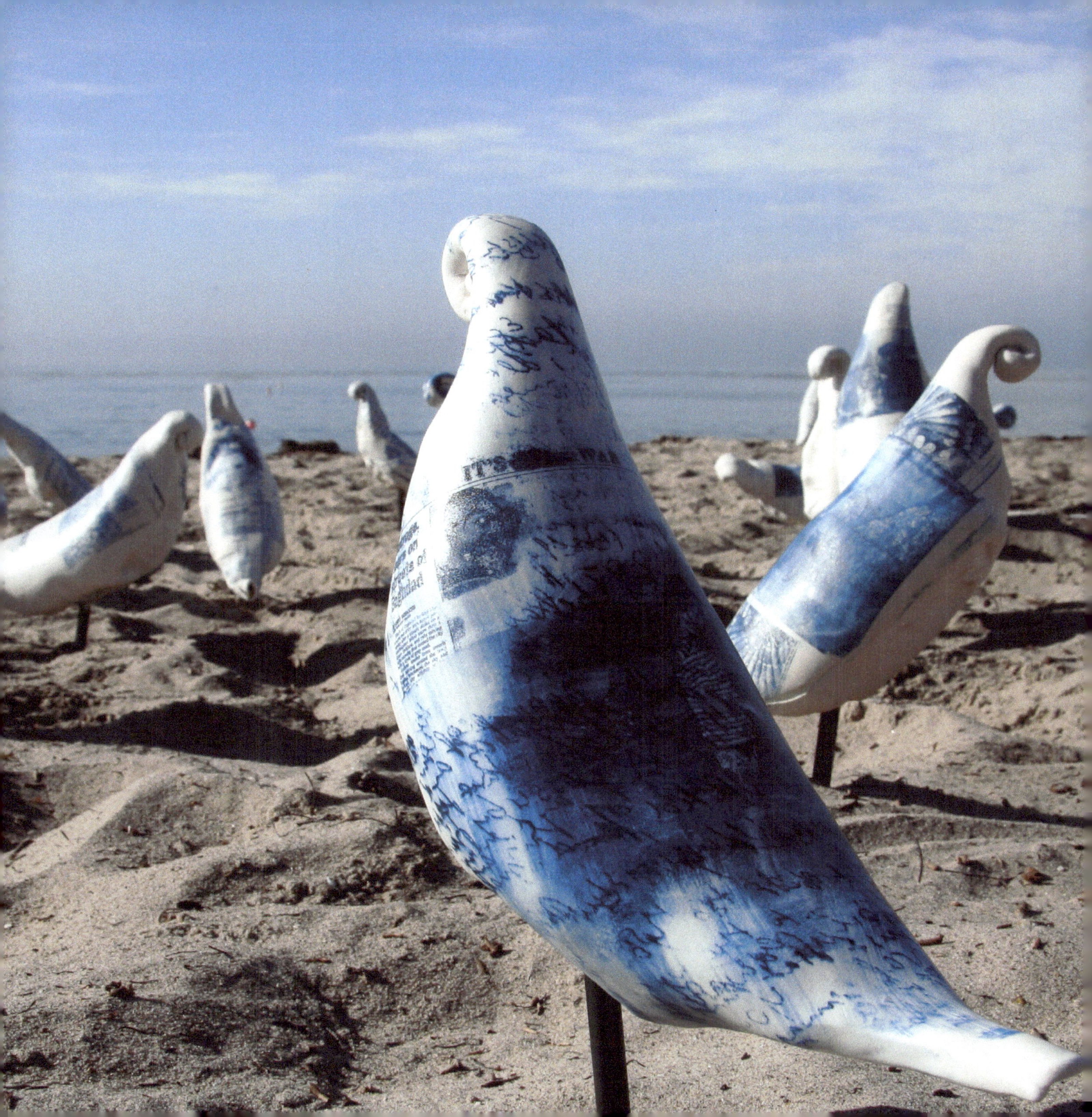
IT'S

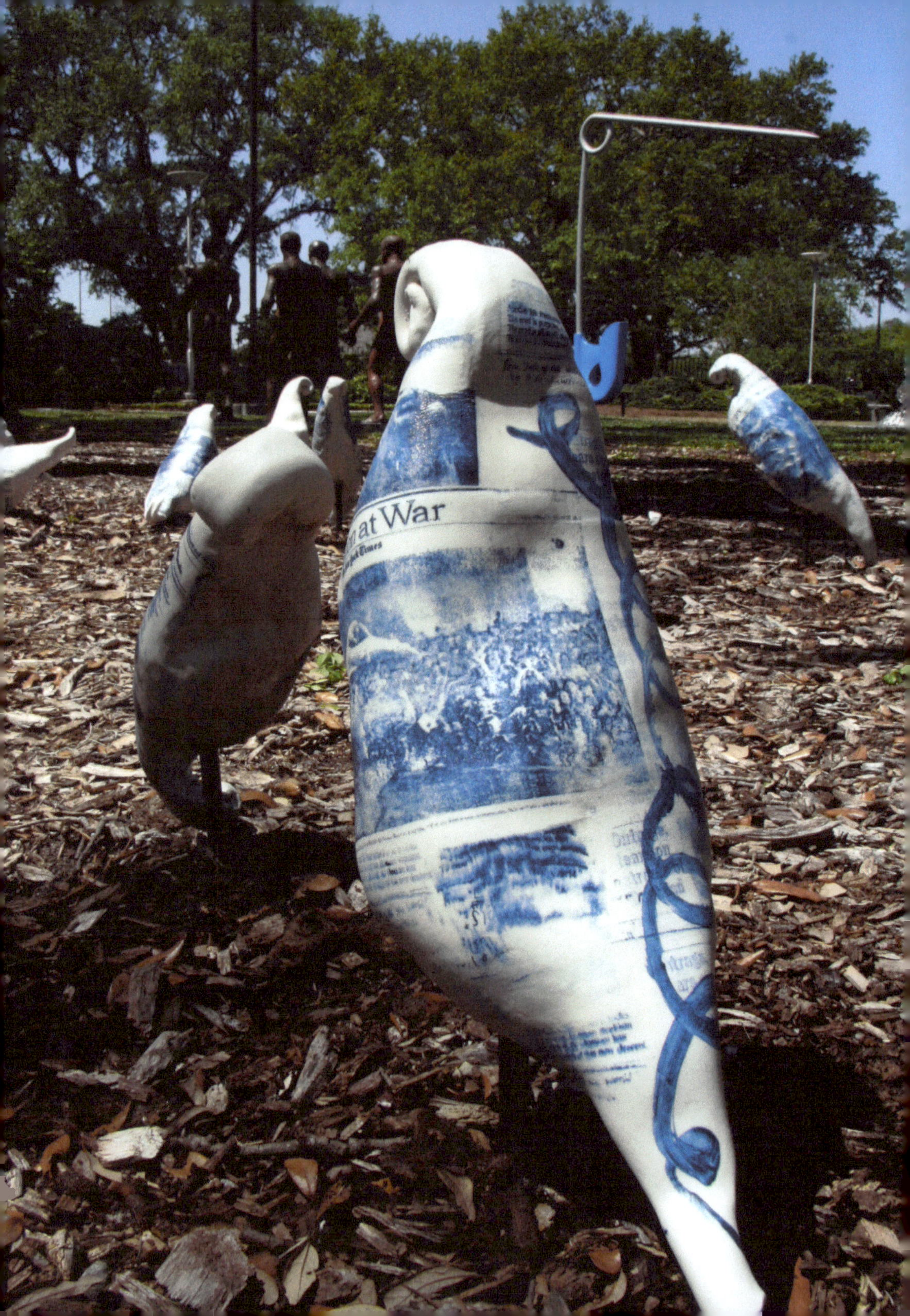
at War

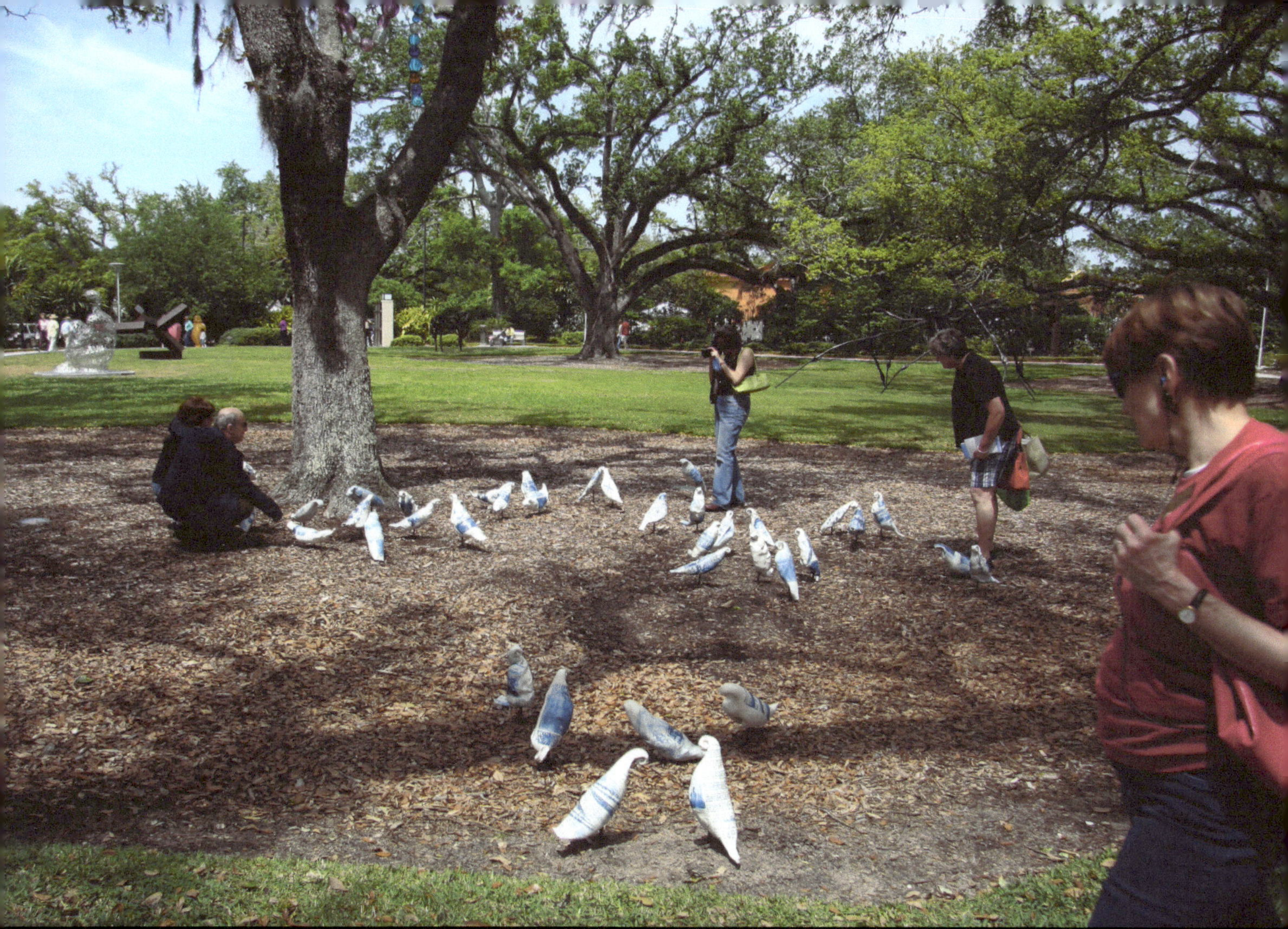

Above and facing page: Besthoff Sculpture Garden, New Orleans Museum of Art, New Orleans, LA 4/4/2009.
This landing was arranged by Sculpture for New Orleans, which places sculpture on loan by artists all around the city.

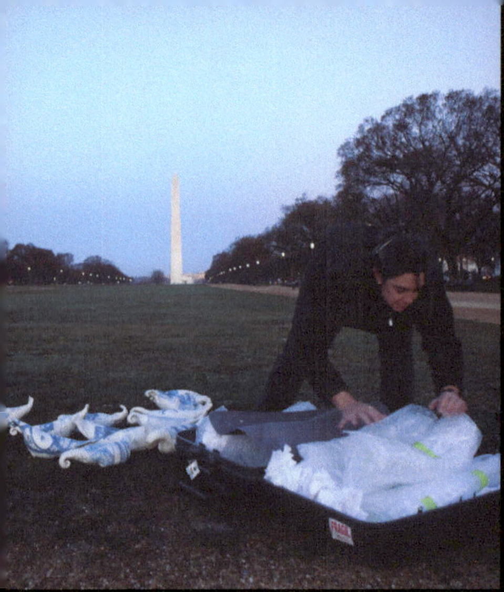

Unpacking.

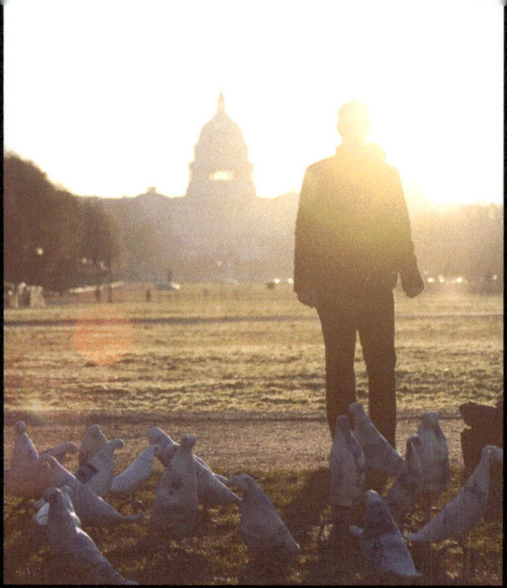

Setting up.

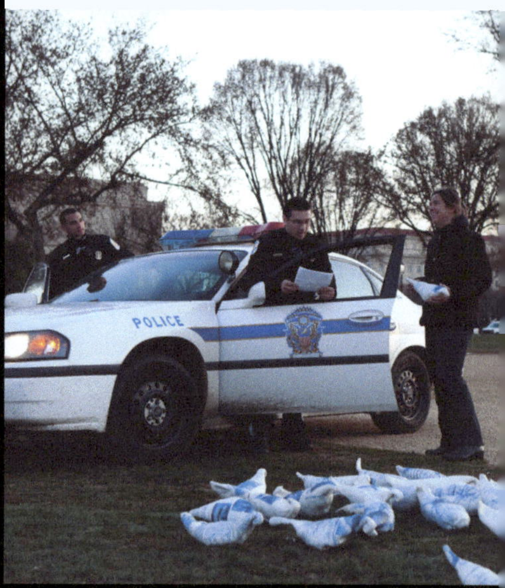

Displaying permit.

This and next three pages: National Mall, Washington D.C. 3/18/2010

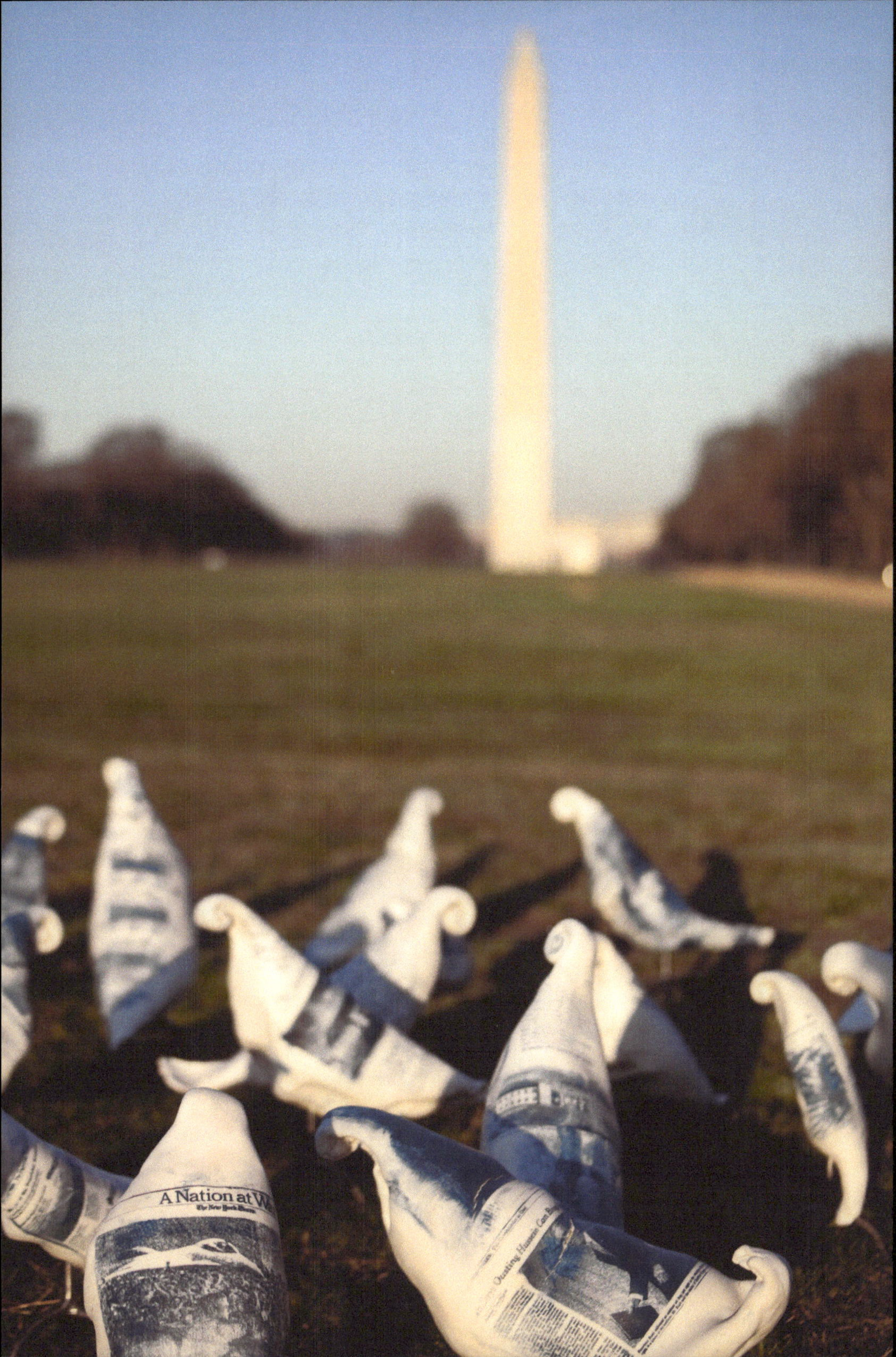

Getting the birds to land on the National Mall in Washington D.C. turned out to be one of the most difficult doors to open. I knew I would need a permit, and started the process online, but with a stated policy of "no art on the Mall" and a particularly vigilant park manager, even my application for an "art picnic" was turned down (it had worked for Central Park!). Finally, after many phone conversations and numerous e-mails with photos to display the mounting methods and the "wind bearing load of the sculptures," I obtained a permit for a "small, and very quiet, political demonstration."

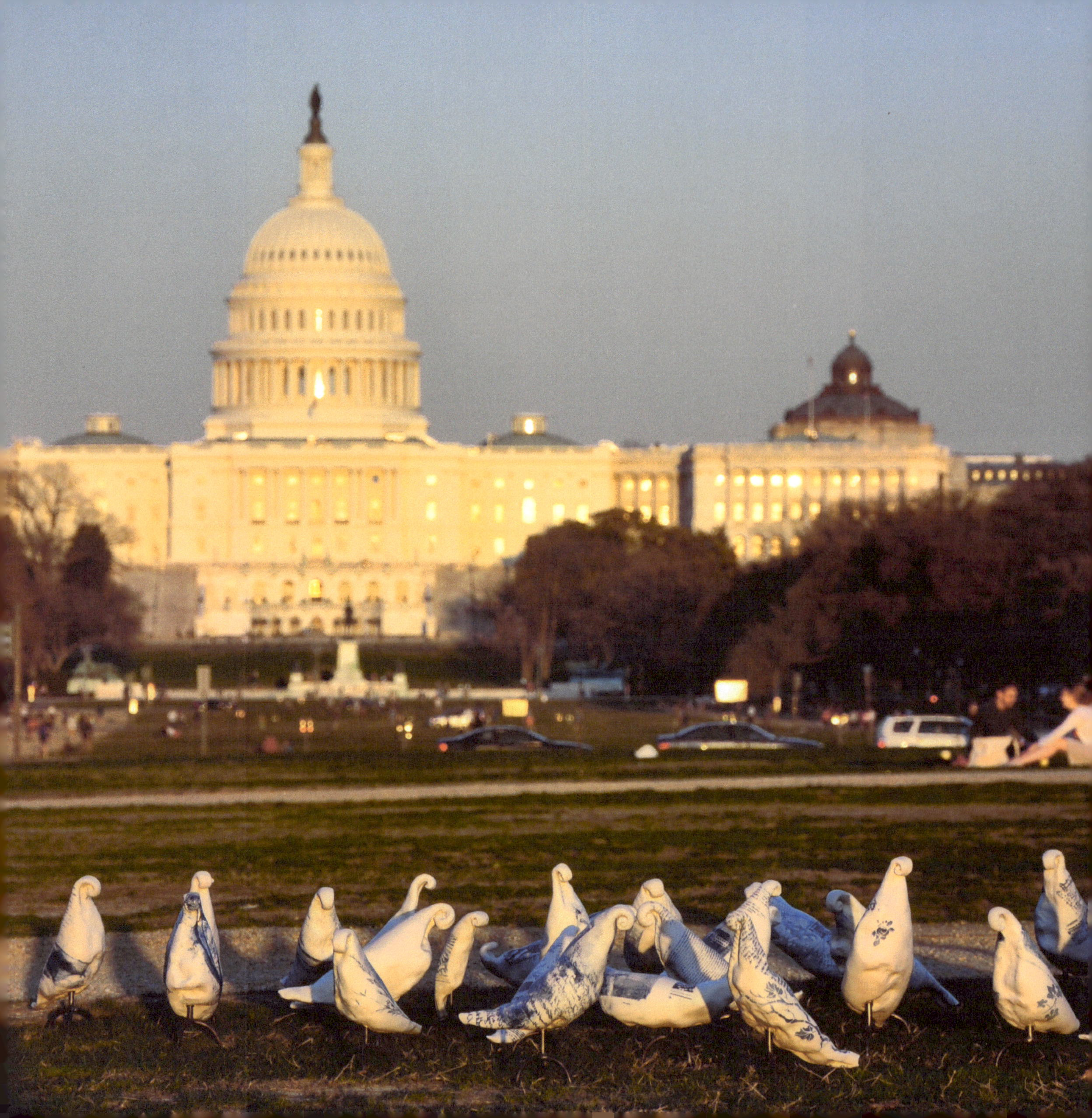

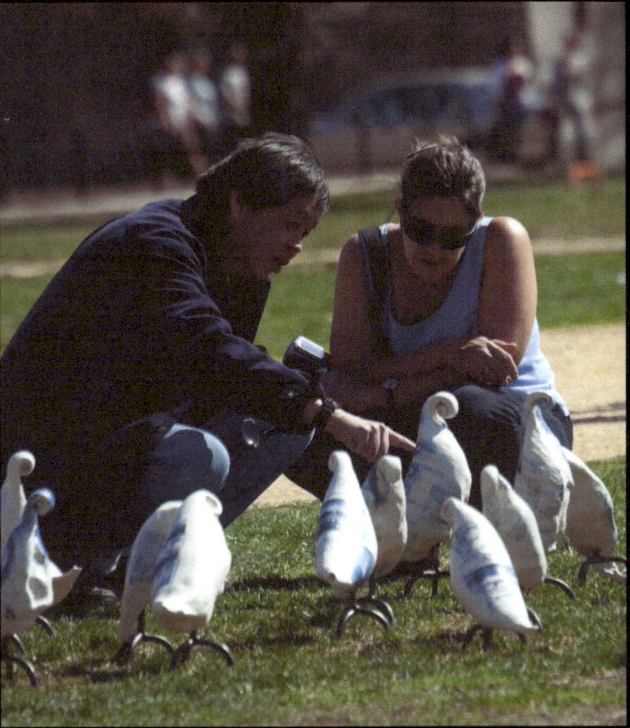

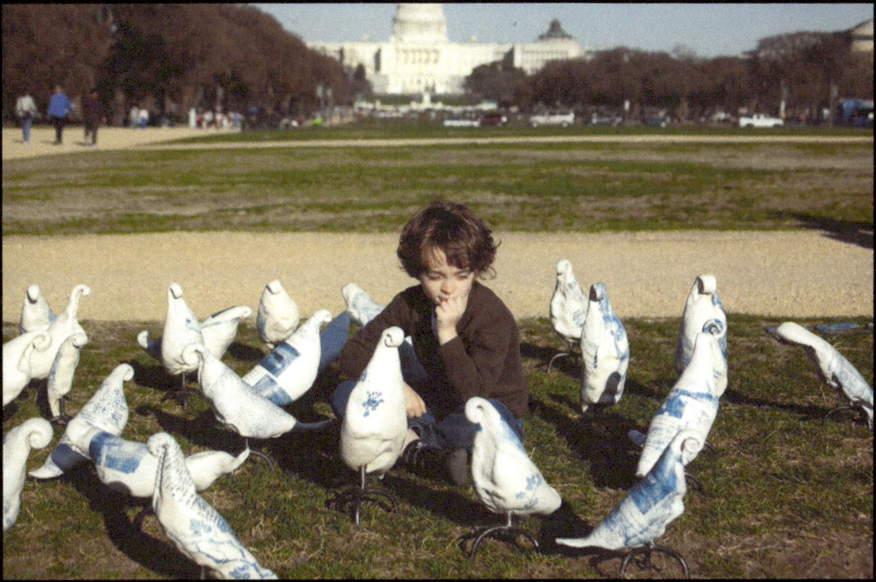

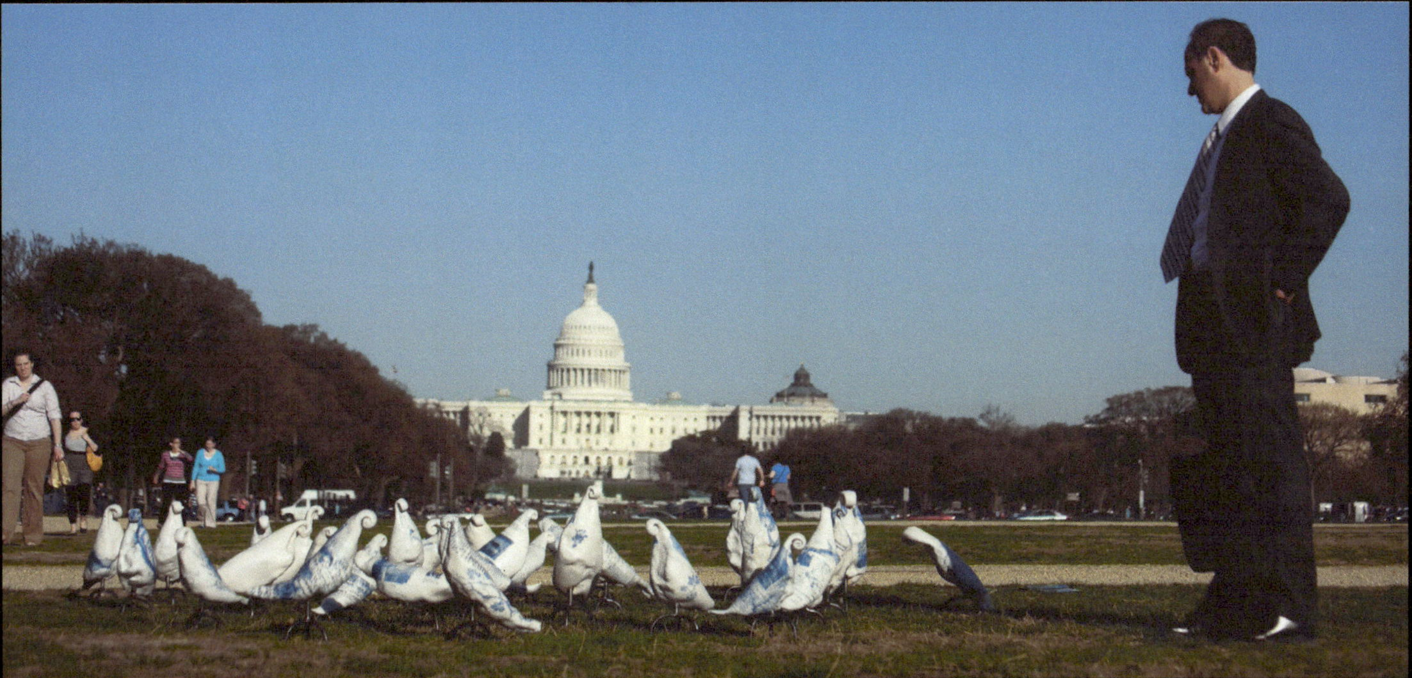

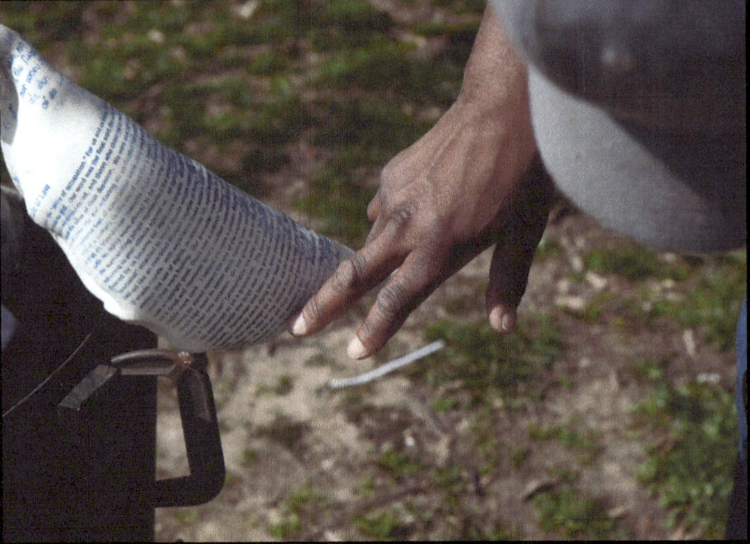

This and facing page: Dupont Circle, Washington D.C. 3/19/2010.

Dupont Circle is one of the places where a significant part of the birds' audience were homeless people. It was a new experience for me to be in a park from early morning until night. I started to realize that there are those who are just passing through, and those for whom I was actually a curious guest in their living room.

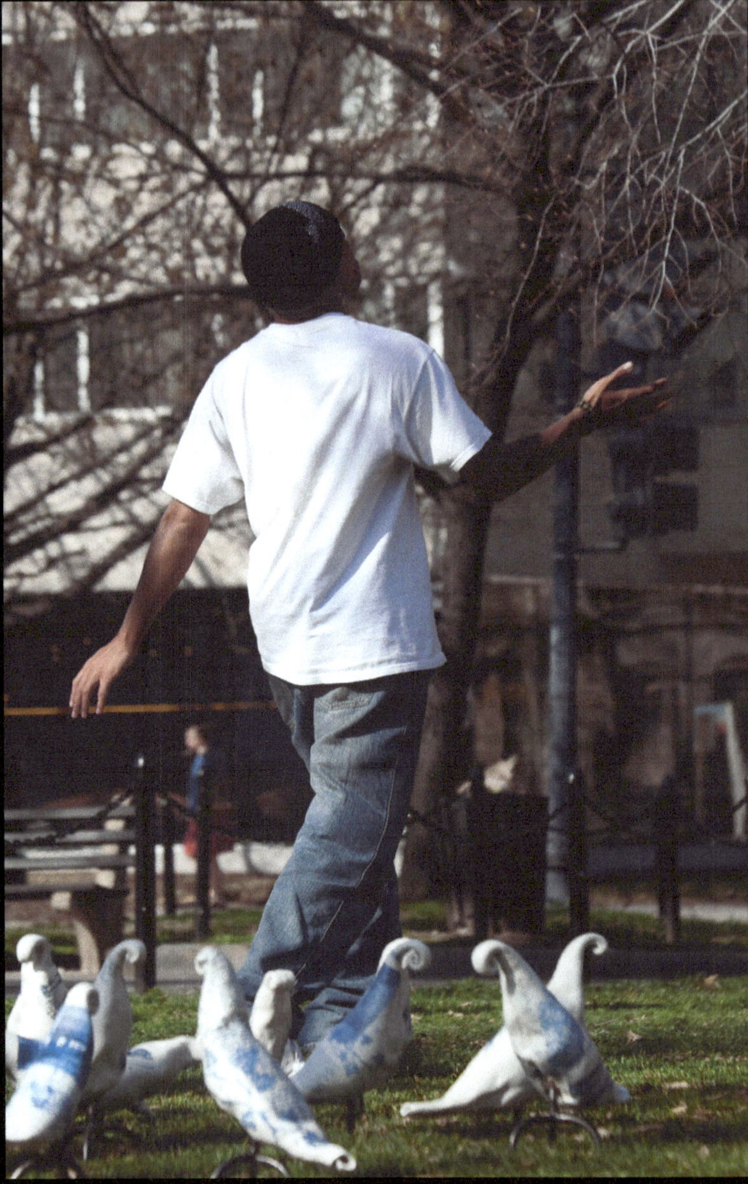

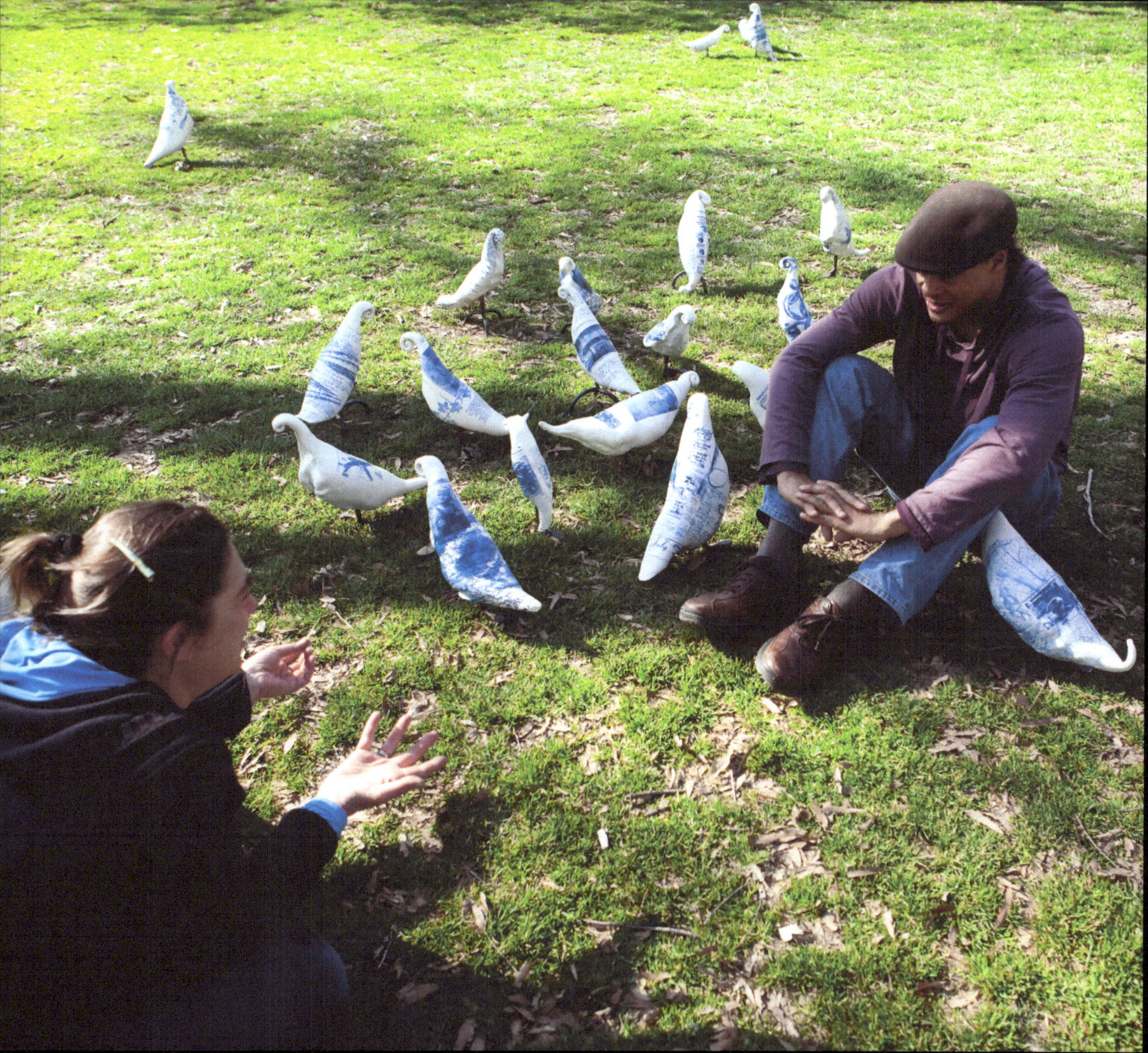

Christy Hengst and musician, Laurence Woodson, discussing the role of the artist in society.

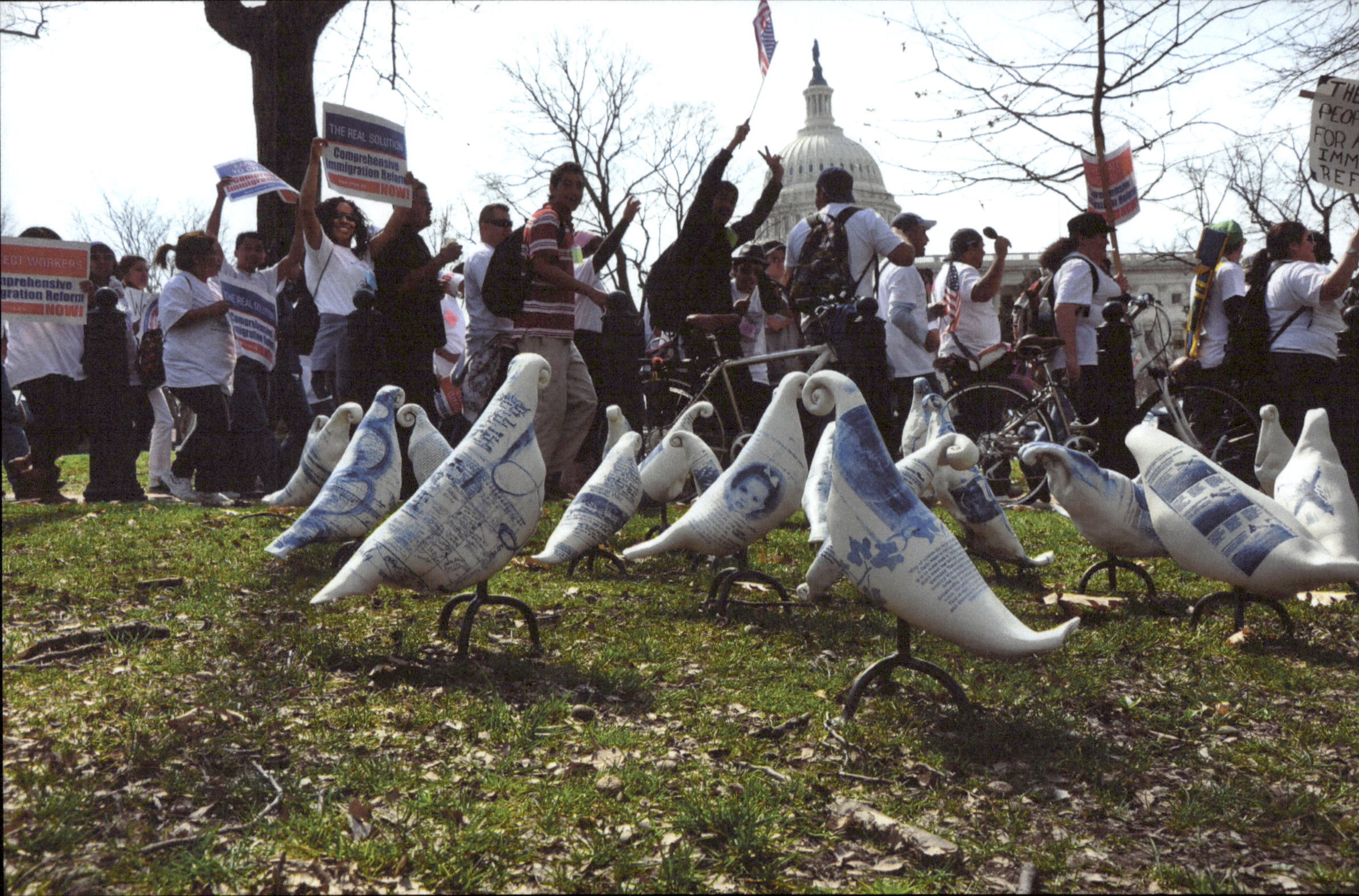

Upper Senate Park, Washington D.C. 3/21/2010.

While the birds landed outside the Capitol building in D.C., there were immigration rallies and health care vote protests going by. Lots of people asked, “What are these birds for, or against?” Although one could say, the birds are against war, this exploration is more complex than that. Some of the questions driving me with this work are “how does war happen?”, “how is it that the same humans can be so loving and so hateful?”, and “is war an unavoidable fact of human existence?” In looking at these questions, I don’t expect to have definitive answers. I think that is one difference between a political demonstration, and art.

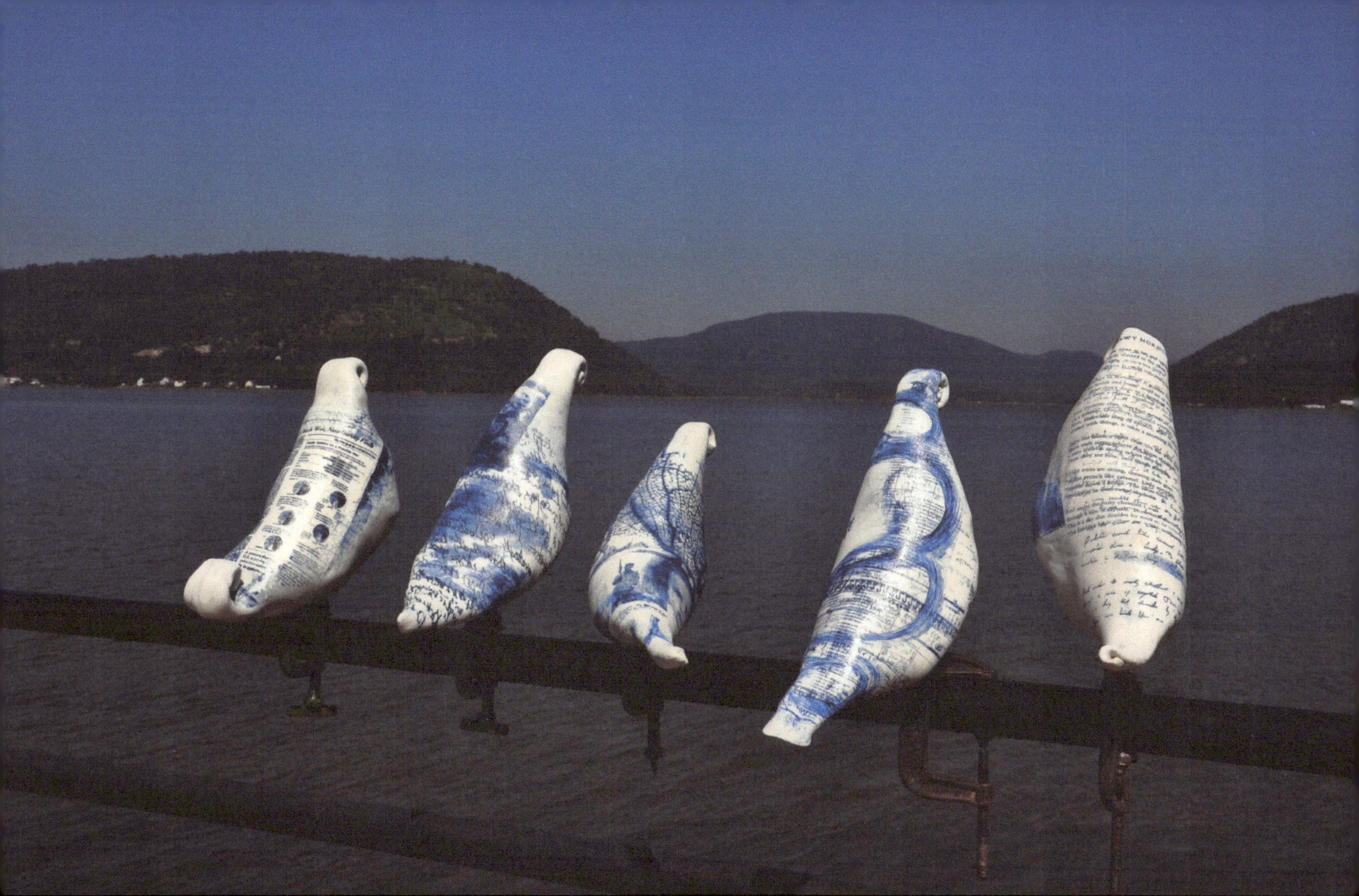

Above and next two pages: Hudson River Waterfront, Peekskill, NY 6/19/2010

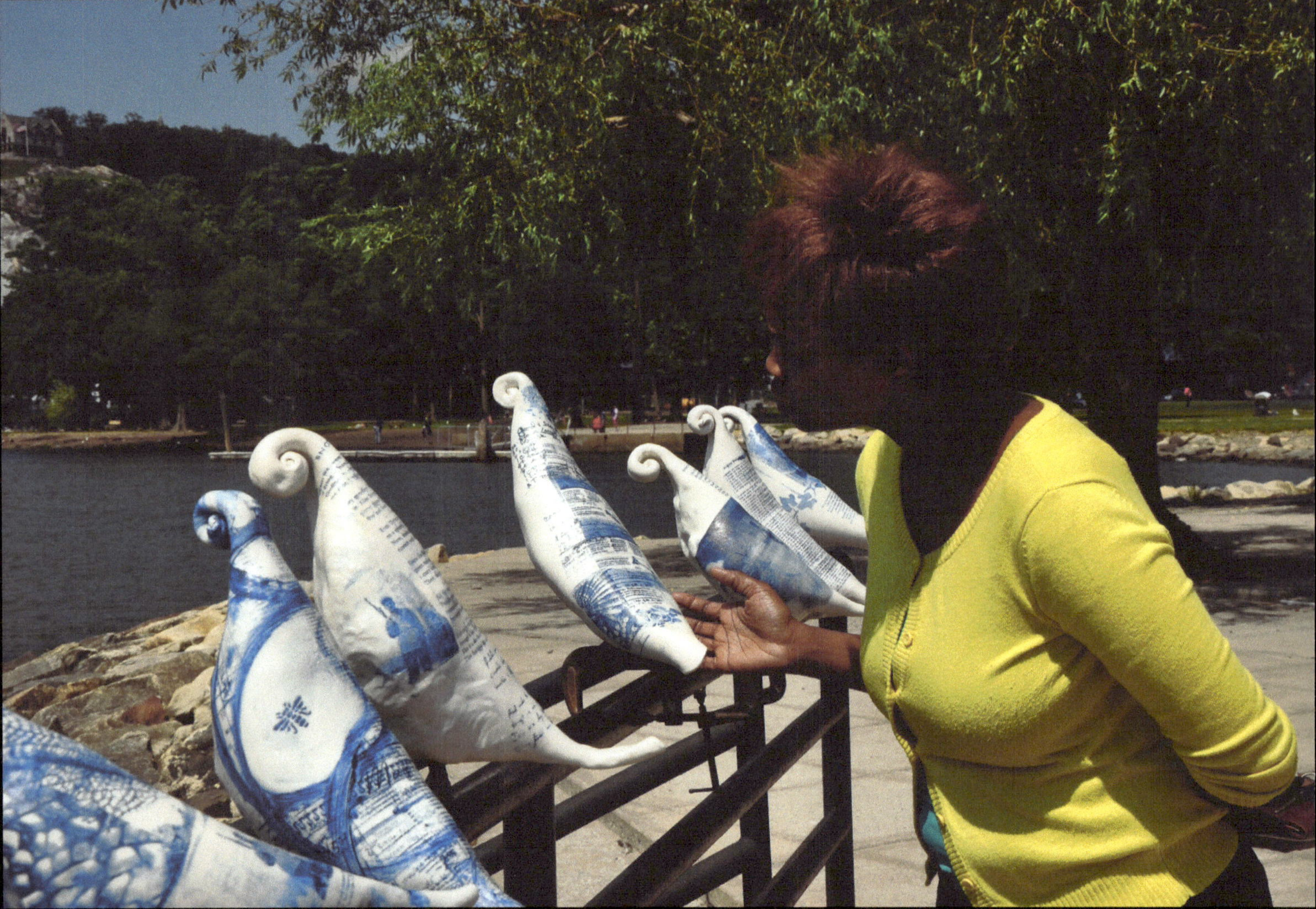

Photo: Oliver Hillenkamp

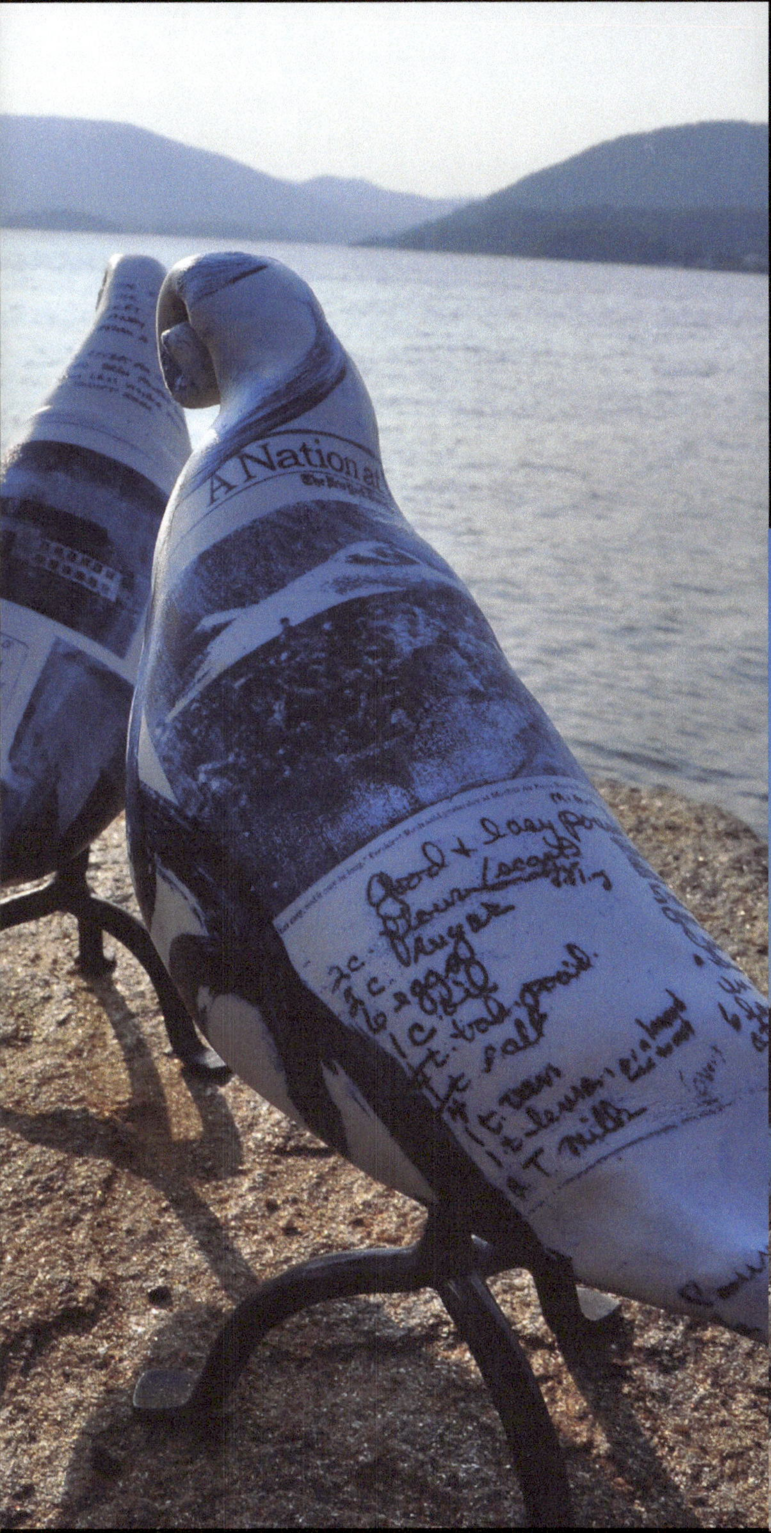

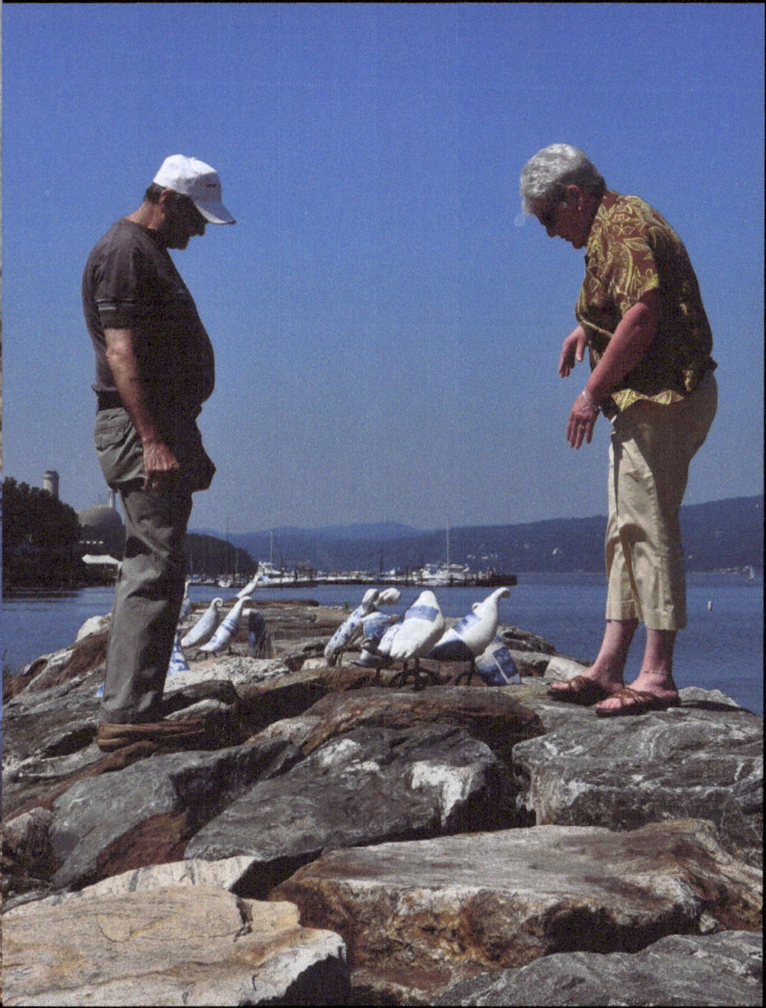

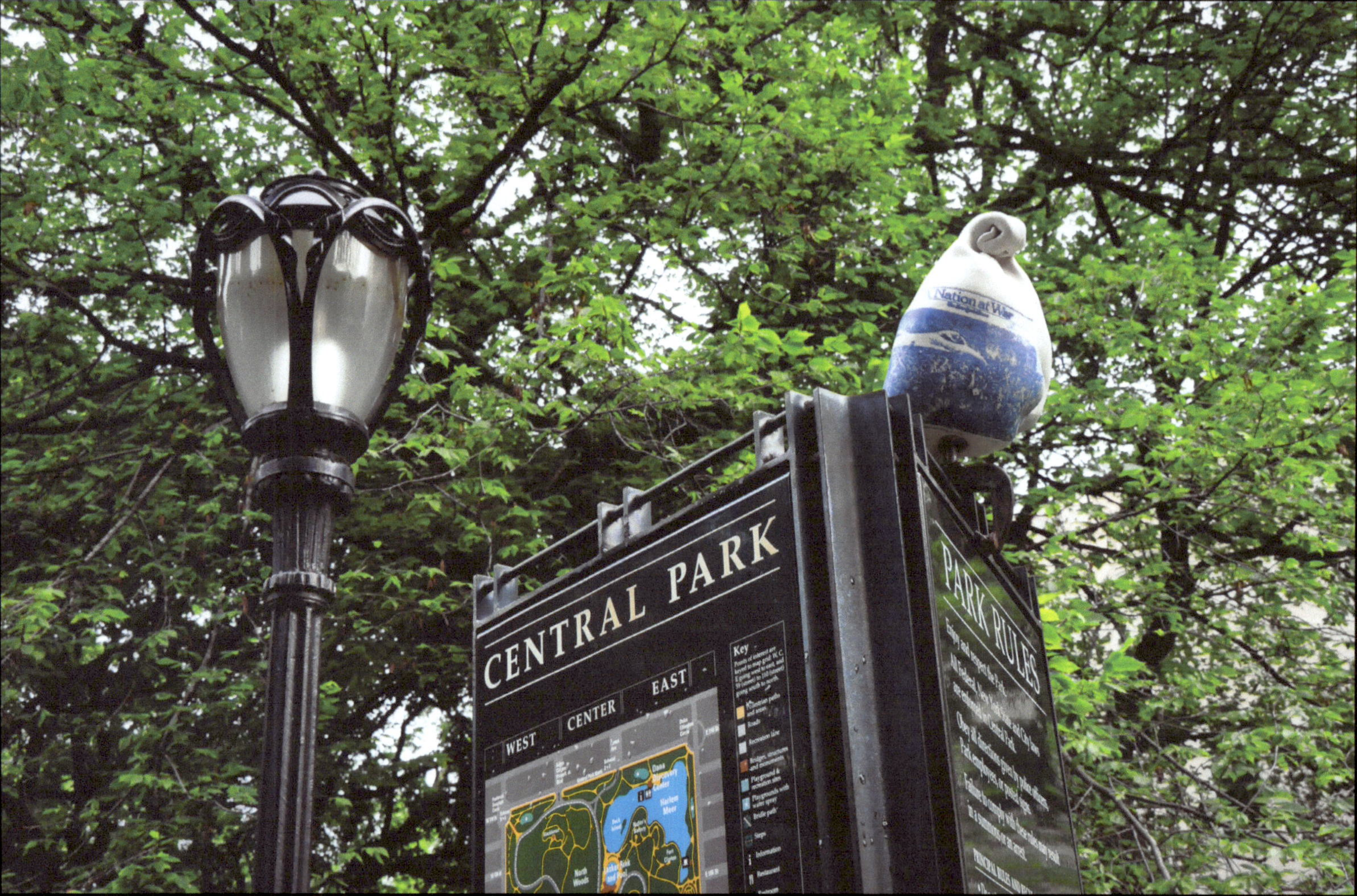

Above and facing page: Central Park, New York, NY 7/2/2009.

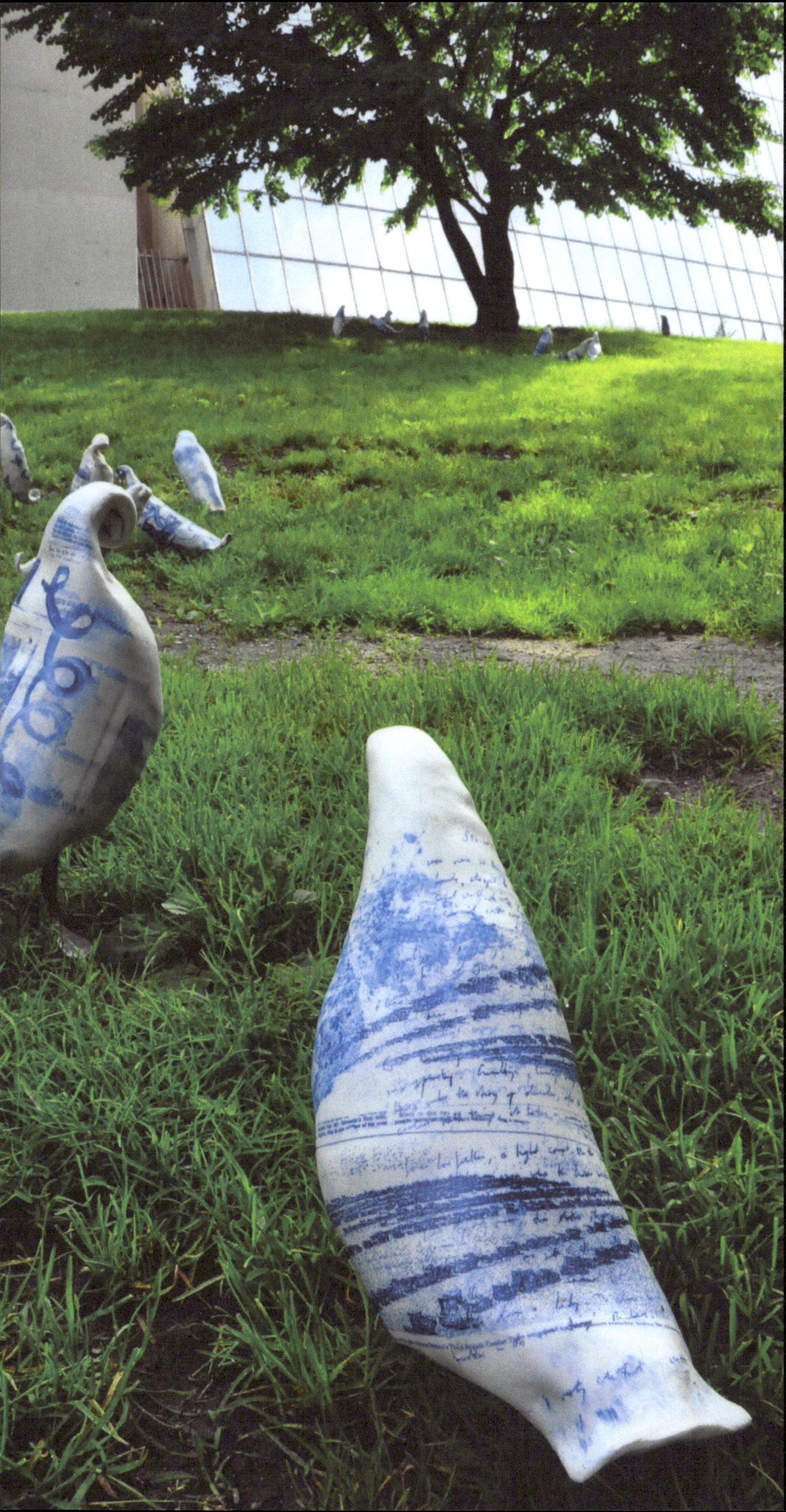

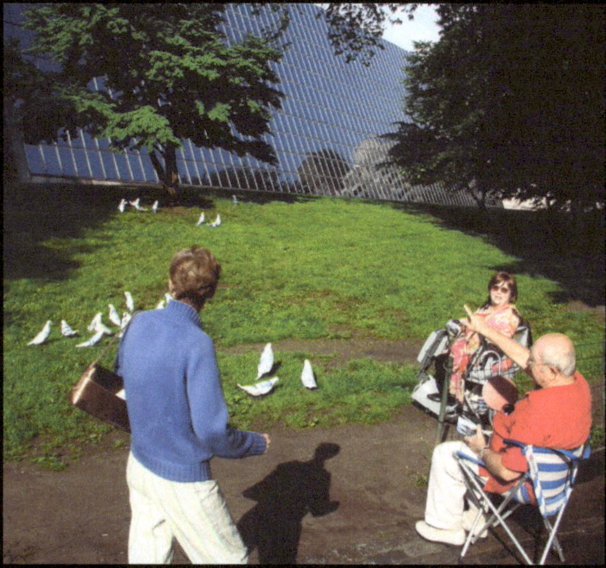

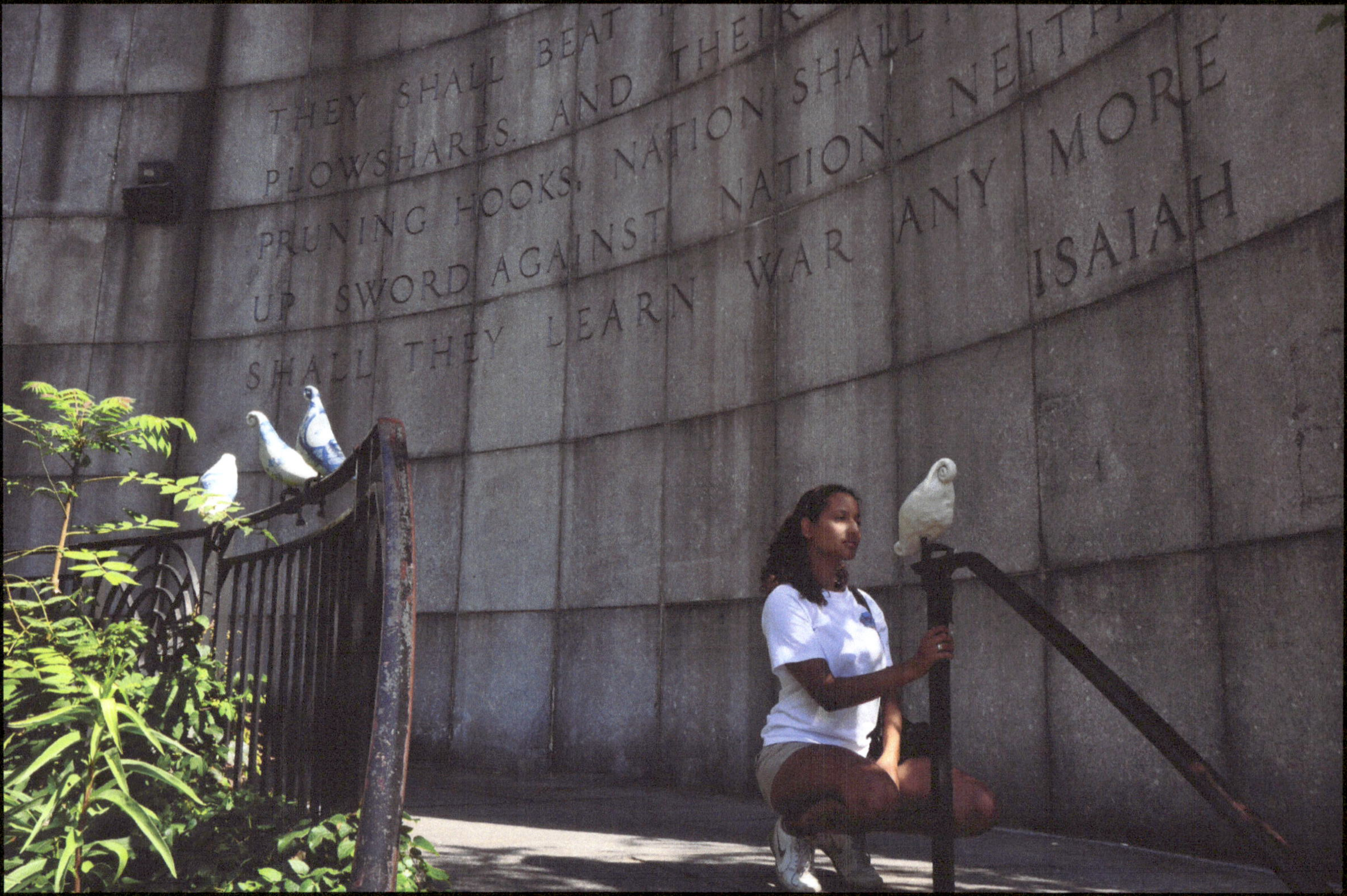

Above and facing page: UN Headquarters/Ralph Bunche Park, New York, NY 7/1/2010.

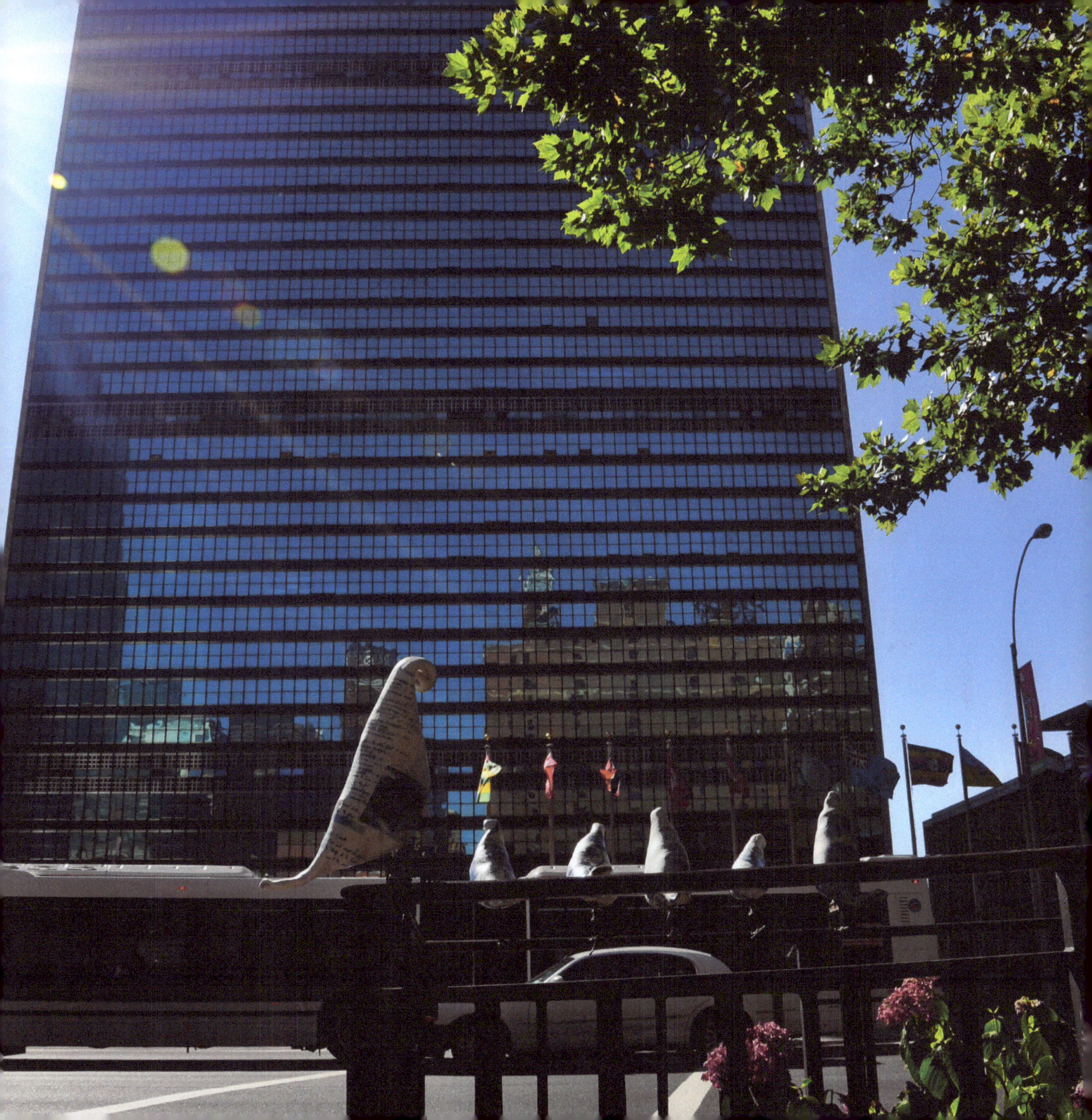

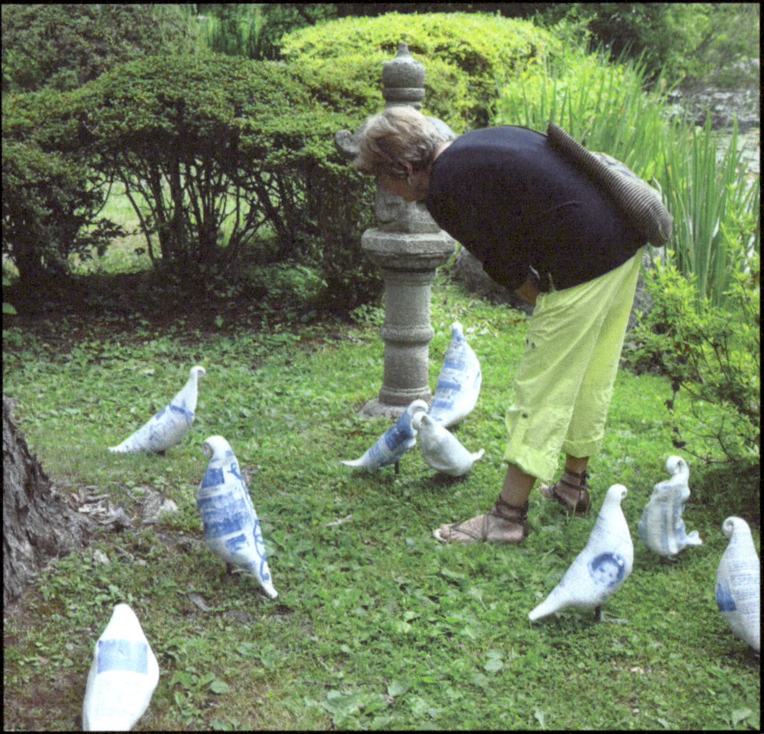

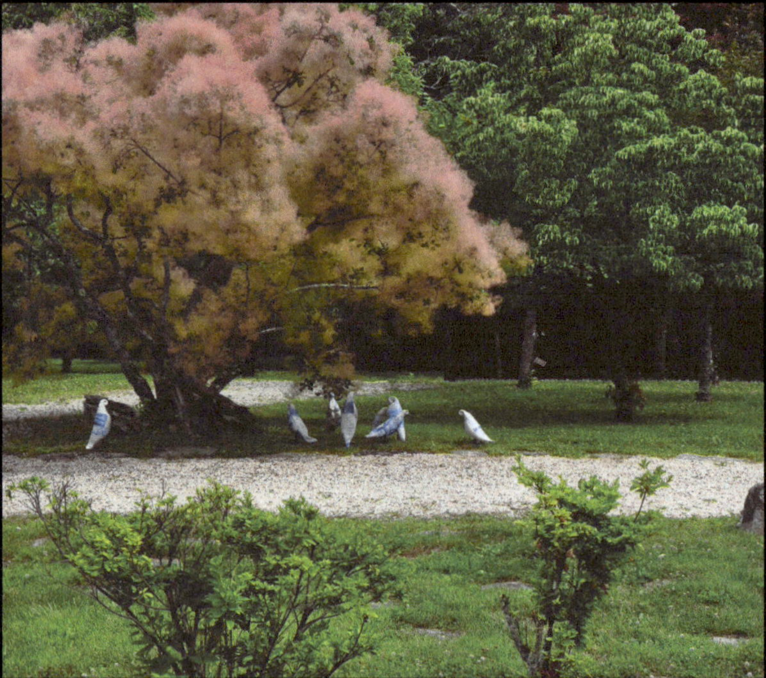

This and facing page: Hammond Museum and Japanese Stroll Garden, North Salem, NY 6/26/2010.

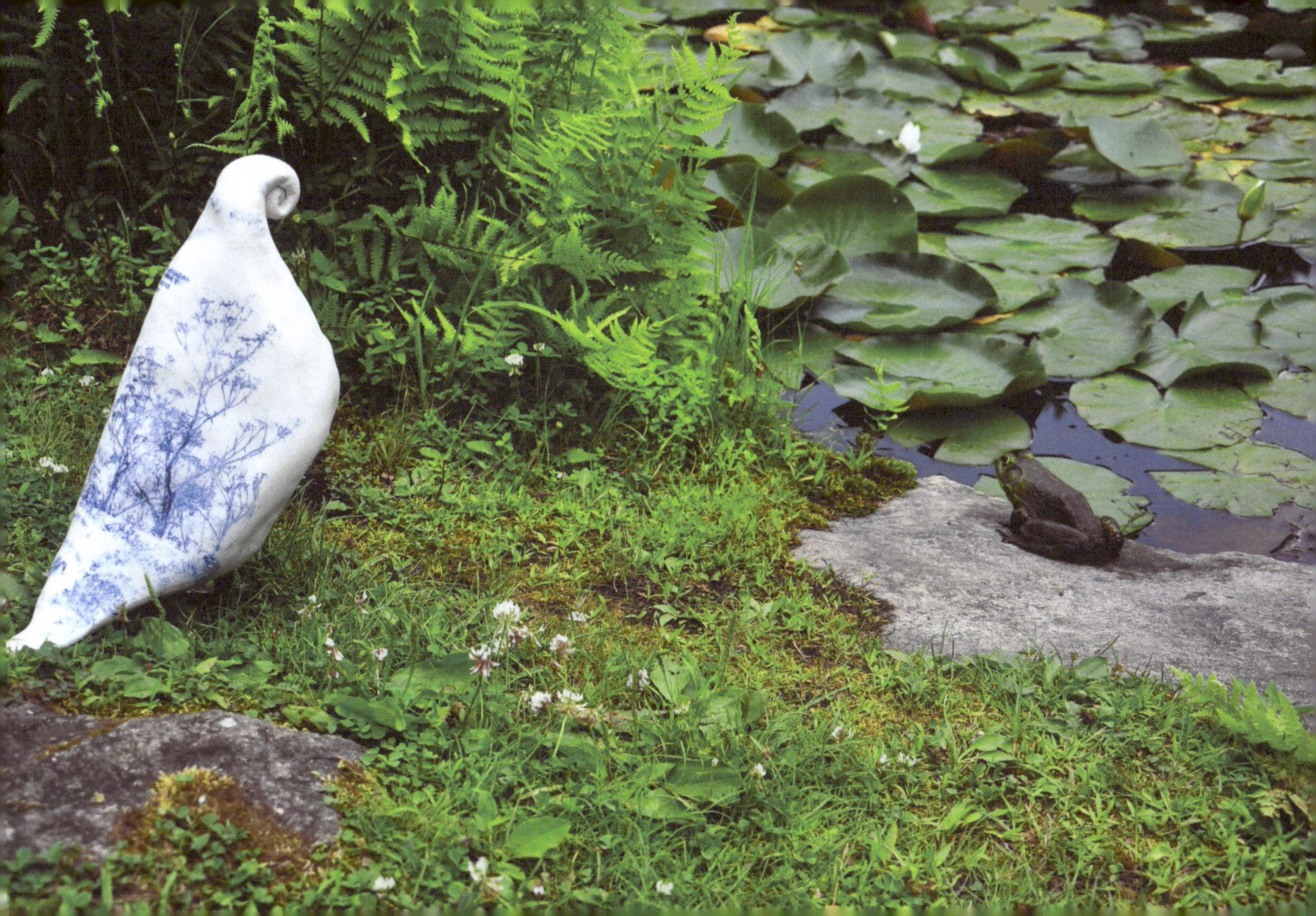

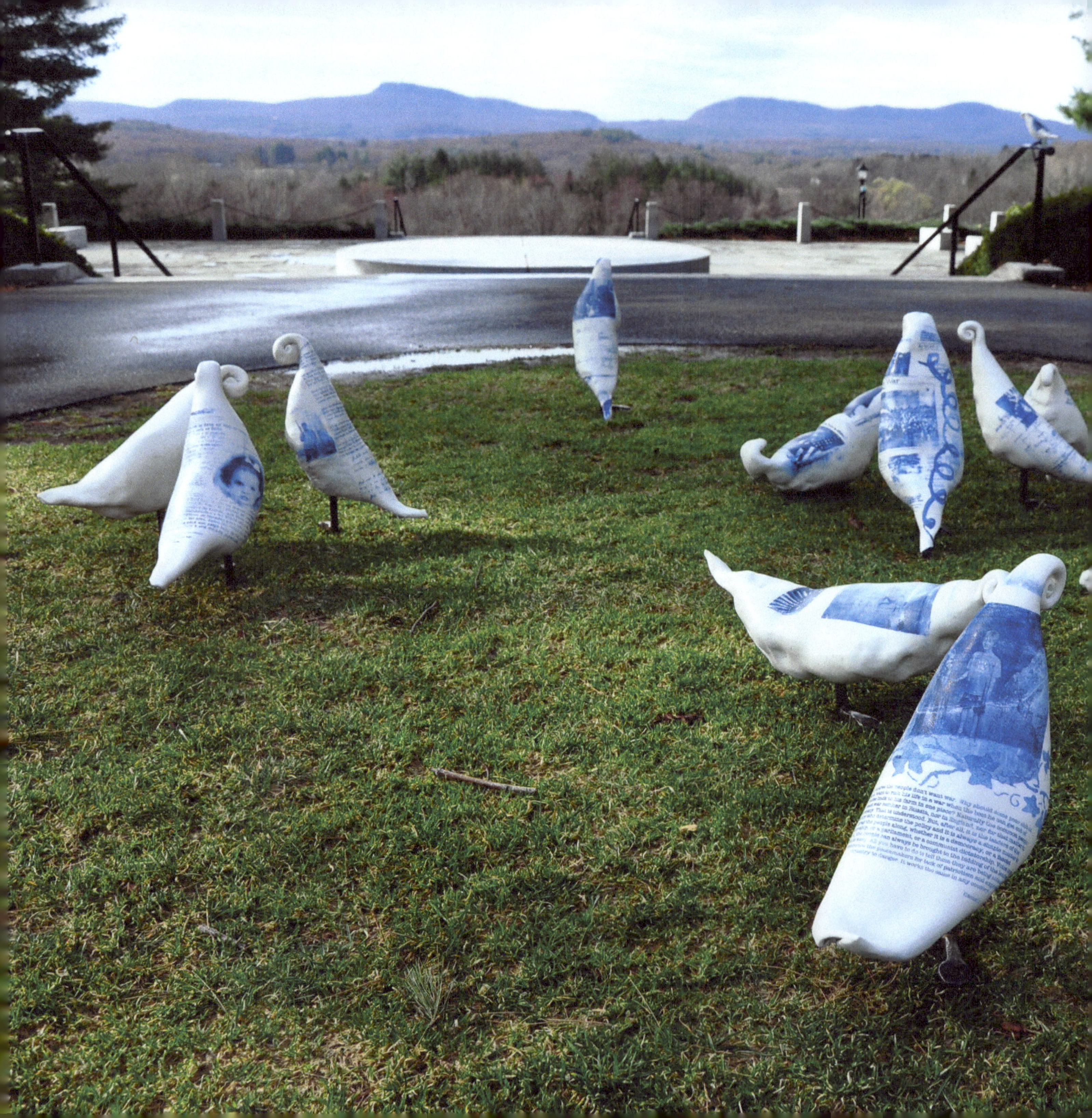

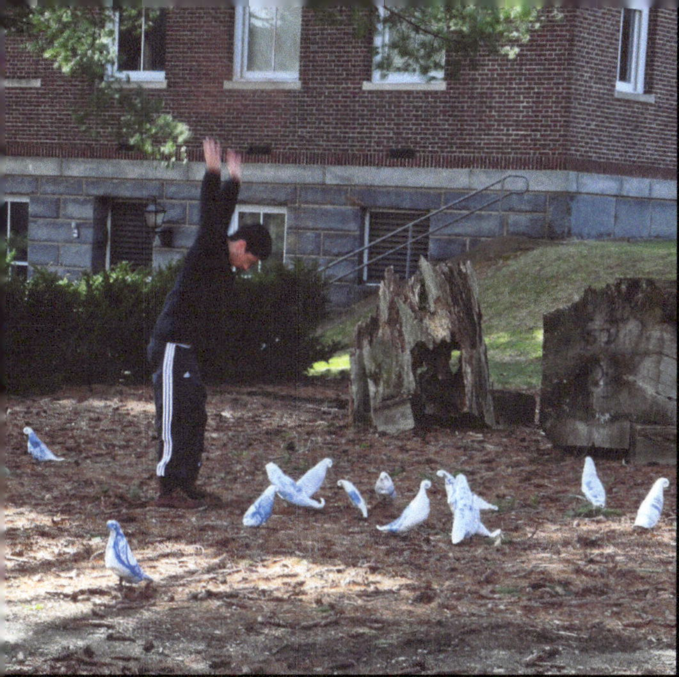

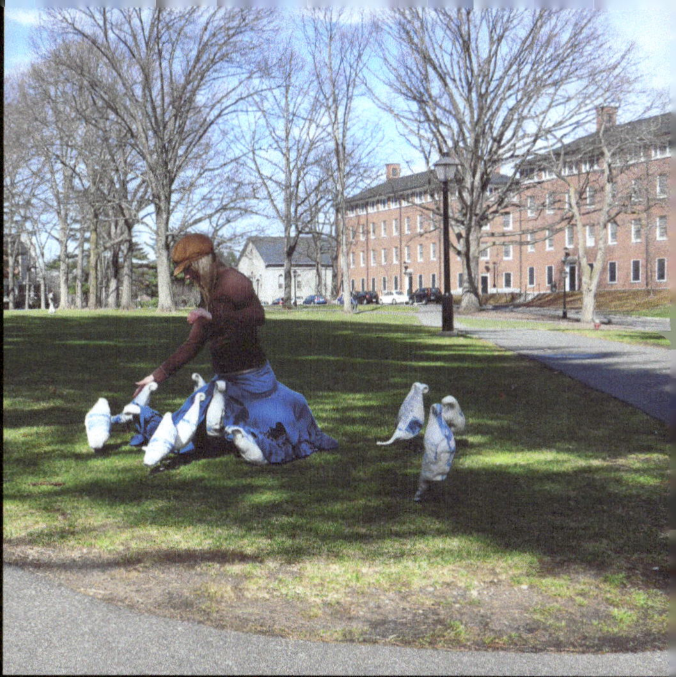

The Amherst College installation was unusual because the birds and I were invited to visit an improvisational choreography/dance class the day before the landing, as subject matter for the dancers to interact with. Some of the dance students then came during the actual outdoor installation and spontaneously performed with the birds.

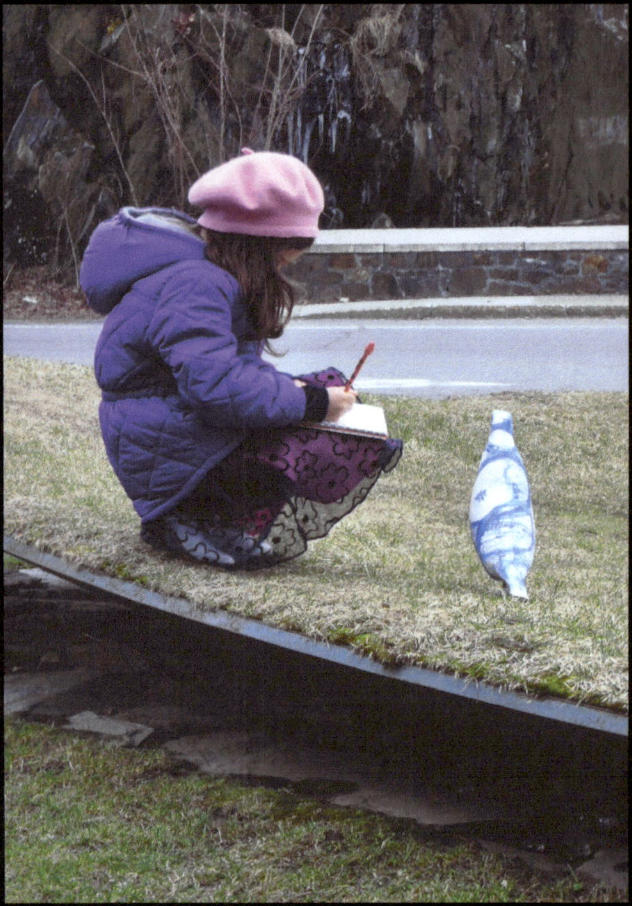

Brattleboro Museum and Art Center,
Brattleboro, VT 3/28/2010.

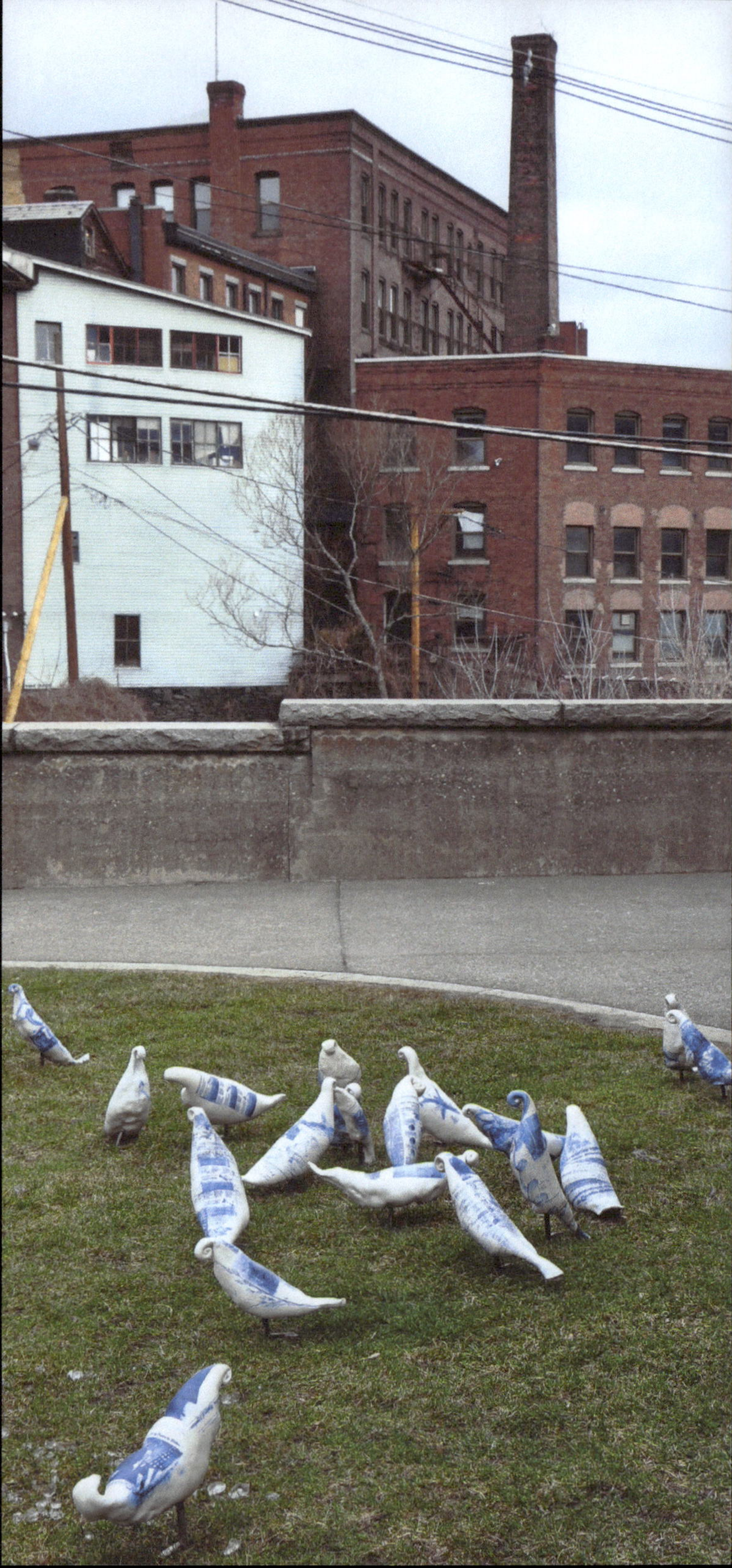

Galapagos, Ecuador

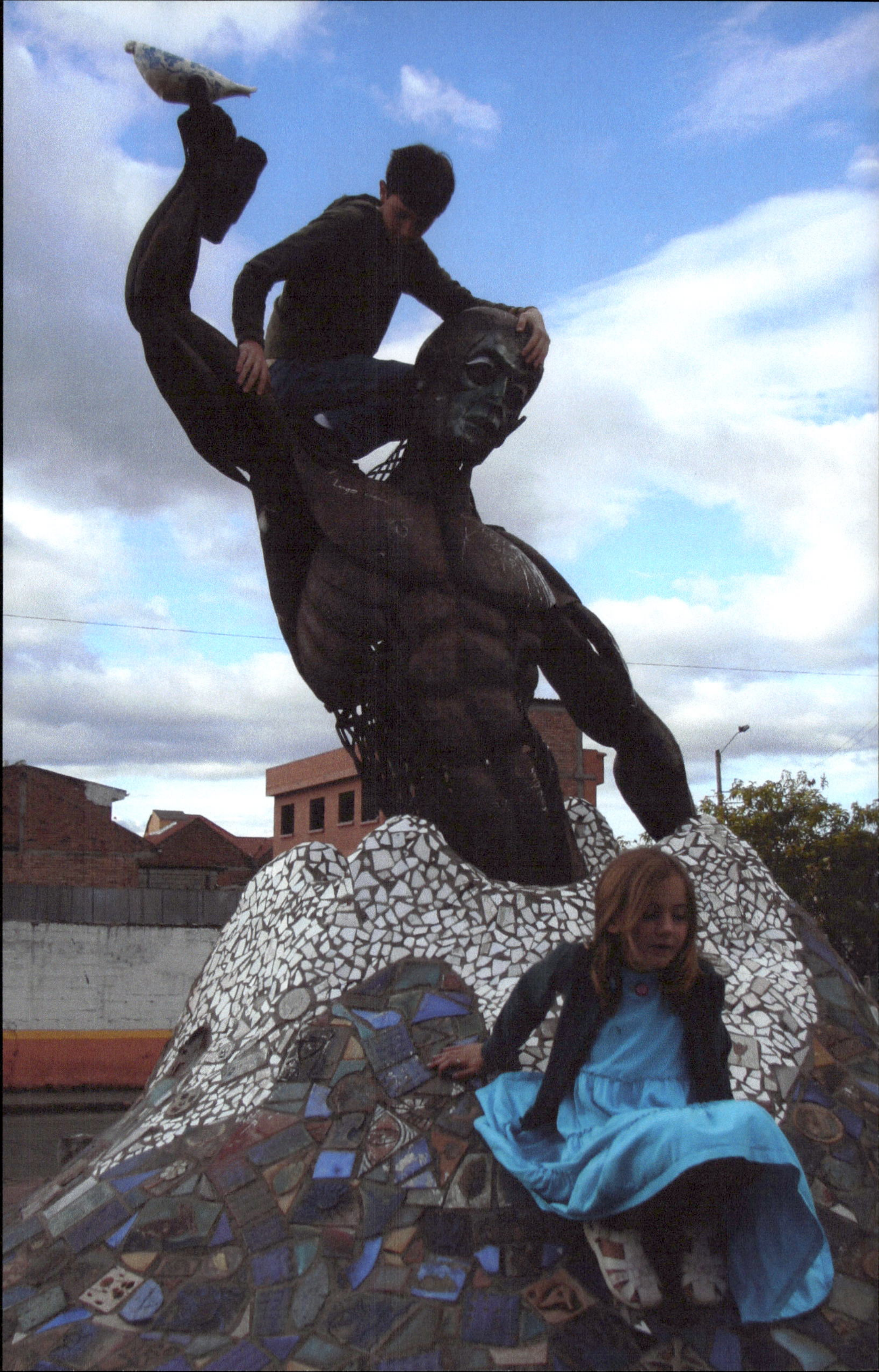

Plaza del Herrero,
Cuenca, Ecuador
8/21/2009.

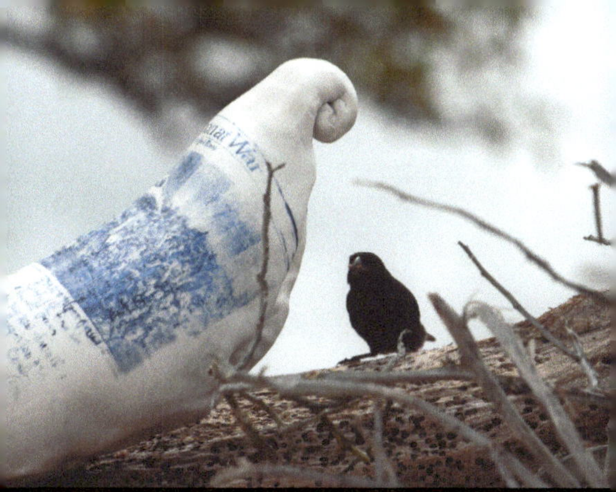

n 1996, Helmut Hillenkamp and I went dowr o Cuenca, Ecuador to build a Monument tc he Blacksmiths for a plaza in the traditiona blacksmithing neighborhood there. We livec n Cuenca for seven months, and became close riends with our collaborator, the architec Fausto Cardoso, and his family.

Twelve years and several collaborations later our two families arranged to go to the Galapagos slands, together with my bird project. There was one official landing of the project for the public, at the main harbor of the island we stayed on, arranged by the Municipio of Santa Cruz. And then there were many informa excursions with impromptu landings, and these became more about the animals. We were fou adults and five children, and all nine of us woulc set out in the morning with porcelain birds ir our backpacks. Exploring destinations by foot we were amazed at how indifferent the animals were to our presence, and it was fascinating tc see, as well, how the feeling of the porcelair bird installation changed in this environmen with so few people; in some ways irrelevant and at the same time even more meaningful, as a harbinger of human culture.

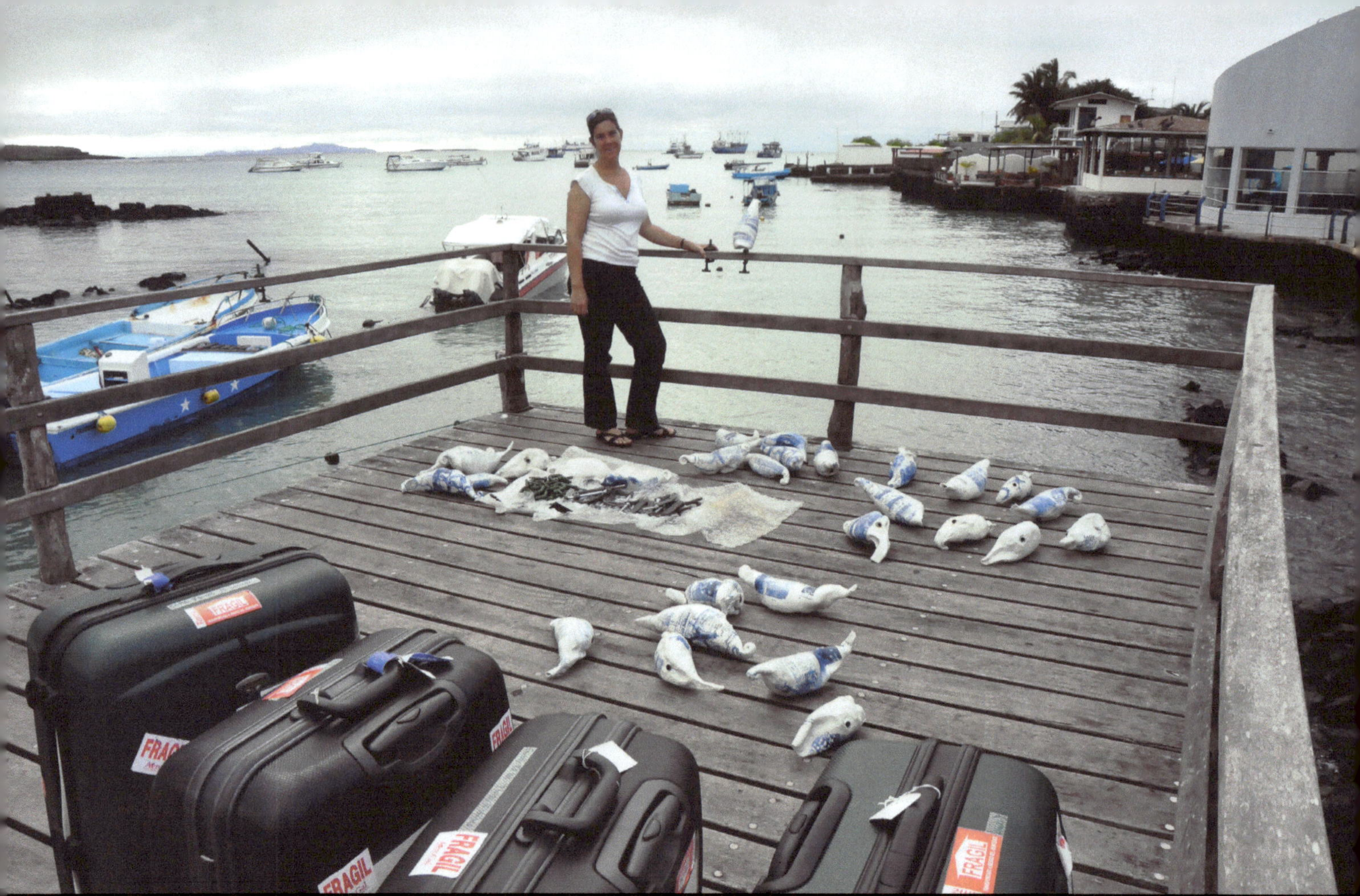

Photo: Helmut Hillenkamp

Above and facing page: Pelican Bay, Island of Santa Cruz, The Galapagos 8/29/2009

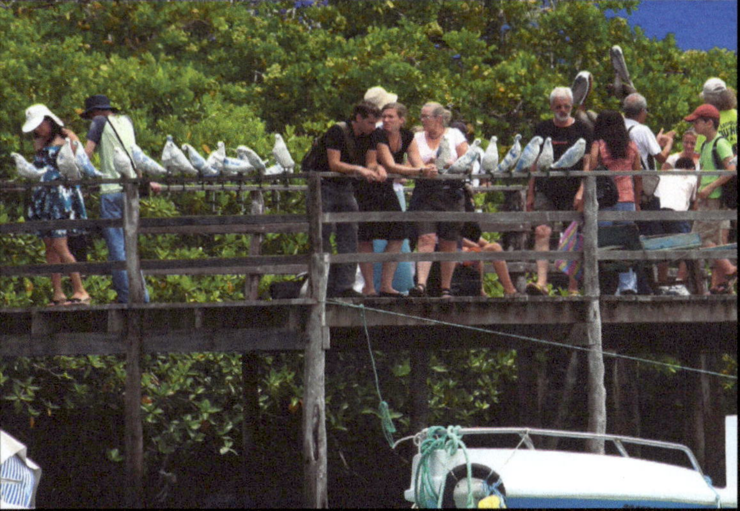

Photo: Fausto Cardoso

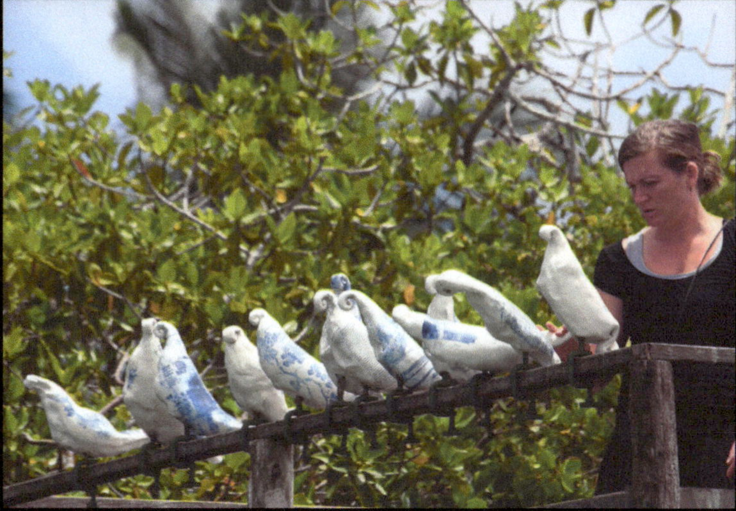

Photo: Fausto Cardoso

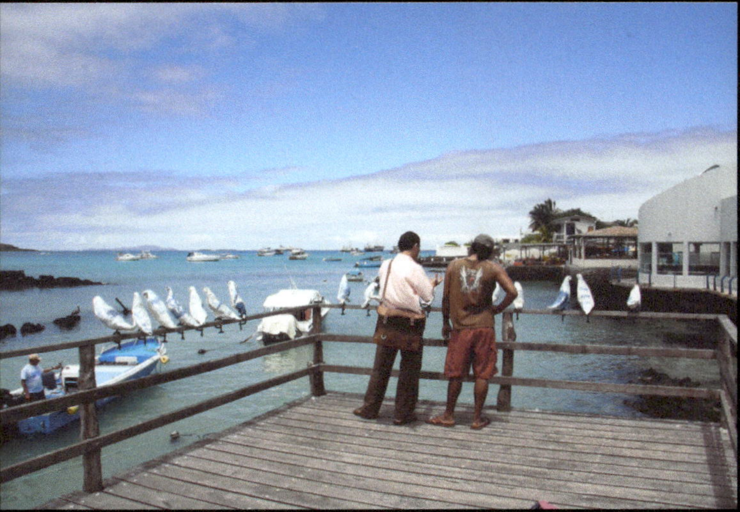

Photo: Helmut Hillenkamp

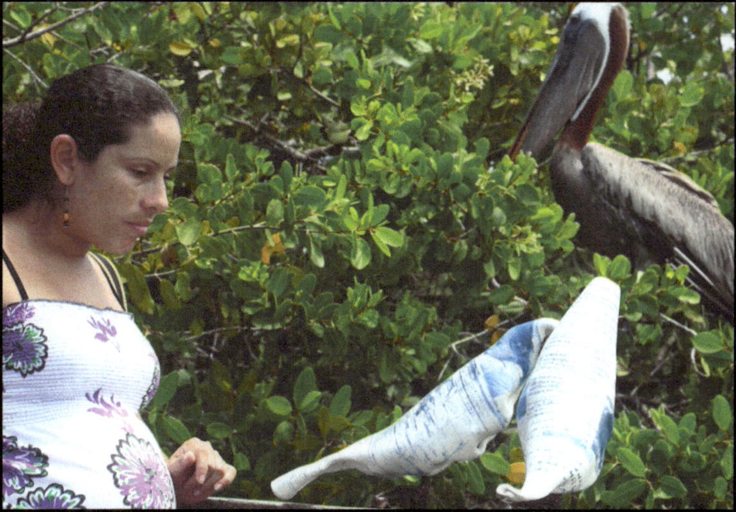

Photo: Fausto Cardoso

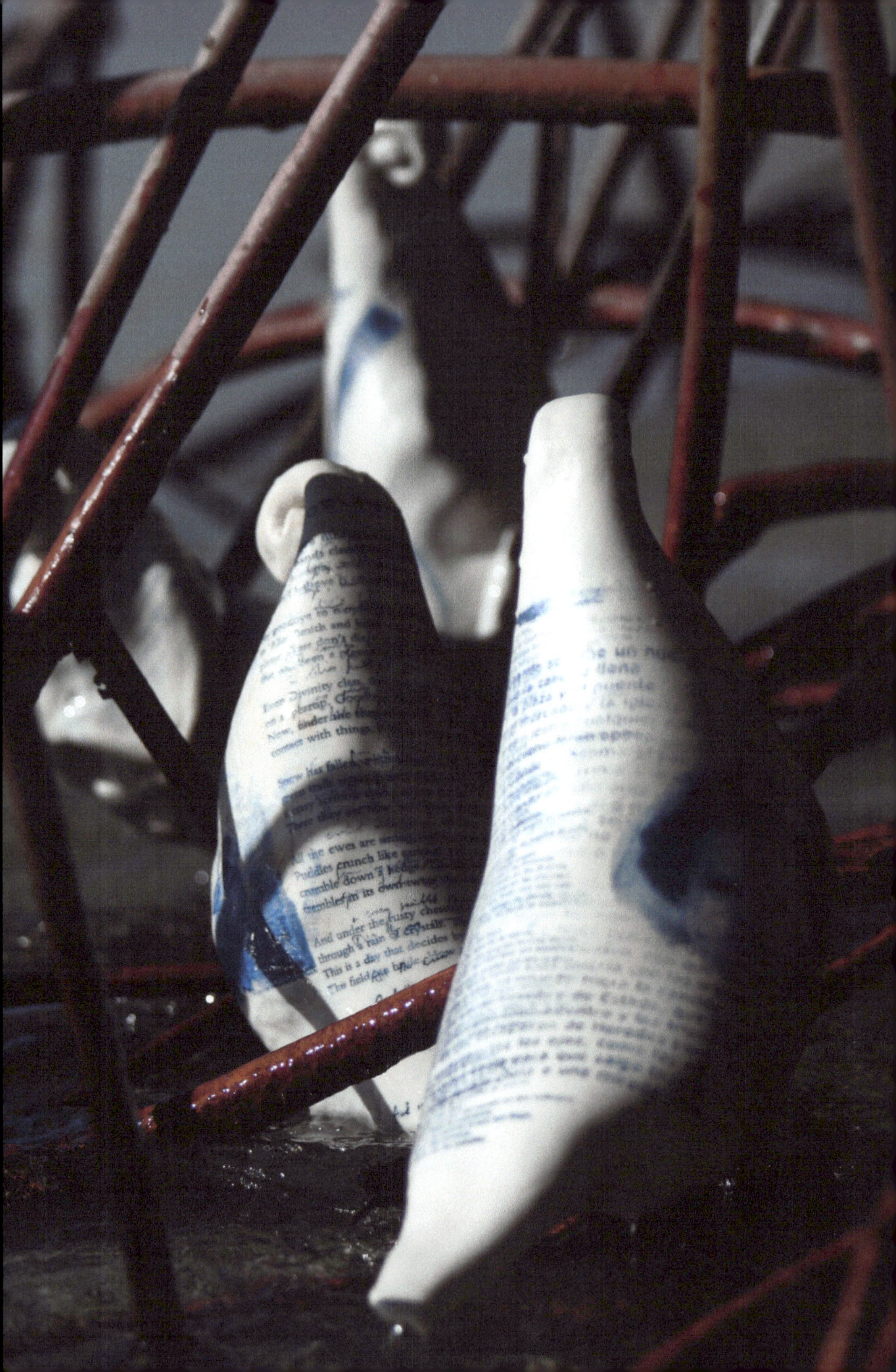

Photo: Fausto Cardoso

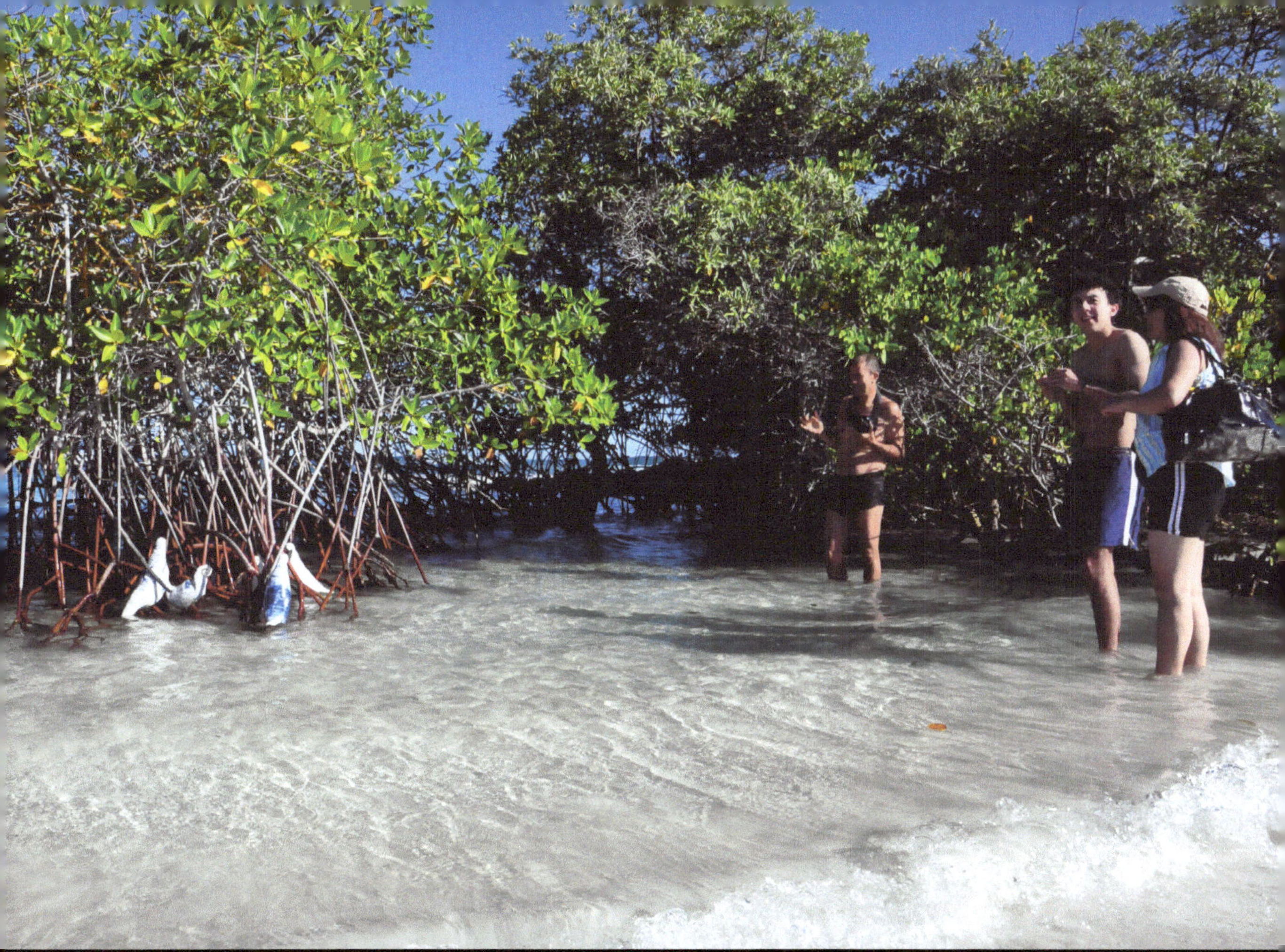

Above and facing page: Tortuga Bay, Island of Santa Cruz, The Galapagos 9/5/2009

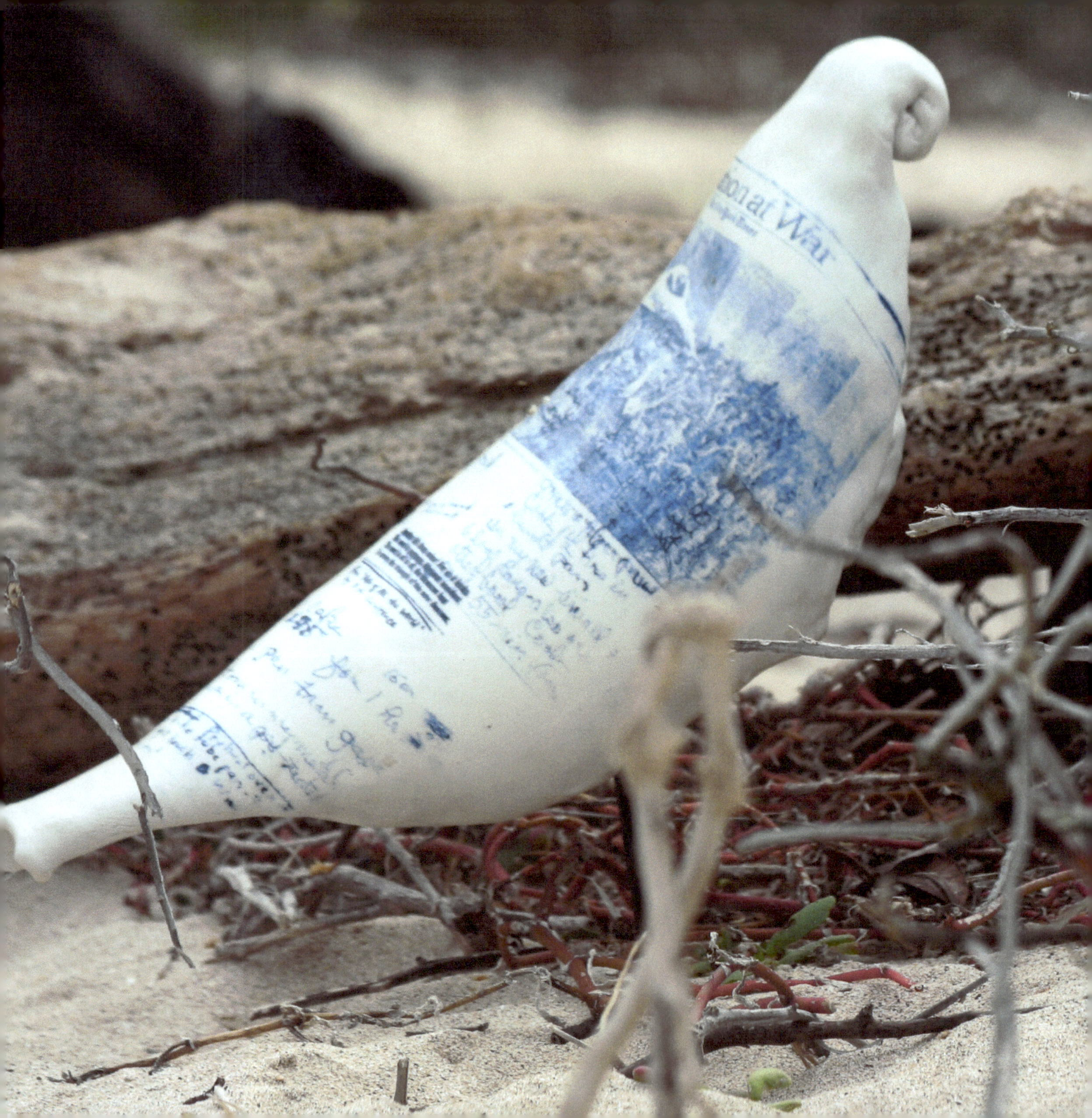

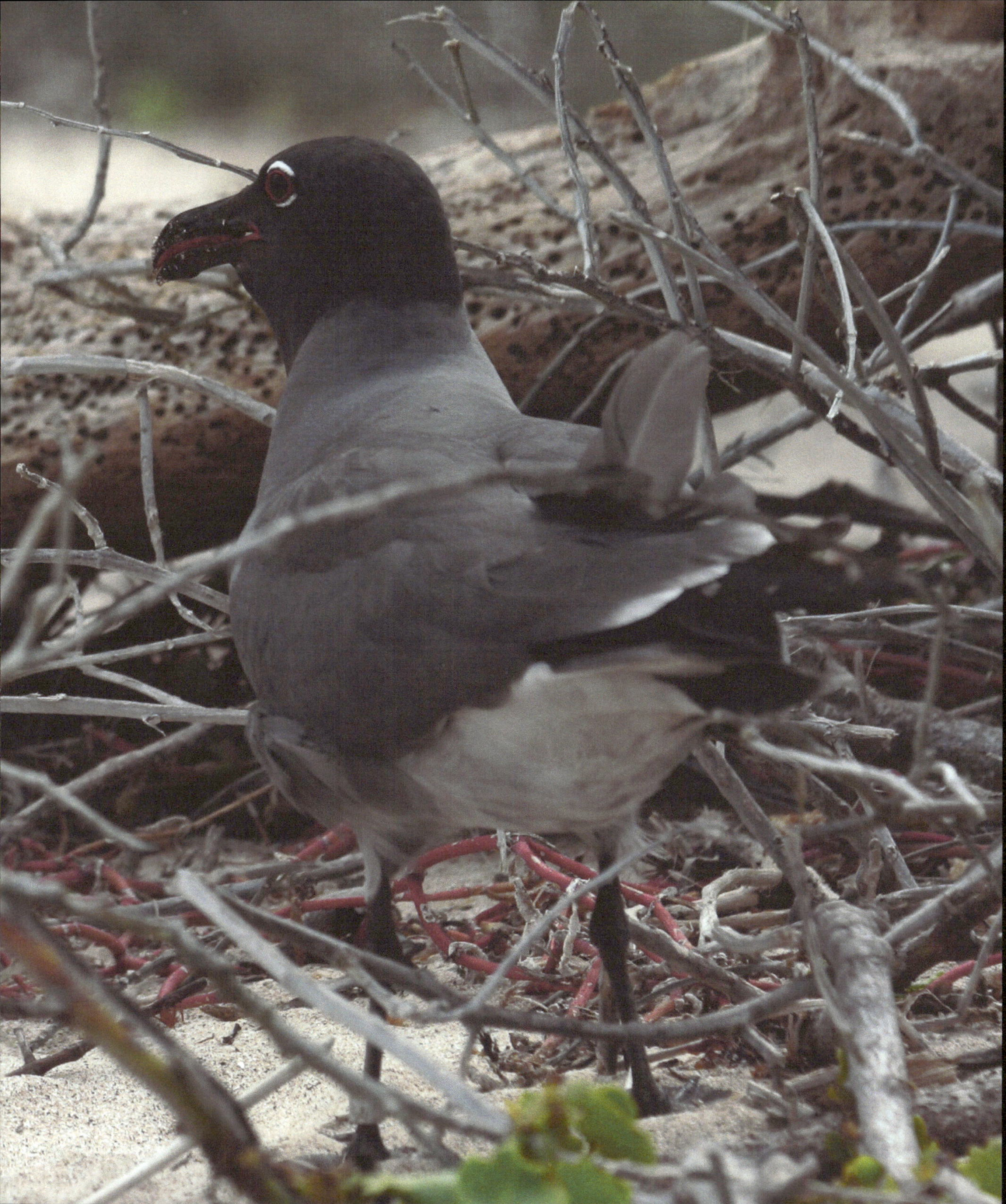

Garapatero Beach, Island of Santa Cruz, The Galapagos 8/31/2009.

Photo: Fausto Cardoso

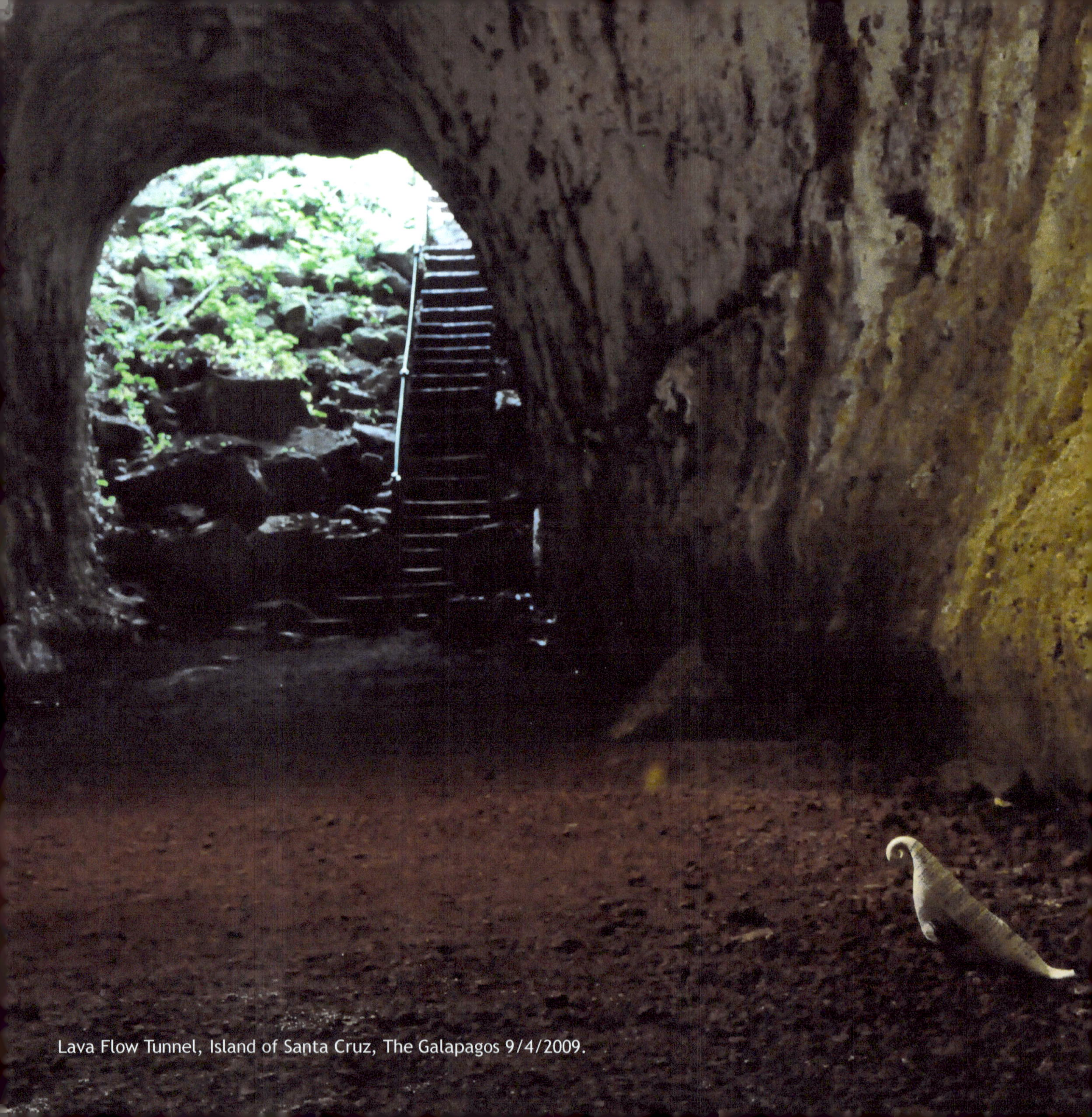

Lava Flow Tunnel, Island of Santa Cruz, The Galapagos 9/4/2009.

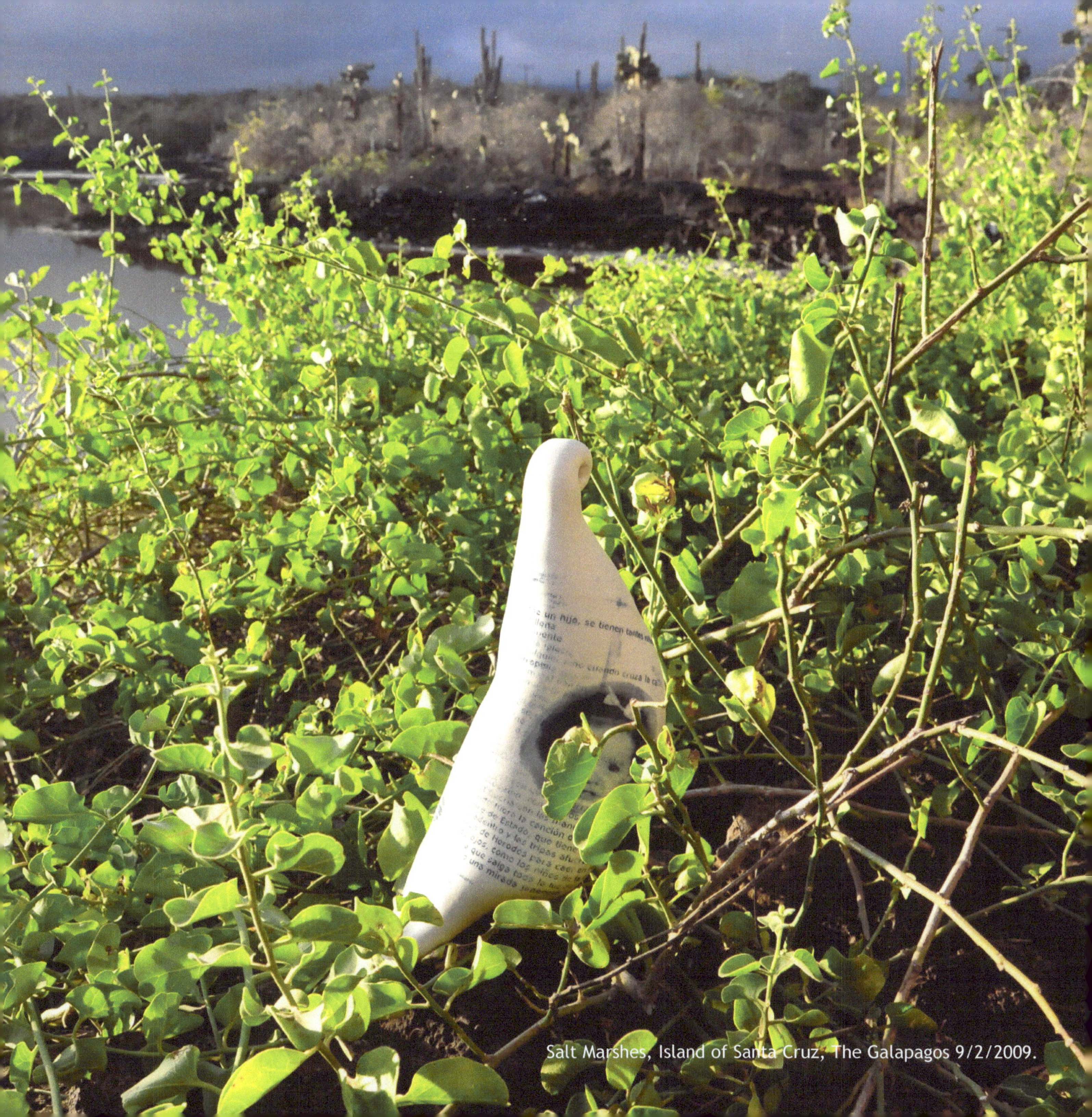

Salt Marshes, Island of Santa Cruz, The Galapagos 9/2/2009.

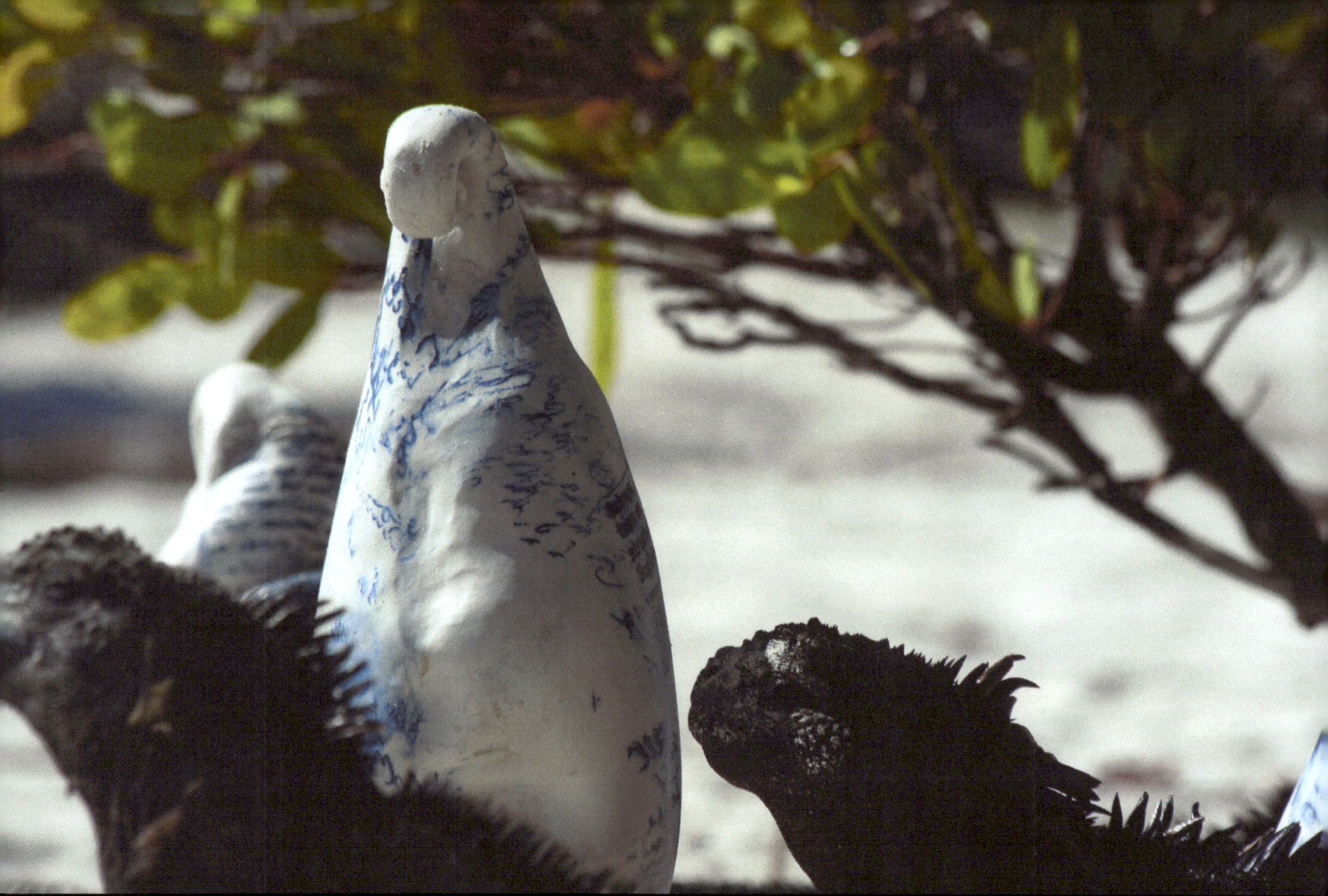

Photo: Fausto Cardoso

Tortuga Bay, Island of Santa Cruz, The Galapagos 9/5/2009

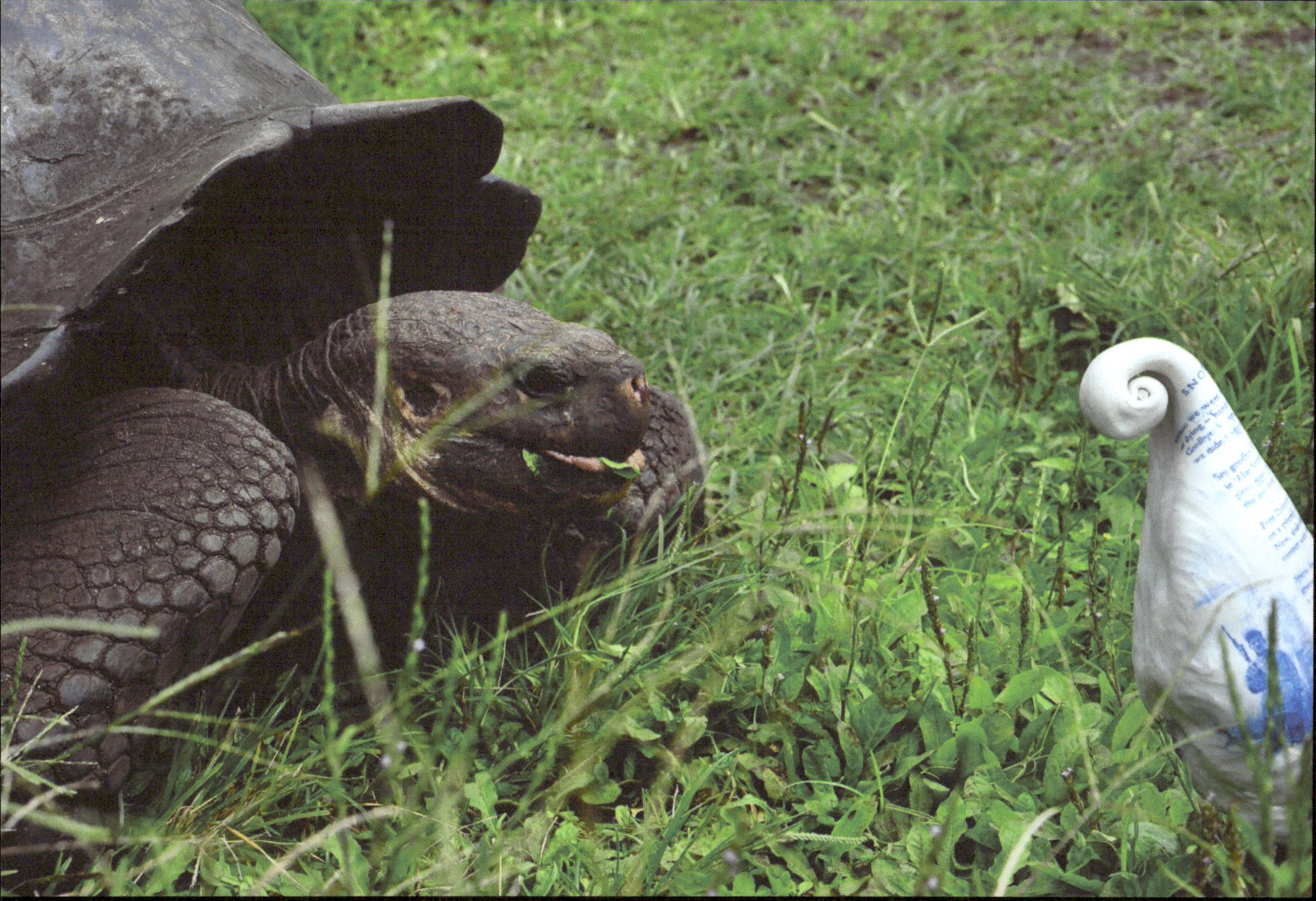

Photo: Helmut Hillenkamp

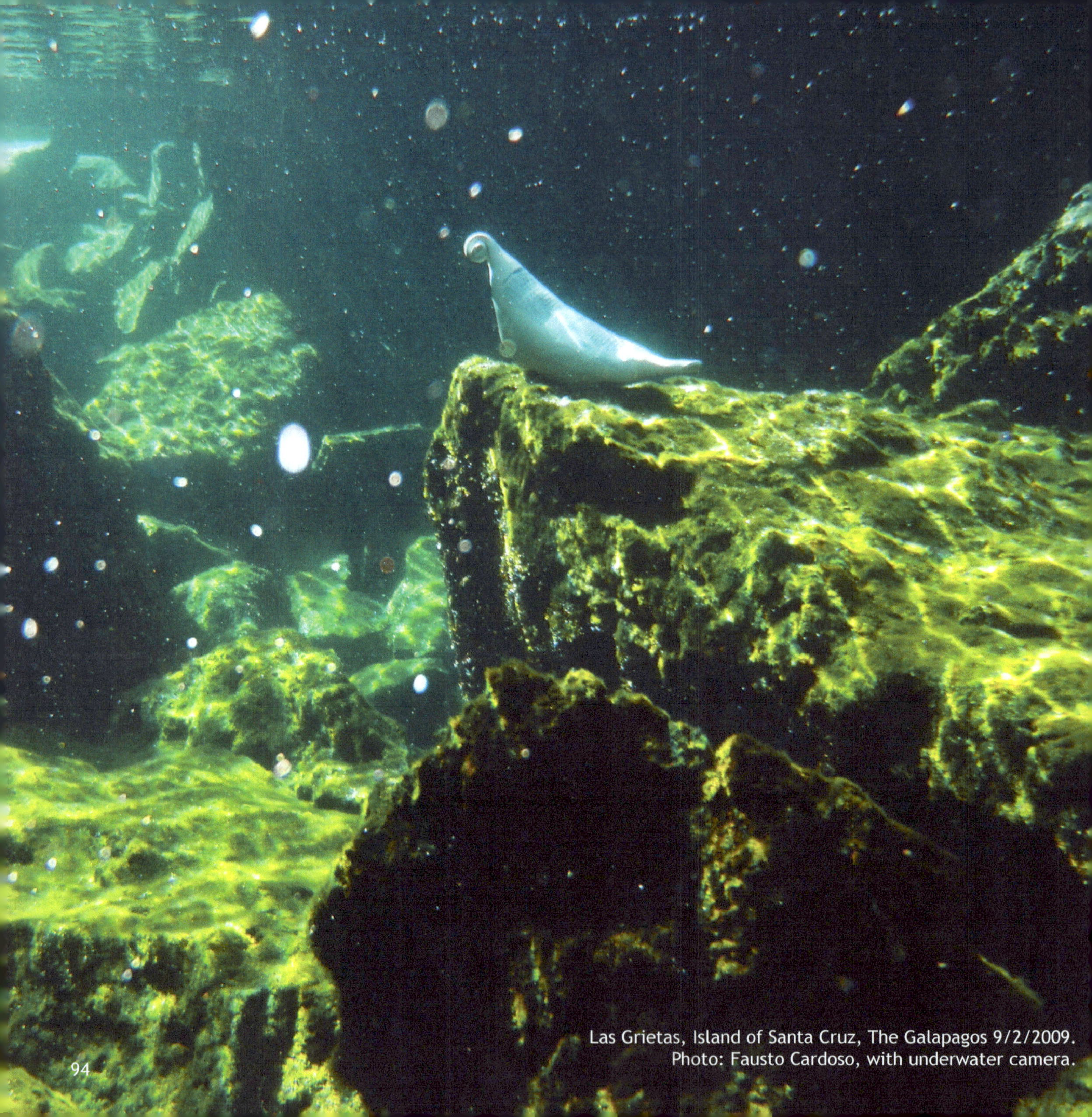

Las Grietas, Island of Santa Cruz, The Galapagos 9/2/2009.
Photo: Fausto Cardoso, with underwater camera.

Europe:

France
Netherlands
Germany

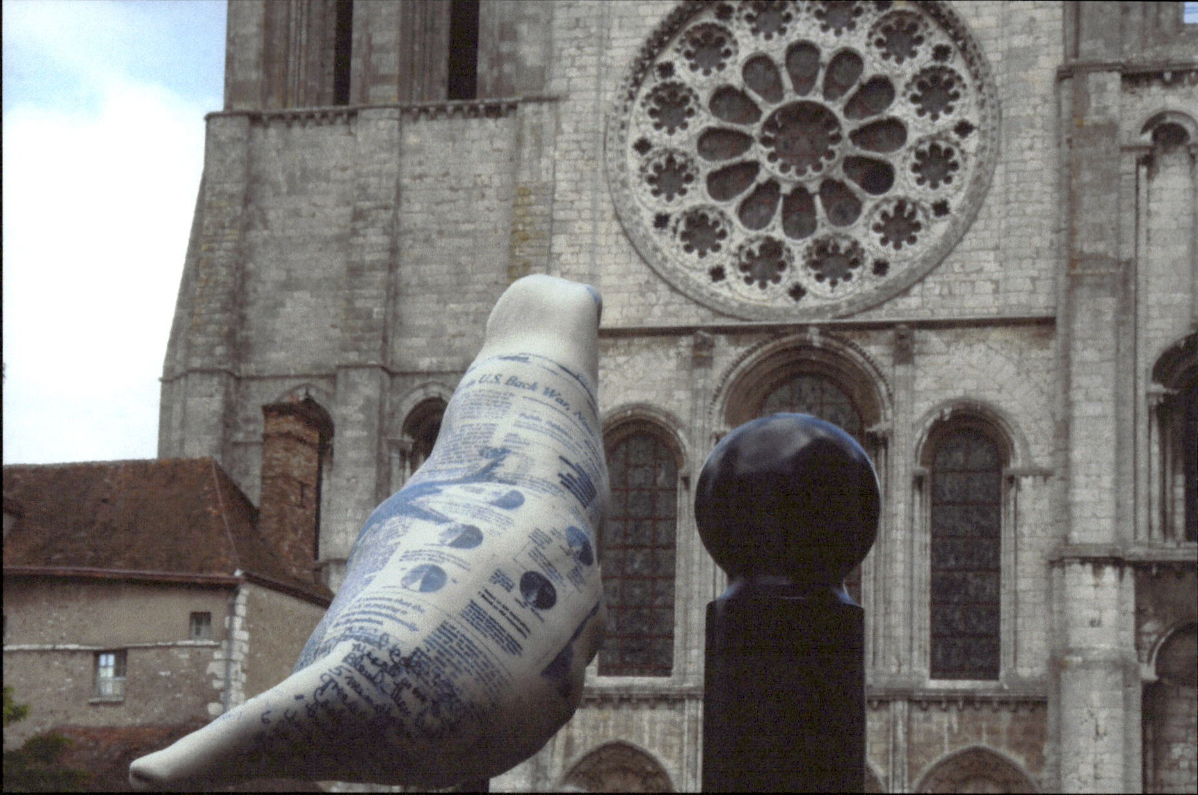

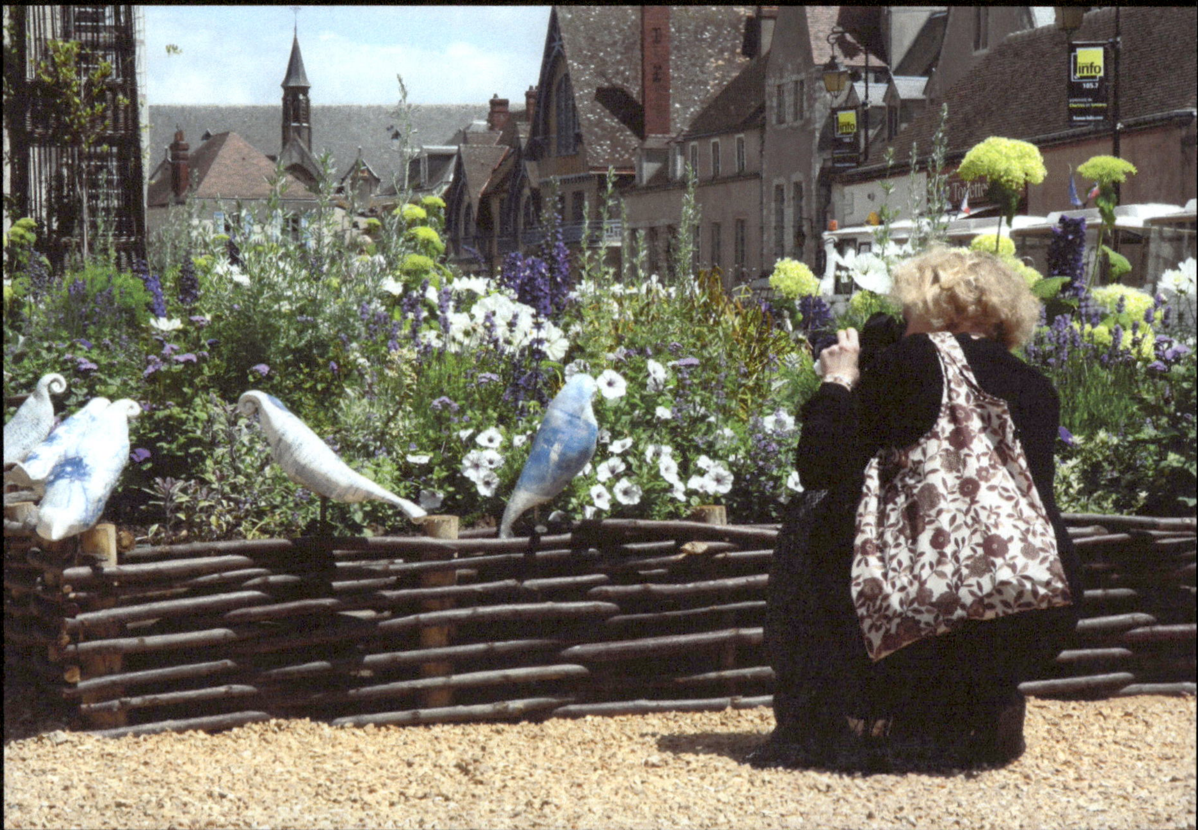

This and facing page: Chartres Cathedral, Chartres, France 6/19/2009.

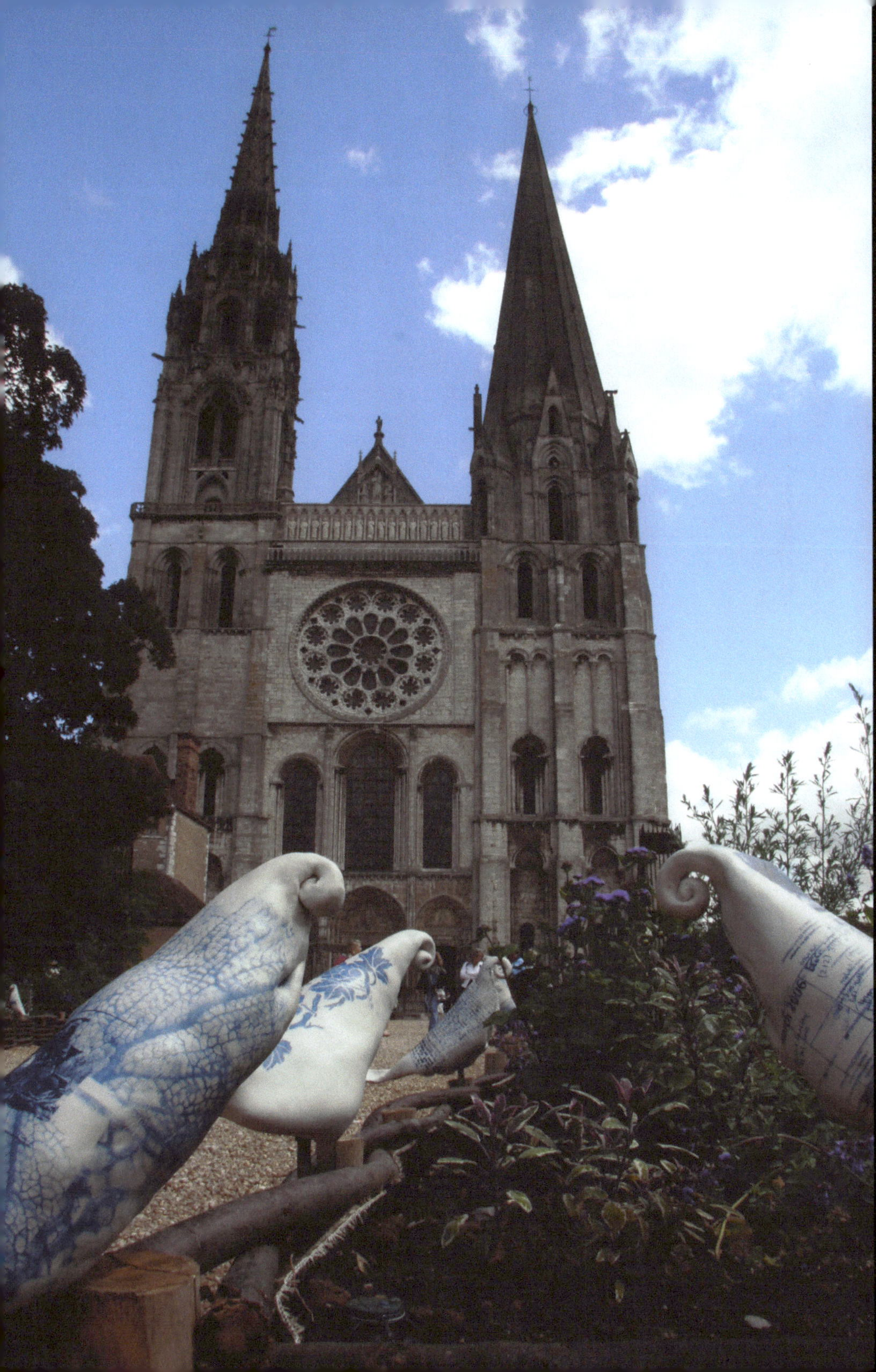

Having decided that we would love to see the birds in front of Chartres Cathedral, we wrote a letter to the Mayor of Chartres, had it translated into French by the friend of a friend, and sent it off. Many e-mails and phone calls later, it still was not clear whether we would get permission, even as we were arriving in France with the birds. A visit to the Musée des Beaux Arts, which is in charge of the space, revealed that it was not possible to put stakes in the ground as we proposed, because of the irrigation system underneath ("C'est impossible!").

Walking away with head hanging, I noticed the flower bed containers with sides of woven branches (see left). A stake could actually thread itself very nicely in between, without damaging anything! I ran back, and we received permission just as the office closed at 5pm, the day before the bird landing.

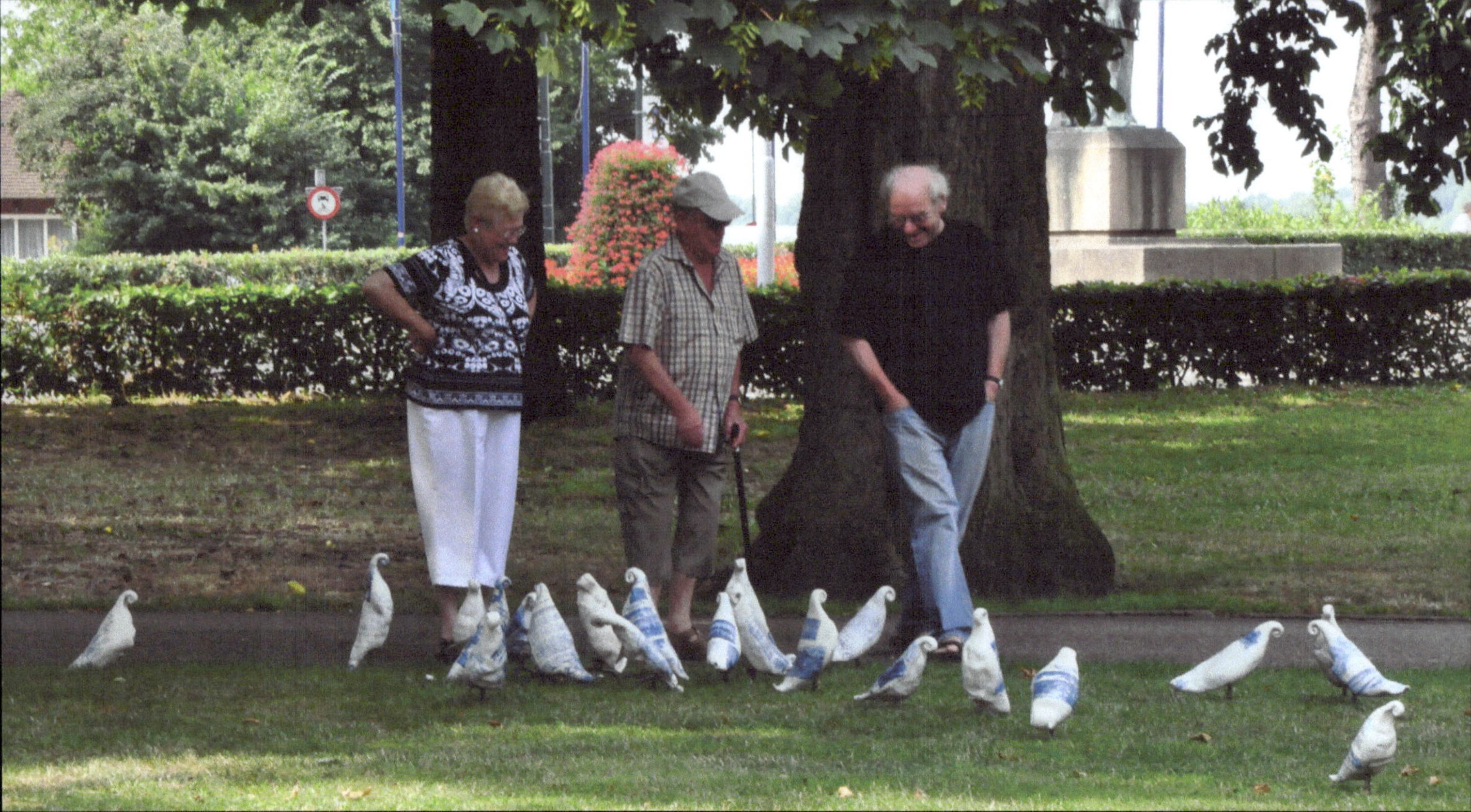

Casino Park, ‘s-Hertogenbosch, The Netherlands 7/21/2010.
This landing was arranged and hosted by the European Ceramic Work Center, pioneers in the field of

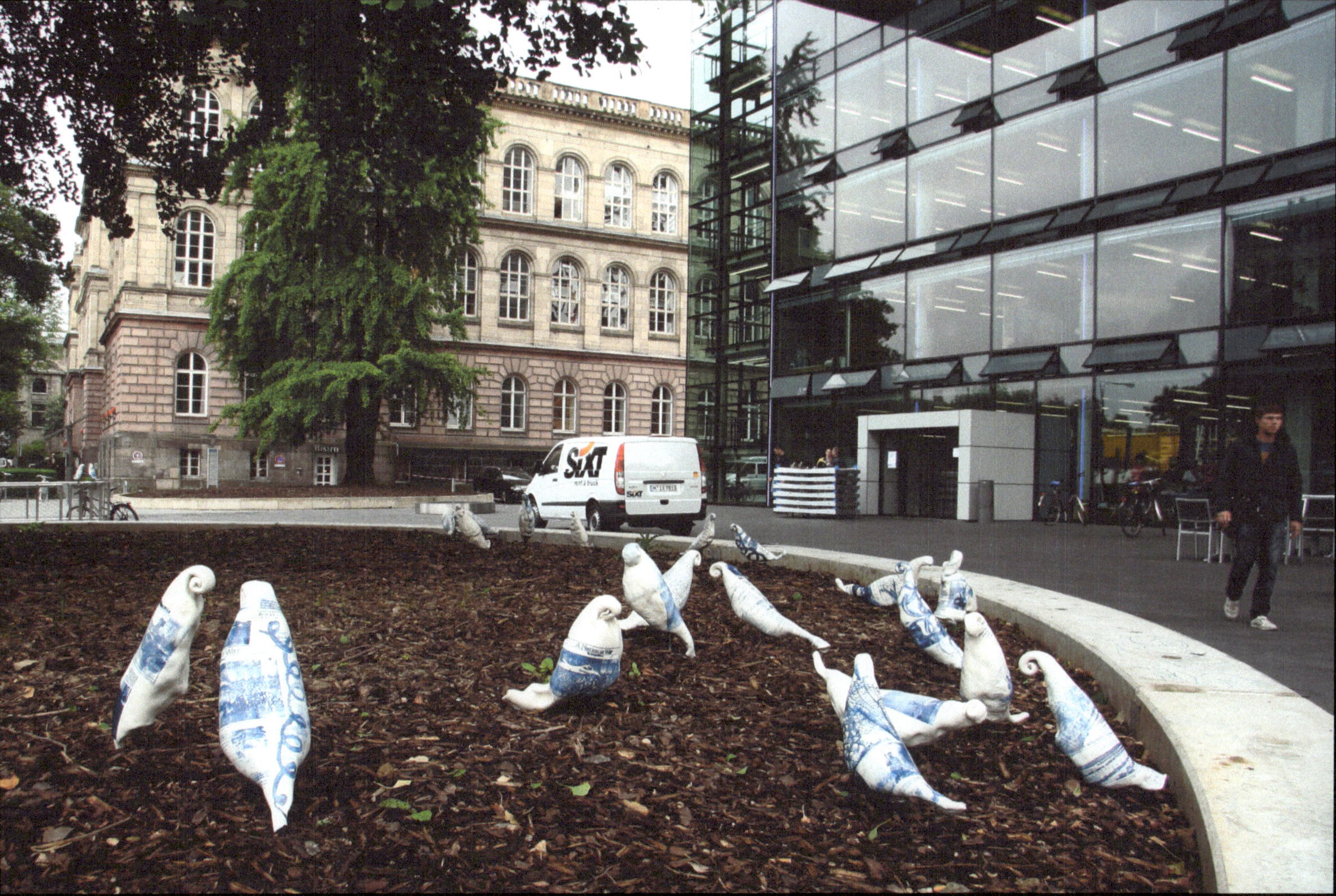

RWTH Aachen University, Aachen, Germany 6/10/2009.

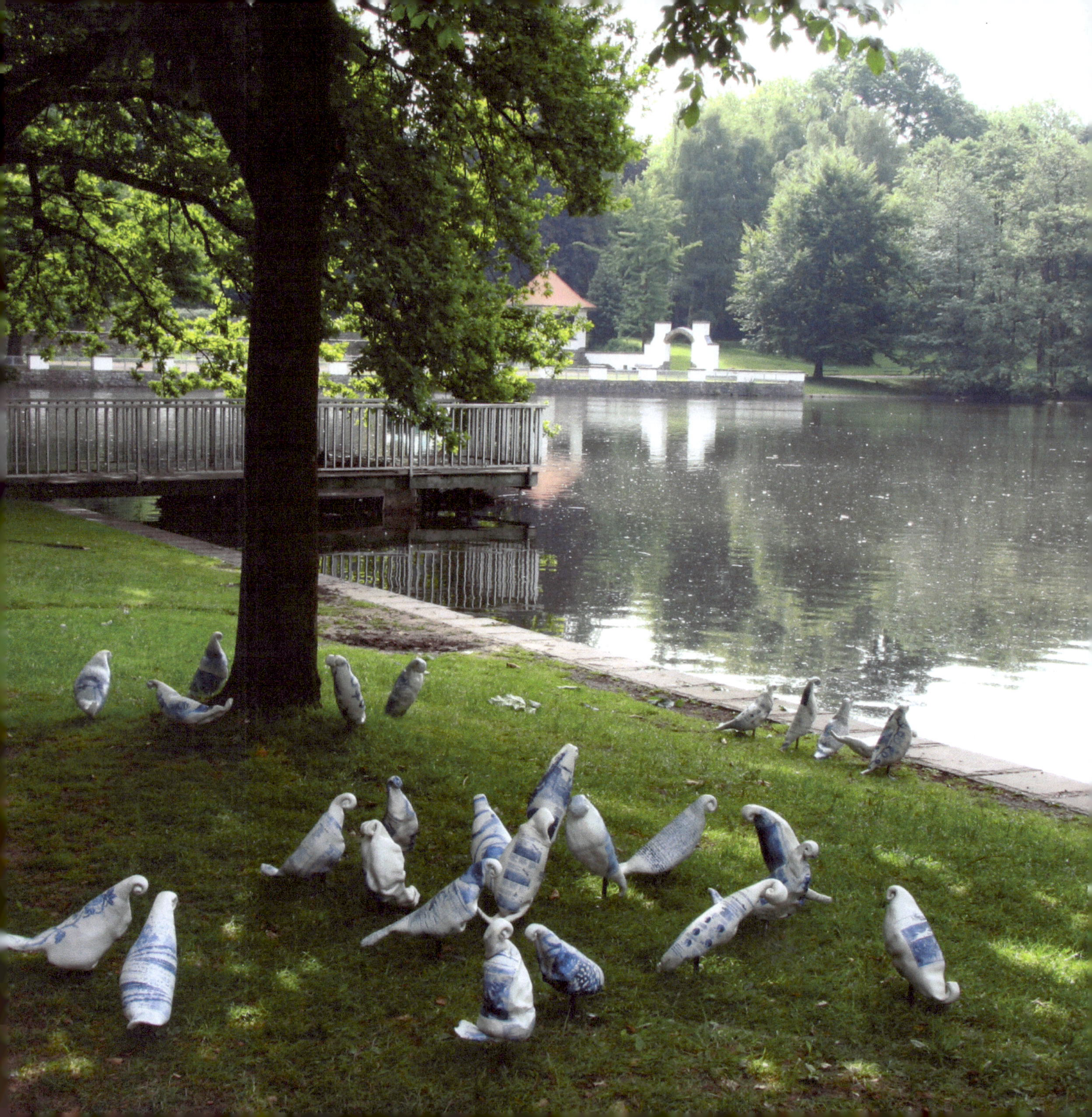

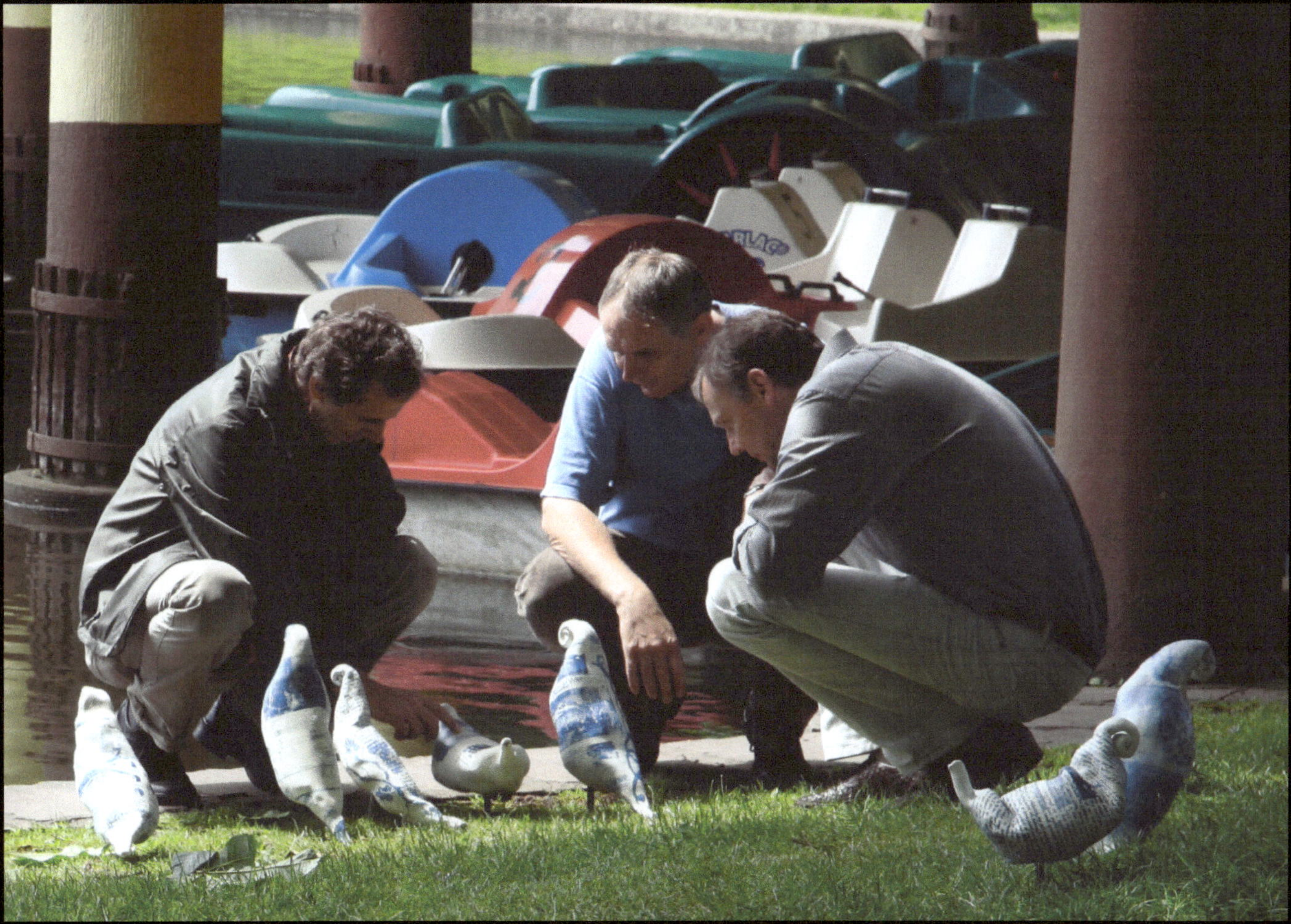

Above and facing page: Hangeweiher Park, Aachen, Germany 6/13/2009.

My father was a child in Germany during WWII. His father was one of the rocket scientists (later to help with the US space program in Cape Canaveral) who during the war was working on the development of the V1 and V2 rockets in Peenemünde, Germany.

When "birds in the park" was well underway, I heard about a new museum that had been built in Peenemünde, focusing on that time in history. I wrote to the director, who invited the birds to land there in the summer of 2010.

It soon developed that my father, who had not been back to Peenemünde since one hour after his house was bombed 67 years earlier, would also come for the bird landing, together with my mother, and give a talk about his memories of that time. Meanwhile, a documentary film about the bird project had begun, and the film makers joined us, with my husband and children, on this island on the Baltic Sea, in the very north of Germany.

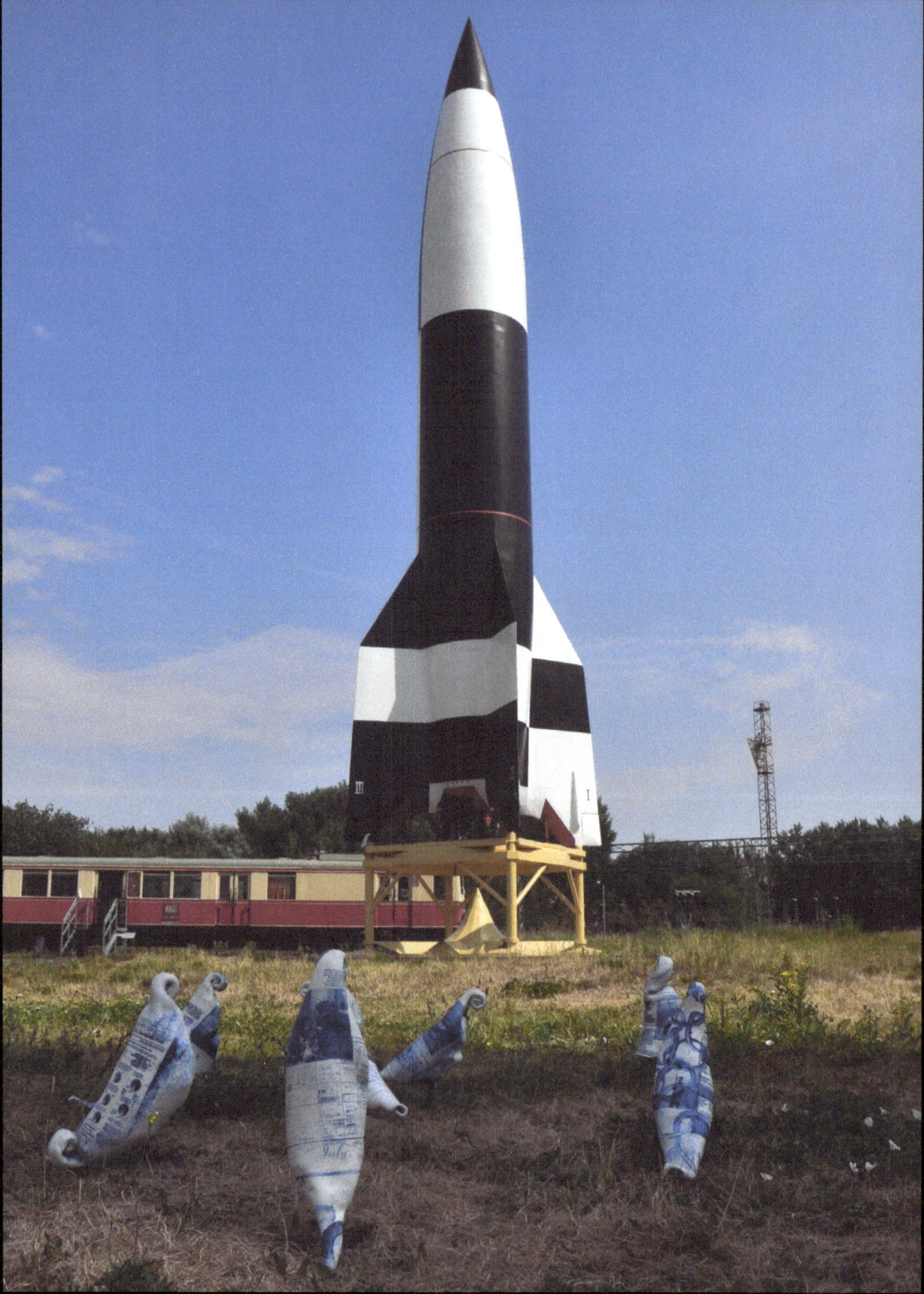

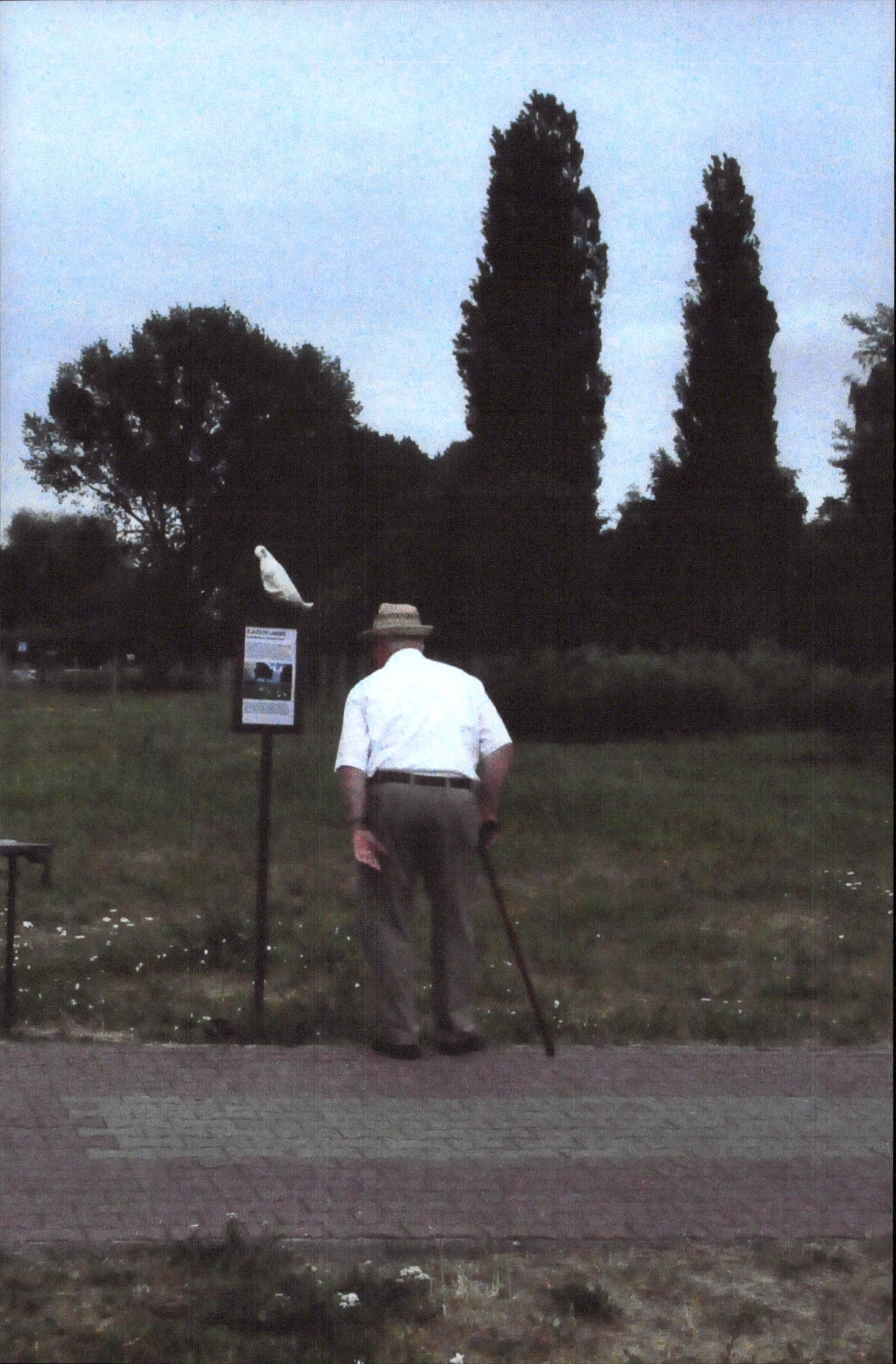

This and facing page: Peenemünde Historical and Technical Museum, Peenemünde, Germany 7/13/2010.

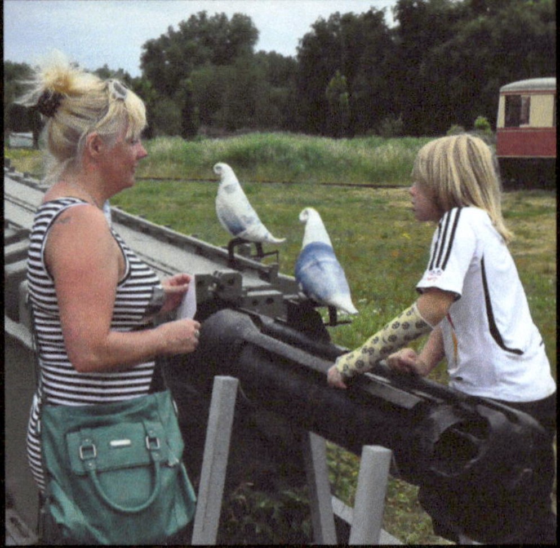

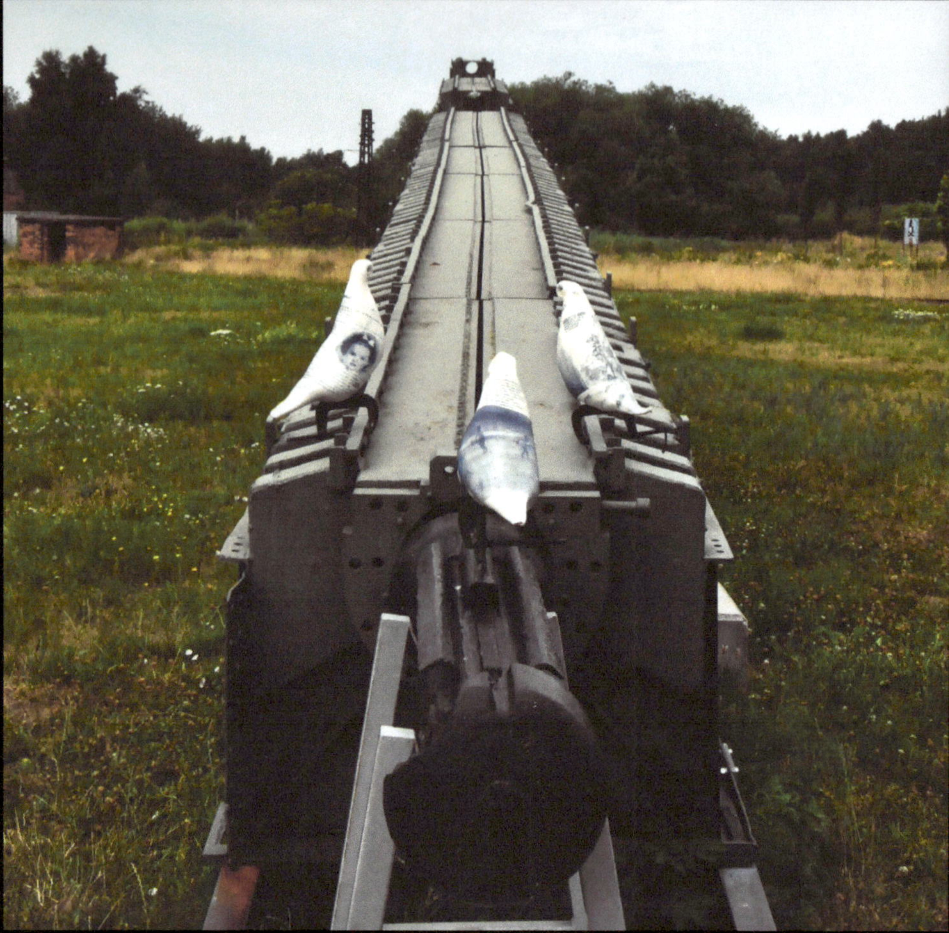

Launch ramp for V-1 bomb,
Peenemünde Historical and Technical Museum,
Peenemünde, Germany 7/13/2010.

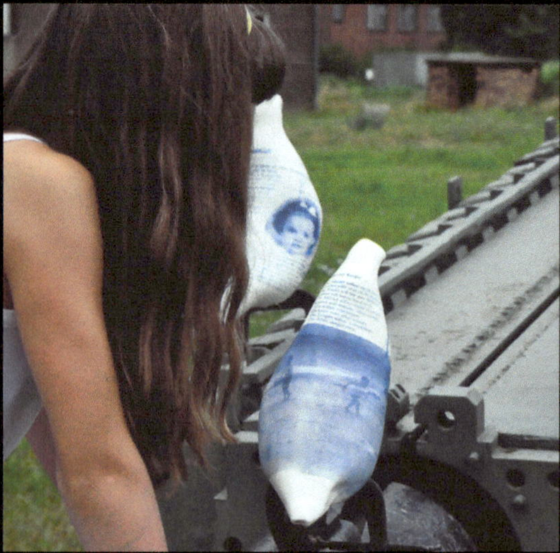

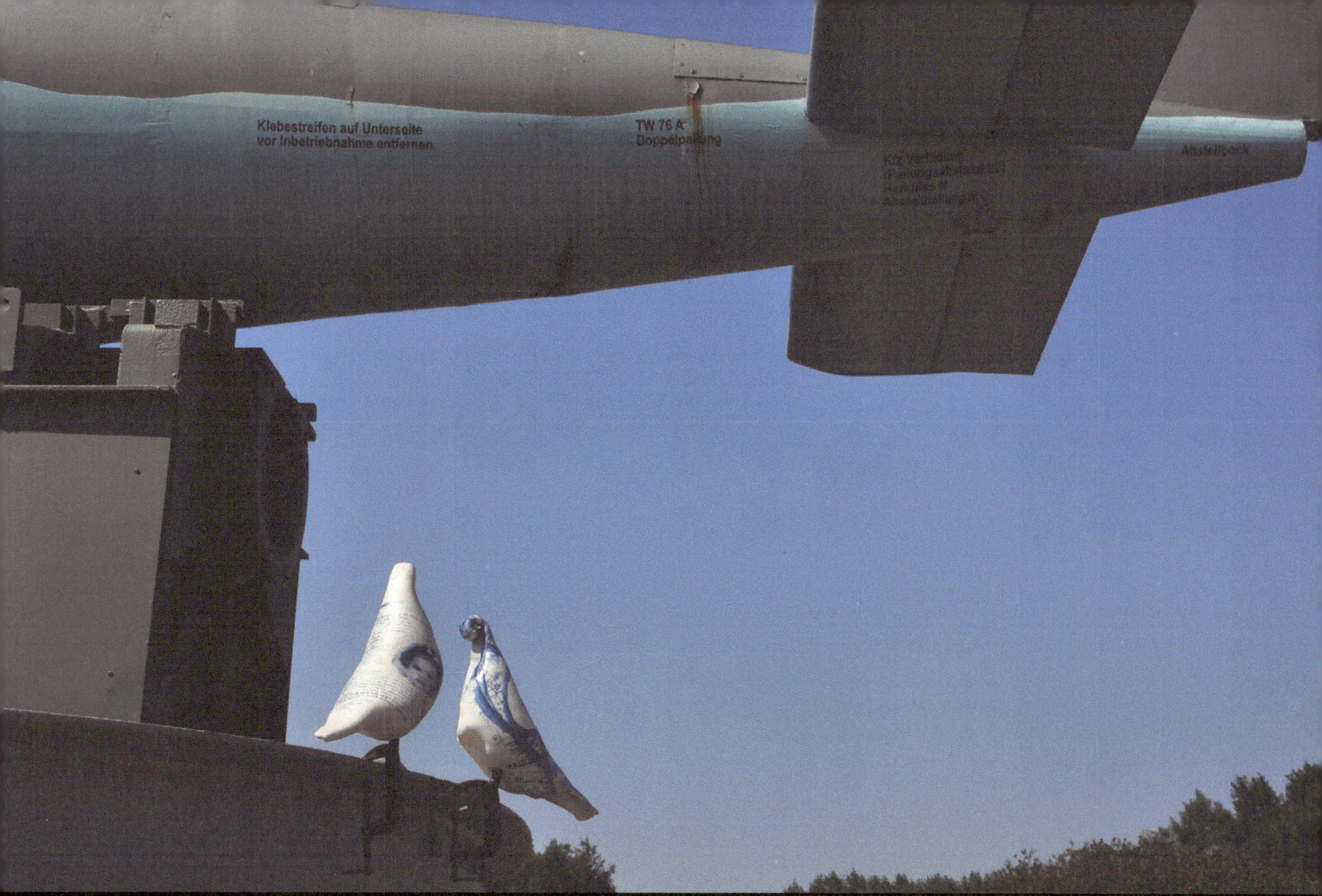

V-1 bomb, Peenemünde Historical and Technical Museum, Peenemünde, Germany 7/12/2010

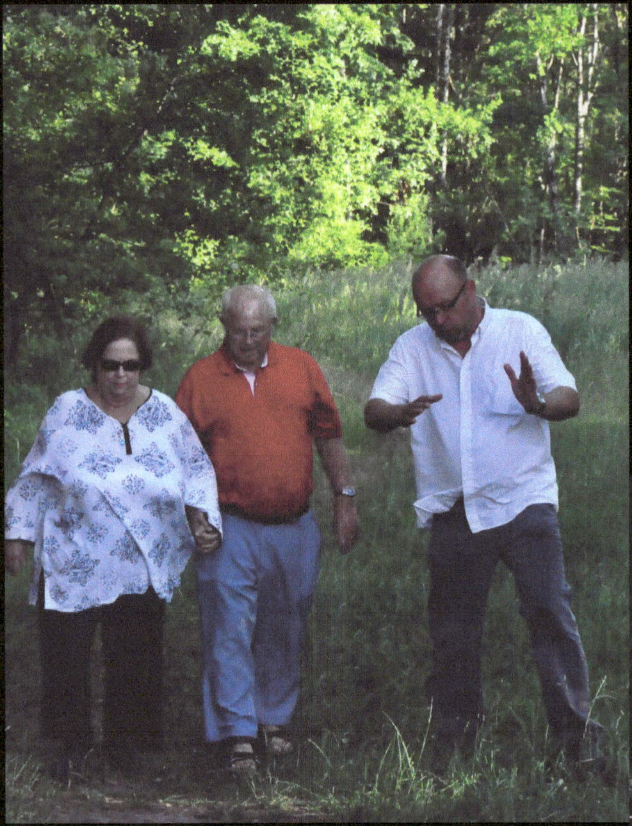

Museum director, Christian Mühldorfer-Vogt, giving a tour to Betty and Werner Hengst of Peenemünde wartime landmarks. Here, at the site of a WWII forced labor camp.

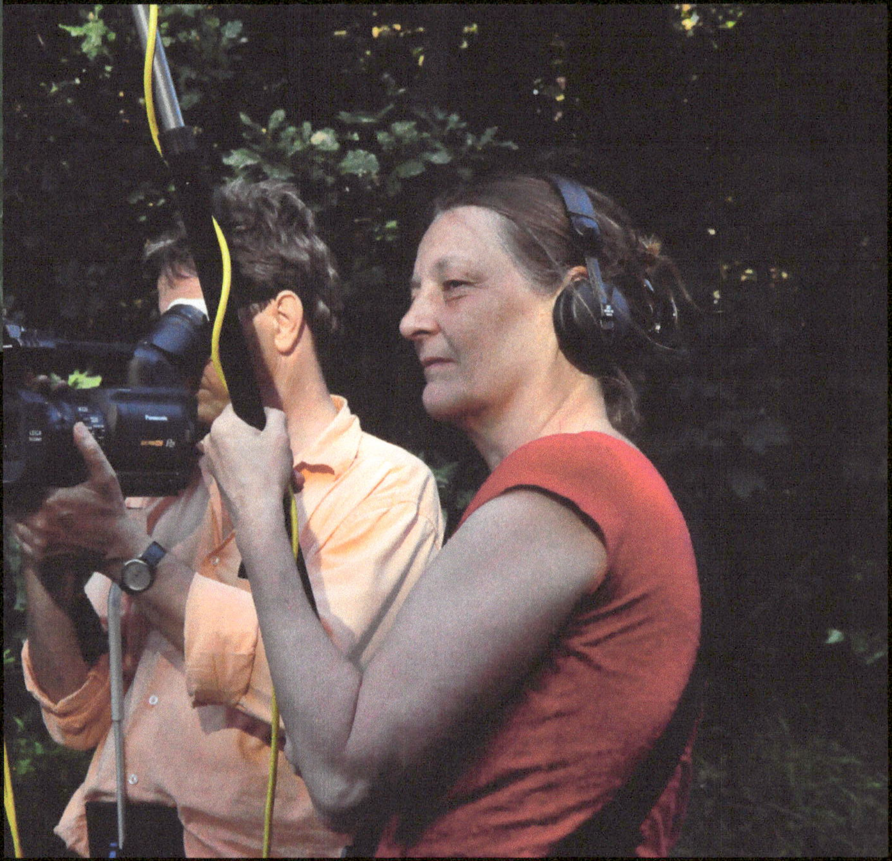

Tom Meffert and Dagmar Diebels filming for a documentary about the bird project.

back home

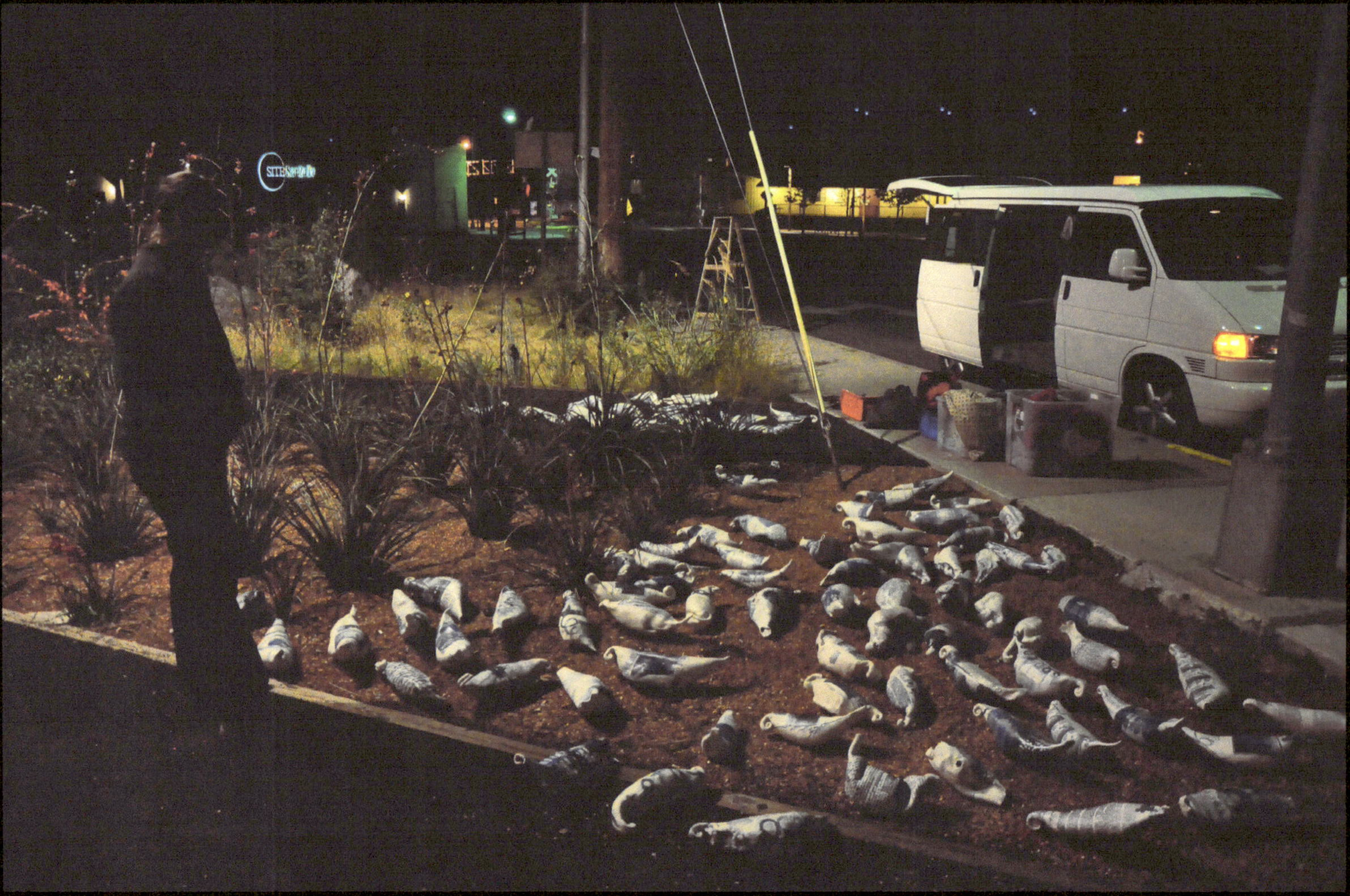

Photo: Helmut Hillenkamp

Setting up at Railyard Park, Santa Fe, NM 9/24/2010.

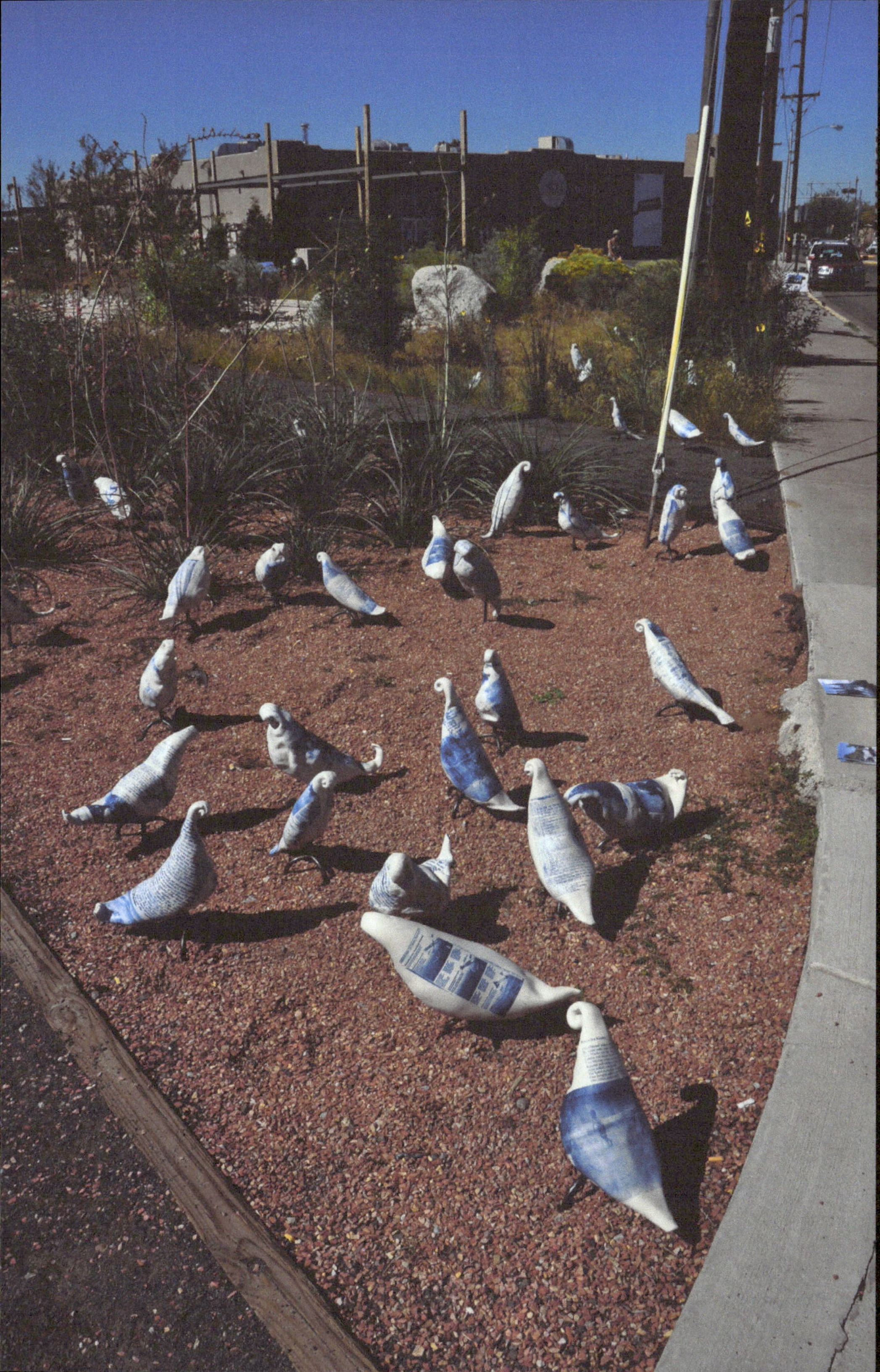

This and next four pages:
Railyard Park, Santa Fe, NM

The Santa Fe Railyard Park, which was just being completed when I started this project, was the inspiration for the idea to see the birds outside in a park, but bureaucracy did not allow it there at that point.

When I decided to wrap up this phase of "birds in the park" after two years of landings, the Railyard Park felt like a good ending spot, and now the door opened easily. It was so fun to be back where I started, in my own community with friends dropping by, having roamed and learned so much!

Now, with the printing of this book and also the documentary starting to travel, this incarnation of public art experiment with birds feels complete. What I take forward, and what I also would like to be an invitation to other artists, is the joy of creating surprising pause and connection through art in the midst of everyday life. We all hope, I know, to have some positive impact in the world, and the leap of faith is that little moments also can be important in the vast interweaving of human culture.

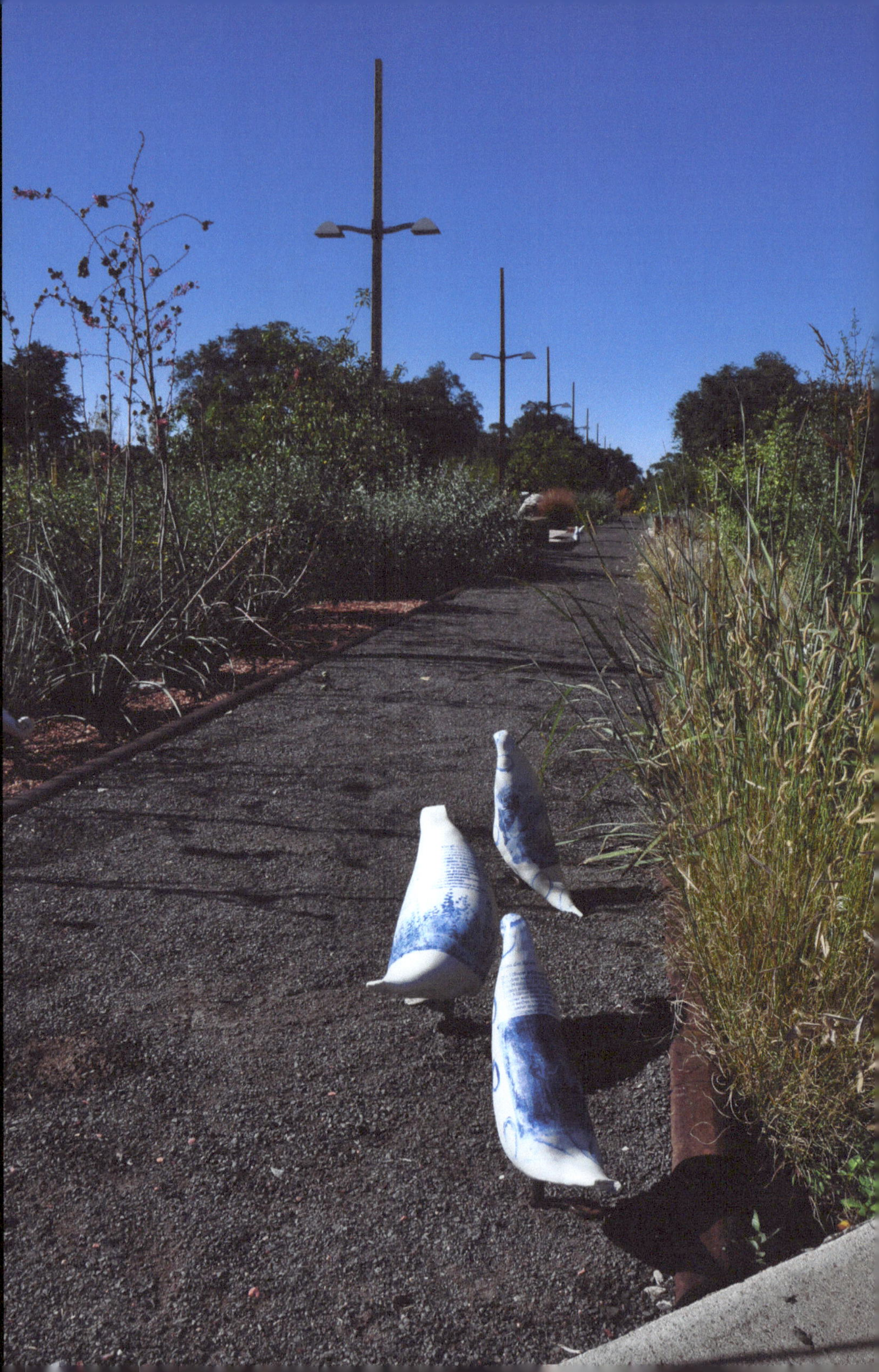

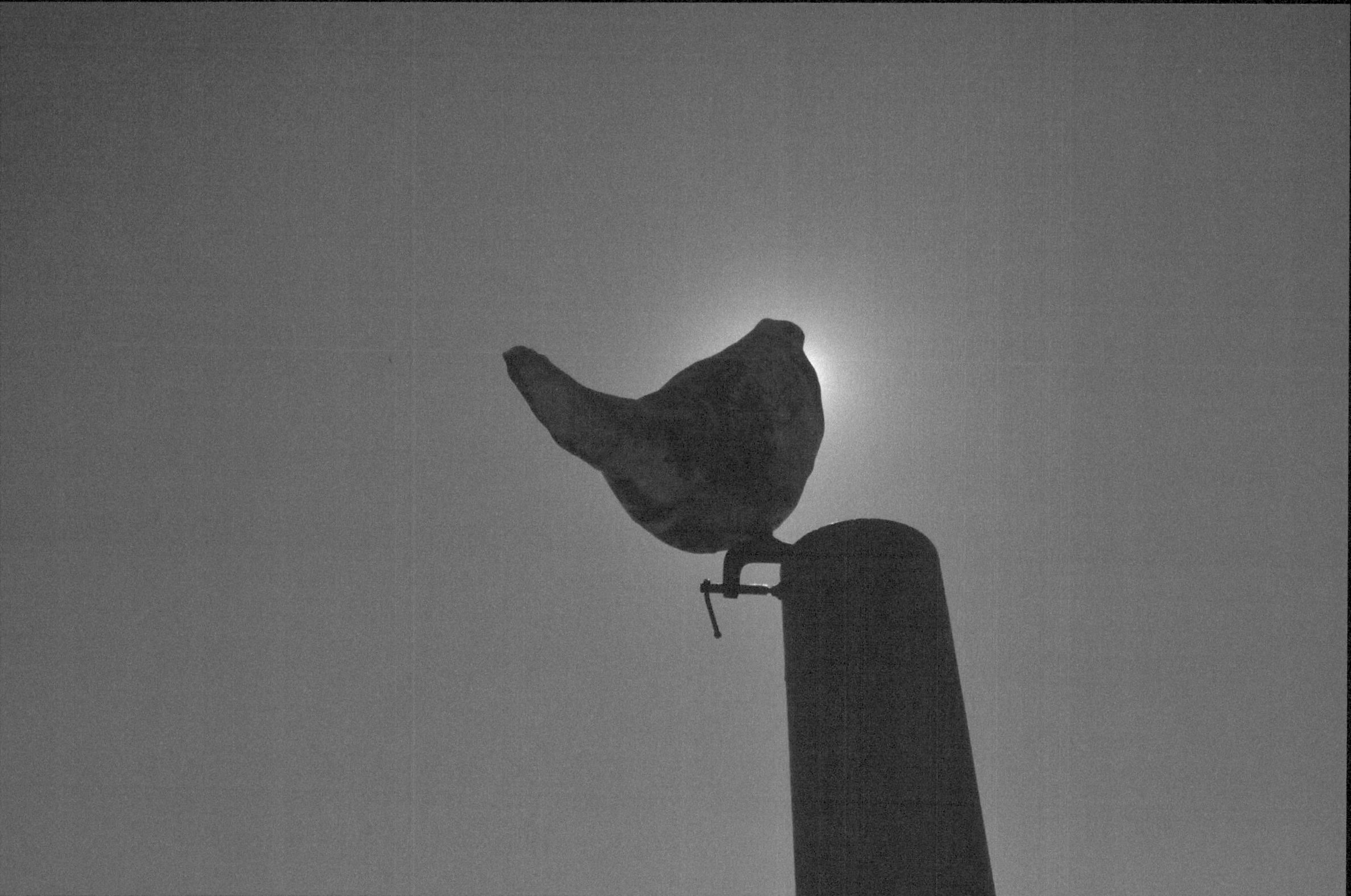

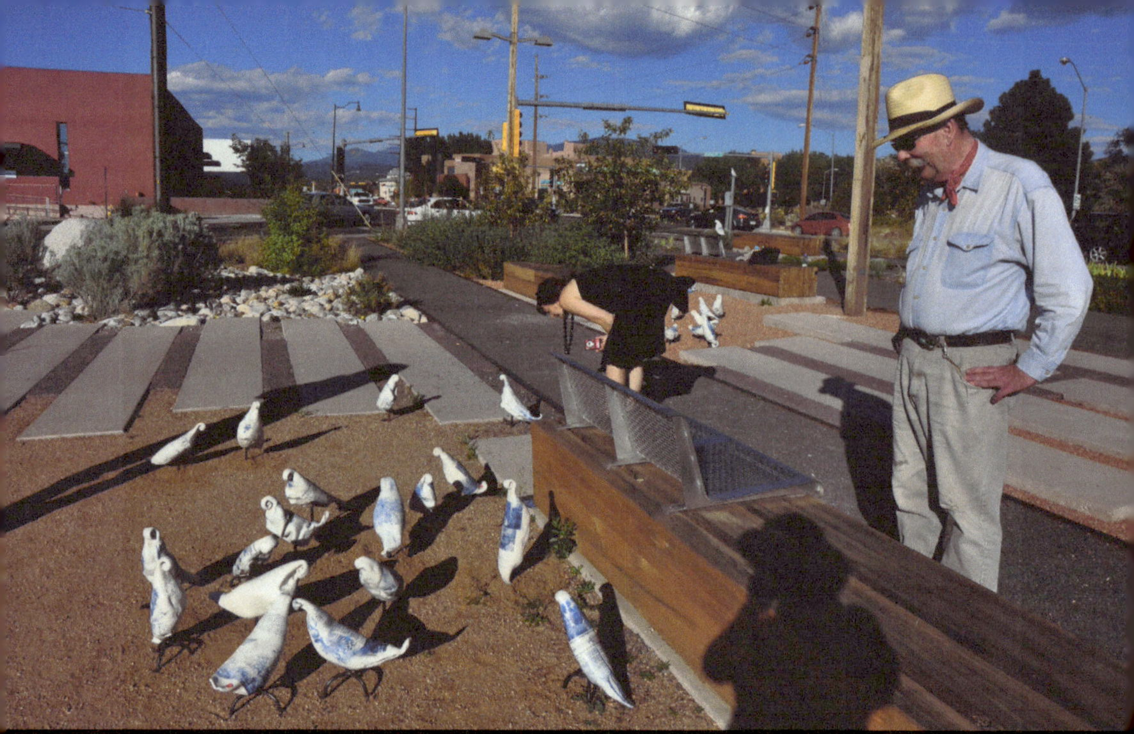

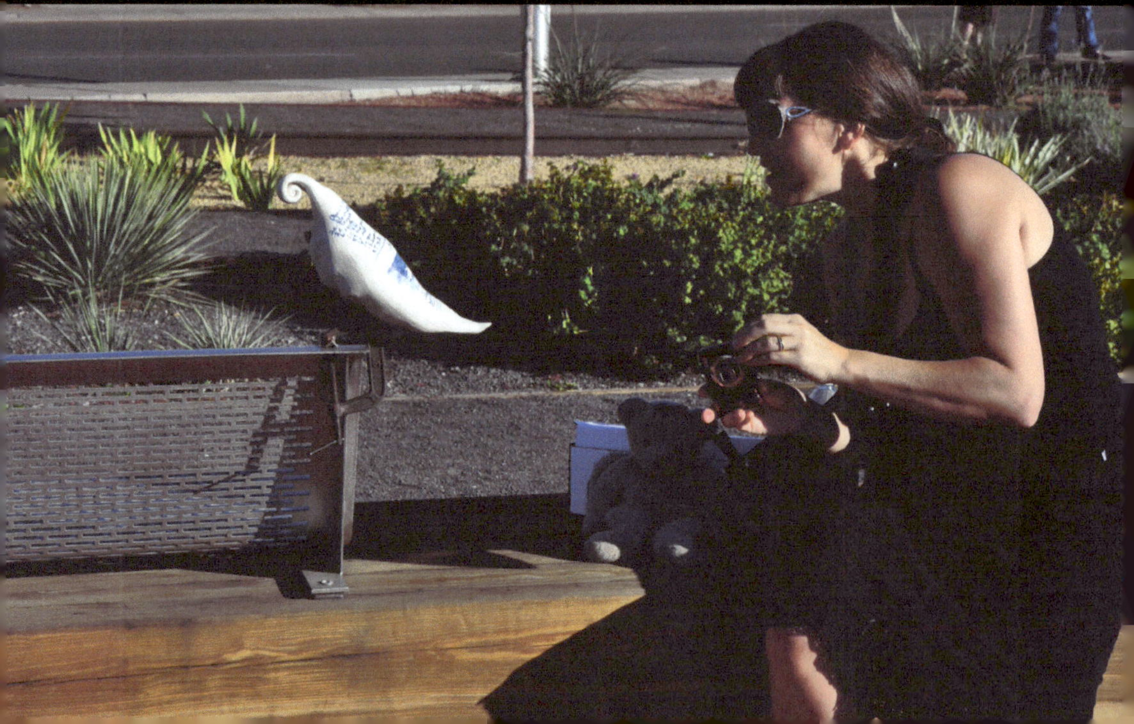

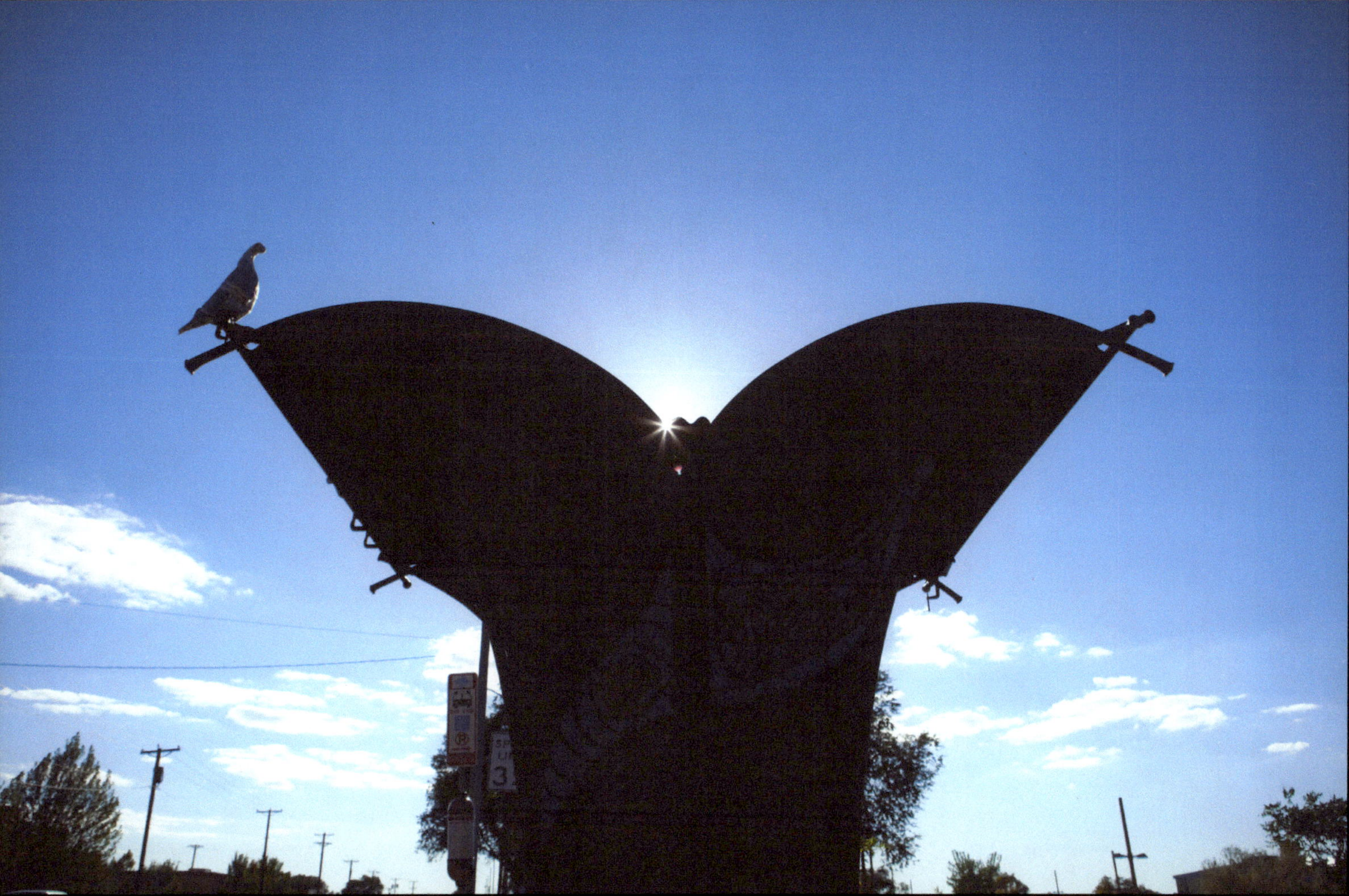

Photo: Genevieve Russell

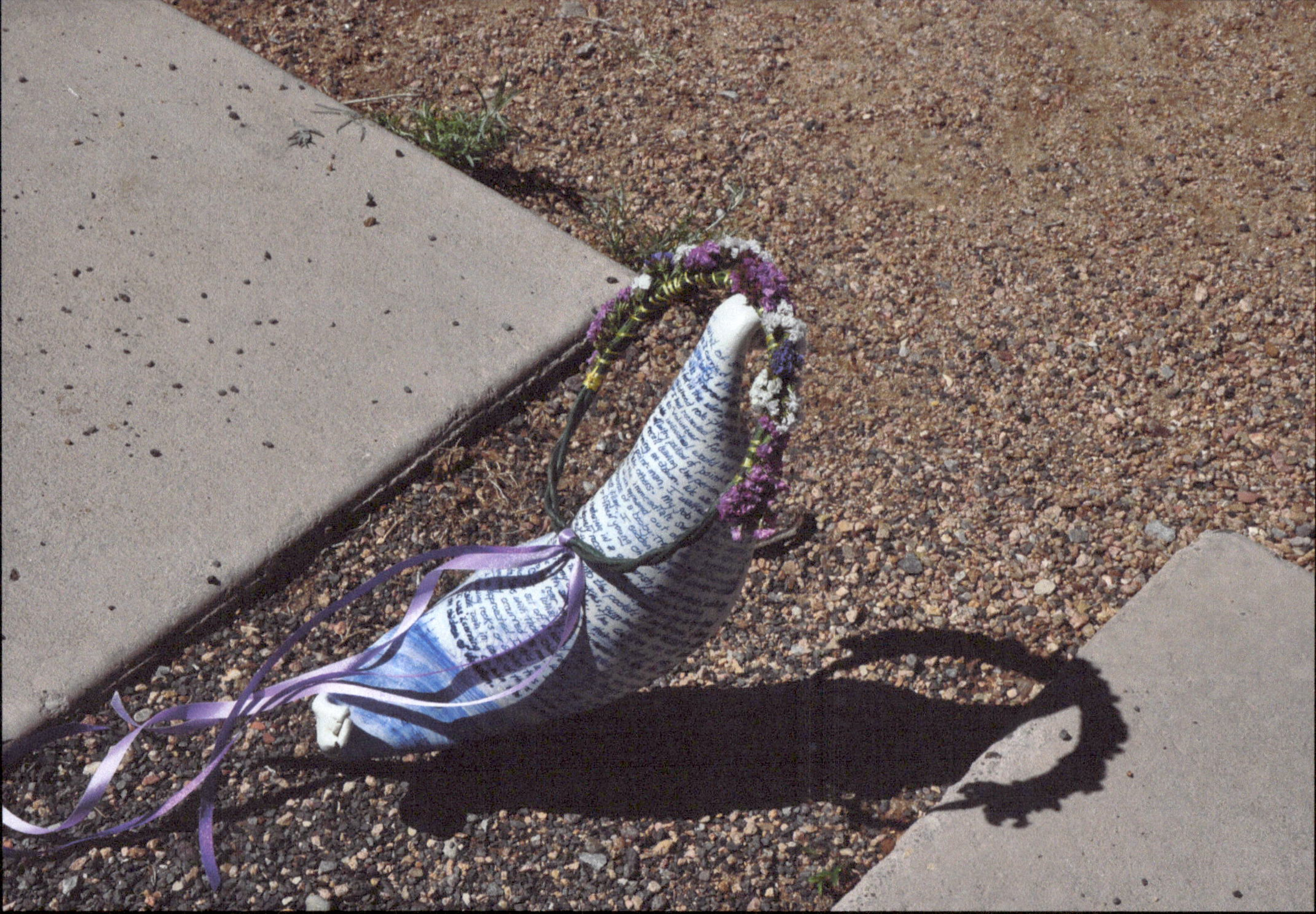

Photo: Oliver Hillenkamp

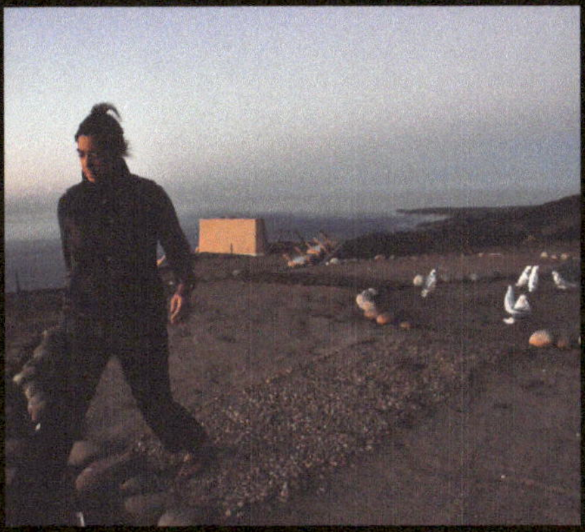

Christy Hengst's art includes site-specific projects out in the public realm as well as wax and porcelain paintings.

The public art projects range from the very temporary to quite permanent. Many have involved travel and/or collaboration with communities.

Born in the US in 1967, Hengst is based in Santa Fe, New Mexico. She is married to blacksmith Helmut Hillenkamp, with whom she often collaborates on projects, not the least of which is their two children.

More information about the artist and her work can be found at www.christyhengst.com

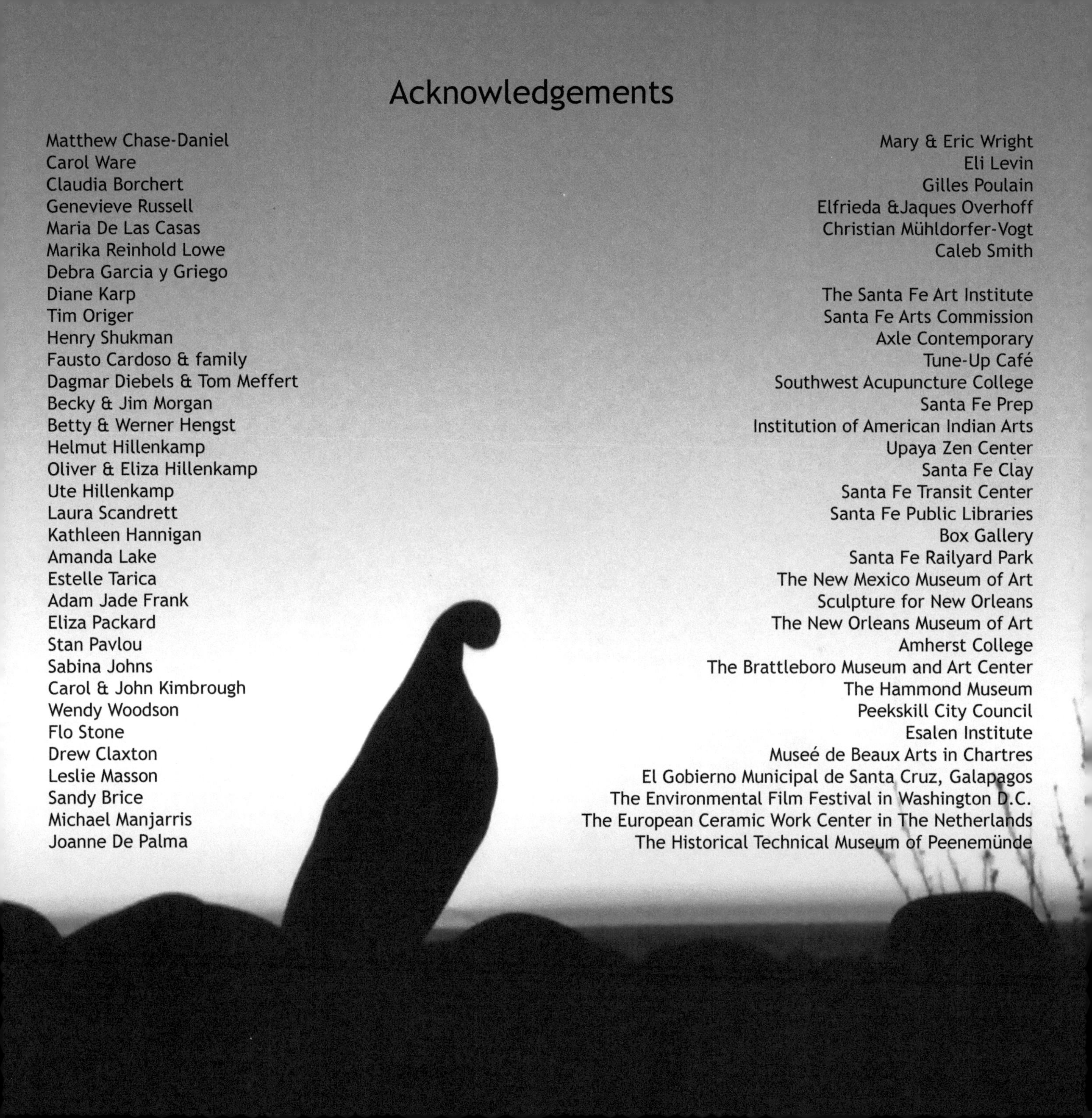

Acknowledgements

Matthew Chase-Daniel
Carol Ware
Claudia Borchert
Genevieve Russell
Maria De Las Casas
Marika Reinhold Lowe
Debra Garcia y Griego
Diane Karp
Tim Origer
Henry Shukman
Fausto Cardoso & family
Dagmar Diebels & Tom Meffert
Becky & Jim Morgan
Betty & Werner Hengst
Helmut Hillenkamp
Oliver & Eliza Hillenkamp
Ute Hillenkamp
Laura Scandrett
Kathleen Hannigan
Amanda Lake
Estelle Tarica
Adam Jade Frank
Eliza Packard
Stan Pavlou
Sabina Johns
Carol & John Kimbrough
Wendy Woodson
Flo Stone
Drew Claxton
Leslie Masson
Sandy Brice
Michael Manjarris
Joanne De Palma

Mary & Eric Wright
Eli Levin
Gilles Poulain
Elfrieda &Jaques Overhoff
Christian Mühldorfer-Vogt
Caleb Smith

The Santa Fe Art Institute
Santa Fe Arts Commission
Axle Contemporary
Tune-Up Café
Southwest Acupuncture College
Santa Fe Prep
Institution of American Indian Arts
Upaya Zen Center
Santa Fe Clay
Santa Fe Transit Center
Santa Fe Public Libraries
Box Gallery
Santa Fe Railyard Park
The New Mexico Museum of Art
Sculpture for New Orleans
The New Orleans Museum of Art
Amherst College
The Brattleboro Museum and Art Center
The Hammond Museum
Peekskill City Council
Esalen Institute
Museé de Beaux Arts in Chartres
El Gobierno Municipal de Santa Cruz, Galapagos
The Environmental Film Festival in Washington D.C.
The European Ceramic Work Center in The Netherlands
The Historical Technical Museum of Peenemünde

www.ingramcontent.com/pod-product-compliance
Lightning Source LLC
Chambersburg PA
CBHW040741200526
45159CB00023B/1101
9780985811617